ROMANTIC POETS AND EPIC TRADITION

Romantic Poets
and Epic Tradition

BRIAN WILKIE

Madison and Milwaukee, 1965
The University of Wisconsin Press

Published by
The University of Wisconsin Press
Madison and Milwaukee
Mailing address: P.O. Box 1379, Madison, Wisconsin 53701

Printed in the United States of America
by the George Banta Company, Inc., Menasha, Wisconsin

Library of Congress Catalog Card Number 65-11199

TO ANN

PREFACE

To the extent that this book has a central thesis it can be put simply: that the epic tradition was alive in the English Romantic age and has some bearing on the meaning of several important long poems of that age. Not everyone would deny this, but many people would do so or would be skeptical, for reasons like those I examine in the first chapter and because of the weight of authorities like E. M. W. Tillyard, whose *The English Epic and Its Background* sees the eighteenth century as the dead end of the epic in England. There is a widespread assumption—it is better to call it that than a conviction—either that the epic was obsolete by the late eighteenth century or that while one can legitimately refer to Romantic "epics," he can do so only by adopting a special, *ad hoc* definition entirely different from the plain and unfancy one applicable to earlier works. This book will make it clear that I do not share these views.

In fact, however, my main purpose is neither to prove nor to disprove this generalization or any other, but rather to discuss individual poems in which the epic intention is central. I wish to treat these poems for their own sakes, not as evidence to be subsumed by a general idea but as statements about life and works of art which are valuable and interesting, each in its unique way. I make some general points about the epic and literary history in the course of the book, and I hope these points are valid and valuable, but to me they are far less important than to determine what the particular poems are doing and saying, especially those with which the last four chapters are concerned. The first two chapters are somewhat exceptional. The first, which discusses the epic tradition in general, is a ground-clearing essay whose aim is to correct what I believe is false in certain familiar approaches to epic. The second, on Southey and Landor, is partly prompted by my desire to give neglected works some of the attention their limited but real merit deserves, but the chapter is more specifically meant to be an extension of my remarks in the first chapter and a convenience by means of which I try to illustrate certain paradoxical facts about epic relevant to the practice of other, greater Romantic poets.

To some extent, then, this book can be read as a collection of separate essays. But they are finally unified, I trust, by a common approach to the poems: I discuss them all in the light of the epic tradition. This common approach is not primarily dictated by the canon of aesthetic unity; surely scholarship ought to be more concerned with what is true than with what is tidy. But to use a common approach facilitates comparison and contrast, without which it is difficult to see clearly what any individual poem is doing. And this is especially true when one is dealing with the epic tradition, which is so markedly derivative, imitative, and generally inbred. Moreover, epic intention is rarely accidental; where it reveals itself it tends to reflect the poet's deepest impulses in writing the poem.

I cannot emphasize too strongly that this book is not a genre study as that term is often understood, that I am only secondarily interested in changing readers' ideas about what a certain literary form really is. I shall be disappointed if readers assume that my general remarks about the epic are the heart of this book. But it is true that I have come to believe that epic is not and never really has been a genre; it is a tradition. Nor do I wish to isolate a definitive art-form to be designated "the Romantic epic," for although the principal Romantic attempts at epic do share some important qualities different from what we find in earlier epics, these differences ought not to obsess or distract us. The basic law of epic throughout its history has been growth, and if we bear that fact in mind we need not see the Romantic approaches to epic as essentially different from earlier ones. *The Prelude* does not, for example, differ from *Paradise Lost* more radically than *Paradise Lost* differs from the *Aeneid*.

More often than not I have assumed that readers of this book will be fairly well read in Romantic literature and criticism of it, and I hope that I have some new things to say to these specialists as to others. But I have also hoped that the book will be useful to students and amateurs of literature who are not specialists in Romanticism, and therefore I have repeated, sometimes at length, a few old and familiar points—for example, that Byron contradicts himself in *Don Juan* and that Wordsworth was obsessed with the problem of reciprocity between the mind and the external world. In an age when scholarly interests are becoming more and more specialized, it seems to me that this approach is warranted.

Readers may wonder why I do not discuss Blake and Scott. In general, the answer is that this book is concerned mainly with individual poems; to "cover" a field is not its purpose. But there are other and more particular reasons too. To discuss in any detail one or more of Blake's long poems in a book that treats six other poets strikes me as impracticable. Blake ought normally to be approached through book-length studies of him, since before examining any particular long poem of his one needs to have cracked his code and persuaded the reader of success in that enterprise, after which one is still only on the threshold of detailed criticism of individual works. As for Scott, one is faced, as with Blake, with a number of poems any one of which might profitably be looked at in the light of epic tradition. One could do little more than generalize about Scott's approach to epic, a procedure that does not accord with my aim to consider individual works at some length. These remarks about Blake and Scott may seem to conflict with my decision to discuss the relatively minor poets Southey and Landor, but I repeat that I am not treating these two entirely for their own sakes; to some extent I am *using* them, to extend points made in the introductory chapter and to help in the transition to later parts of the book.

One general note on my practice in quoting: Where I have cut off a quotation of verse or prose before the end of a sentence of the original text, I have generally allowed myself to omit ellipsis dots, but only where I have felt confident that the omitted words do not affect the applicability of the quotation in my context.

Where the omitted concluding words might make a difference in contexts other than mine I have used the final ellipsis dots. Omissions in the *middle* of quotations I always indicate, of course.

For their advice during early stages of this book's composition I should like to thank Professors Ricardo Quintana and Alexander Kroff, more especially Professor Alvin Whitley, and above all Professor Carl Woodring, who over several years gave me kind and painstaking advice which was never once other than constructive. I have received research grants from the University of Wisconsin and have been helped with manuscript expenses by Dartmouth College and the University of Illinois. My wife worked hard at a multitude of tasks, including most of the typing; of even greater value to me were her many helpful observations on style and tone and her general encouragement of my efforts.

B.W.

Urbana, Illinois
September, 1964

CONTENTS

CONTENTS

ROMANTIC POETS AND EPIC TRADITION

One: THE ROMANTICS AND THE PARADOX OF THE EPIC

But sometimes things may be made darker by definition. I see a cow, I define her, Animal quadrupes ruminans cornutum. *But a goat ruminates, and a cow may have no horns.* Cow *is plainer.* SAMUEL JOHNSON

I T is commonly assumed by historians of literature that the epic, moribund in the late eighteenth century, was dead by the beginning of the nineteenth. This generalization prevails notwithstanding an actually increasing tendency to apply the word *epic,* usually in some loose sense, to certain long Romantic and Victorian poems. True, Keats's first *Hyperion* has always been regarded as a true if relatively minor epic, but we know that Keats had to abandon the poem because the strain was too great for him; the abortive exception would seem to have proved the rule. One is tempted to see in Keats's surrender an emblem of Romanticism trying heroically to keep the past alive and being forced finally to recognize that, like so much else that was old and noble, the epic was no longer feasible.

The critical essays in this book depend on a very different set of premises: that the epic tradition was alive in at least the early nineteenth century, that this tradition is important to an understanding of certain important poems of the period, and that therefore we can profit from reading these poems in the light of that tradition. Since many readers will be disinclined to grant these premises out of hand, an "enabling" essay seems in order; its function is to clear the ground for later essays by correcting what I believe is an oversimple view of what epic is and the way it has developed. I do not intend to redefine the epic in eccentric or unfamiliar terms, for, as I shall try to show, valid epic theory

3

depends more on the techniques of identification than on those of definition. On the contrary, I shall maintain that, although they were radically original, the Romantic poets, to the extent that they were heirs of the epic tradition, used that tradition much as earlier poets had done.

In any case, it should be understood that this book is not a genre study in the usual sense; except in the treatment of Southey and Landor, who figure in the study primarily because they illustrate so well certain general points made in this introduction, my final concern is not with epic theory but with seeing the poems I discuss for what they are in themselves. Thus the reader, especially if he does not share the view that the Romantic epic is a contradiction in terms, may be able to read the later chapters sympathetically even if he is unpersuaded by my preliminary generalizations. For they are in the strictest sense *introductory* remarks; they are meant to clear the ground for what follows rather than to advance a thesis for subsequent documentation.

II

"If no one asks me, I know: if I wish to explain it to one that asketh, I know not," says St. Augustine about time. A similar sense of frustration is experienced by almost everyone who tries to define the epic in terms which are true to his experience of it and yet not utterly subjective. Theorists over the last three centuries have agreed on only two things: an epic must be long (though how long is moot), and it must be narrative. Even in an age of comparative orthodoxy like the early eighteenth century there was much disagreement, and where significant consensus prevailed it was often on matters which later ages have considered marginal (for example, the Aristotelian doctrine of the probable and the possible) or on pious truisms equally applicable to many other literary forms (an epic should have unity of action).[1]

There are many reasons for this confusion, most of them fairly obvious. One is the very small number of specimens from which to generalize. From our vantage point in history we can count about half a dozen works which virtually everyone would concede to be epics: Homer's *Iliad* and *Odyssey*, Virgil's *Aeneid*, Milton's *Paradise Lost*, Tasso's *Jerusalem Delivered*, and Camoën's *Lusiad*. (I have in mind the so-called "literary" or "artificial" epic, not the "primitive," "authentic," "oral" epic, whose rules are as much the business of the anthropologist as of the literary scholar. And, while it may be preferable to consider the two Homeric poems oral epics, their long-established status as models places them in the line of literary epic.) Two centuries ago even this canon would have seemed lax, because of the three moderns included in it. In various centuries and critical traditions, theorists have accepted Dante, Spenser, Ariosto, or Boiardo, but more self-consciously; it is often necessary to argue these poets and their poems into the select circle. And, in general, epic theories help substantiate that, as the statistician might put it, the smaller the number of samples the more uninhibited and eccentric the inferences which can be drawn from them. It is partly to this danger of hasty generalization that Addison alludes when, Aristotelian though he generally was, he expresses regrets that Aristotle's rules were written in ignorance of the *Aeneid*.[2]

The exclusiveness of the epic canon is chiefly attributable to the tendency, even among rigidly formal theorists, to demand of an epic not merely formal credentials but greatness as well. Just as most epic theorists in our own day would hesitate to adduce the works of, say, Glover in support of generalizations about epic, so critics in earlier ages have often excluded minor ancient poets like Lucan, Statius, and Apollonius Rhodius, sometimes with a sneering implication that such writers are impostors. The effect is to treat epic poets as candidates for a literary pantheon. Addison once more provides an illustration; in describing Milton's imitativeness he writes, "I might have inserted also several Passages of *Tasso*, which our Author has imitated; but as I do not look upon *Tasso* to be a sufficient Voucher, I would not perplex my Reader with such Quotations, as might do more Honour to the *Italian* than the *English* Poet."[3] When Shelley declares that "none among the flock of Mock-birds, though their notes were sweet, Apollonius Rhodius, Quintus Calaber Smyrnetheus, Nonnus, Lucan, Statius, or Claudian have sought even to fulfill a single condition of epic truth,"[4] we may wish to dismiss his statement as typical Shelleyan iconoclasm. But Aristotle himself shows the same sensitivity; on a number of important points he seems to accept Homer's practice as authoritative but unique. Among epic poets, he tells us, Homer alone "is not unaware of the part to be played by the poet himself in the poem . . . Whereas the other poets are perpetually coming forward in person," Homer advances his action by introducing objective characters. In an epic poem the Thought and Diction must be good and in these Homer's epics "surpass all other poems." Homer is the only epic poet who understands the distinction between chronicle-history and unified action.[5] Here and occasionally elsewhere in the *Poetics* Aristotle betrays something like impatience at having to consider works other than the master's; it is only a slight exaggeration to say that Aristotle's epic rules are based on the *Iliad* and the *Odyssey* alone. Like many later critics Aristotle seems to be saying that although there have been many epics only a few really count. In recent criticism we find E. M. W. Tillyard taking this same traditional view when, as the very first of his requirements for epic, he lists "the simple one of high quality and of high seriousness."[6]

Surely this is a strange situation, very different from common practice in defining or legislating for other literary forms. Scholars generally assume that the study of Peele, Dekker, and Gascoigne (not to mention writers far more obscure) helps us understand Elizabethan comedy and comedy in general. They may even feel that greater figures like Shakespeare and Jonson obscure the underlying pattern by the very exceptionality of their genius. Romance, tragedy, satire—all these, we feel, can be defined and investigated with the help of second-rate works. Not so with epic; here it is the great, qualitatively exceptional work that is definitive.

The criterion of greatness is one of several signs that the epic is not simply a literary genre if by that term we mean a literary category adequately defined by general rules or traits. As Karl Kroeber has pointed out, "The Augustan discussions of the rules and techniques of epic (largely derived from Le Bossu) make tedious reading today not because they are silly (they are not) but because they never come near the experience we feel when we read epic poetry."[7] The same holds true, I believe, of all theorizing about epic as a genre. Prescriptive rules seem arbitrary. Inductive generalizations seem vague and nebulous, even when the generalizations are based solely on the few long-canonized epics and the waters are not muddied by the recognition of such works as *Orlando Furioso, Tom Jones,* or *Moby Dick.* In some ways we encounter even greater problems if we shorten our list. The *Iliad* and the *Odyssey* are surely epics, yet how much, after all, do they have in common, in form or in spirit or in any other way? Aristotle, while virtually identifying epic with the two Homeric models and them alone, finds it necessary to make a formal distinction between them,[8] and there has long been a tendency to see in these poems two basic, alternative views of human experience, like tragedy and comedy. It is not surprising, then, that when theorists try to generalize about these epics and a handful of others to boot they can reach consensus on nothing as common to all the poems except length and the use of the narrative mode.

Most of us remain convinced, and I think rightly so, that we know what an epic is; on the other hand, we sense the irrelevance of most abstract formalism like that of Le Bossu and the inadequacy of inductive generalizations based on form, content, or mood to describe even the small number of undoubted epics. One familiar way out of this dilemma is to generalize, not about what the epics are or what is in them, but about their relationship to the world which produced them; this has been a standard approach since the latter half of the eighteenth century. Thus Tillyard, rather like Shelley, sees as one of the few constant marks of epic its "choric" quality, the fact that it voices the commonly shared

values and aspirations of a large group of men in a certain place
and age.[9] This type of approach, like the inductive approach in
general, would surely seem more realistic than abstract formalism,
and it is. Yet in some ways the inductive and social definitions, as
usually formulated, violate our *Gestalt* of epic even more than neoclassic formalism does; the formalists seem in touch with the unmistakable texture, at least, of epic; they recognize as most of us
do that the literary epic always threads a maze of conventions more
elaborate than can be found in any other literary form. It may ex-
asperate us to have the grandeur and power of the great epics explained myopically in terms of apparently accidental things like
the *medias res* convention or the descent into the underworld, but
at least the mention of such things reassures us that we are concerned with the *Aeneid* and the *Odyssey* and not with, say, Thucy-
dides' *Peloponnesian War* or *The Mirror for Magistrates.*

The discussion would seem to have come full circle and left us
with a problem like St. Augustine's. Neoclassic formalism, which
was usually a combination of rules drawn from Aristotle and Horace and of prescriptions directed toward an ideal which, in theory, need not ever have been realized, seems narrow, arbitrary,
and beside the point; more inductive methods arrive at excessively
vague, nondescript criteria—unless, that is, we wish (as no one
does) to exclude one or more of the already tiny number of acknowledged epics.

The best way out of the dilemma, I believe, is neither to define
epic through generic rules nor to do so through common characteristics induced from the standard epics, but to use a different approach which emphasizes that epic is a tradition, "something
handed on or transmitted." For a certain type of word, writes the
philosopher Richard Robinson, "examples are the best method of
definition"; what words of this type mean is "primarily certain
cases. There is a feeling that these are the cases of some one general connotation; but it remains obscure what that connotation is,
and in any conflict between the examples and a suggested connotation the examples will win."[10] (*Connotation* as used here means,

approximately, "defining attributes.") The term *epic* provides a perfect example of this type of word; it means those "cases" which we all wish to call epics.[11] Consider, for example, the prevalent attitude toward *Paradise Lost*. Addison found it necessary to argue for the poem's epic legitimacy (not everyone was willing to call the work an epic, as Addison himself pointed out[12]), and he did so according to formal neoclassic rules. But once Milton's canonicity had been firmly established it became unnecessary, indeed irrelevant, to justify *Paradise Lost* as an epic. If today we habitually think of the poem as an epic, we are not, I believe, adverting unconsciously to Addison's argument or to any other in particular; it would just be impossible now for any epic theory whatever to get a sympathetic hearing if it denied that *Paradise Lost* was an epic. The poem has simply become one of the defining cases, and this despite the immense differences between it and other acknowledged epics.

All this, however, is not to say that the great literary epics are related to one another only through verbal habit; we could say of that statement too that it belies our experience of epic, which for all the diversity of its exemplars conveys an unmistakable impression of intramural cohesiveness. It has few if any universally common traits or devices, but it has many frequently recurring ones. The most obvious is an exemplified ideal of human conduct—that is, of heroism. Usually the hero has a divinely sanctioned mission, to accomplish which requires fortitude and resistance to temptation, including sensual temptation. More often than not the action concerns some crucial episode in the history of a nation or other homogenous group. There is a strong tendency for the epic to be etiological, to find the seeds of the present in the past; the action is "influential." Almost always the general tone is lofty and serious, and there is almost always a sense that human life is enacted in a setting of mystery, that somehow life derives urgency and poignancy from the darkness or vastness which surrounds and impinges on it. (The response to this spiritual or supernatural tone is almost certainly what has prompted all the seemingly su-

perficial critical discussion of "machinery.") Furthermore, as
everyone admits, an epic is a long narrative work. But, although
it is largely from things like these that our sense of epic derives,
and although every definitive epic illustrates a number of them,
no single one can be shown to be essential and many of them are
very general.

The present study assumes that we can best understand epic not
as a genre governed by fixed rules, whether prescriptive or inductive, but as a tradition. It is a tradition, however, that operates in
an unusual way, for although, like any tradition, it is rooted in
the past, it typically rejects the past as well, sometimes vigorously
and with strident contempt. The great paradox of the epic lies in
the fact that the partial repudiation of earlier epic tradition is itself traditional.[13] Nor is this situation fortuitous; the paradox is
closely related to the peculiar nature of the epic tradition and has
had a special usefulness for the great poets who have contributed
to it.

We may perhaps understand the epic paradox more easily if we
compare it with another tradition in many ways analogous: the
tradition of the Old Testament prophets. The great Hebrew prophets are very different from one another in their emphases and
tones; they strike us as individualists. Yet it is clear that they fall
into a distinct pattern. Typically the prophet places himself, along
with the message of God which he is commissioned to deliver, in
dramatic opposition to the corrupt beliefs and practices of his
time. He calls for a thorough revolution in the attitudes and behavior of the nation, and in doing so he often adds consciously a
radical new dimension to faith and ethics. This new religious ideal
is sharply opposed to the corrupt version of orthodoxy which the
prophet finds all around him; thus he seems dangerously radical
to his contemporaries and is persecuted and rejected by them and
their leaders. Yet the touchstone for his teachings is always traditional; the prophet sees his task as that of renewing the vital values of the Covenant, of which the prevalent orthodoxy is merely

a legalistic stereotype. In the name of true orthodoxy he rejects the specious orthodoxy that obtains. And although the prophets appeal to the ancient Covenant because they sincerely believe in the historical marriage contract between God and His people, they also find in the Mosaic tradition a powerful rhetorical device for emphasizing the relevance and centrality of their own new codes, for these are to be seen as occupying in the regenerated lives of the people exactly the same place as the rigidified orthodoxy to which the people have come to pay at least lip service. And as this prophetic pattern is repeated, and the prophets themselves become aware that they are the inheritors of the pattern, a rich symbiosis develops between the progressive and conservative emphases.

Incidentally, it is in precisely this spirit that Shelley compares the revivifying function of poetry to the "trumpet of a prophecy" which, like the revivifying "clarion" of the spring blown over "the dreaming earth," is to usher in a new life both antithetical to the dead past and conditioned by it. (This interpretation might also explain the self-pitying tone which critics have often complained of in the "Ode," for rejection and persecution are part of the prophetic pattern.)[14] Similarly, in *The Prelude* Wordsworth refers to "Poets, even as Prophets, each with each / Connected in a mighty scheme of truth," where each has "his peculiar dower, a sense / By which he is enabled to perceive / Something unseen before" (XII.301–5, 1805 text). This passage aptly summarizes the prophetic paradox, the interdependence in the prophetic messages of original individuality and a sense of shared tradition.

These two examples of direct influence notwithstanding, I must emphasize that in my general comparison between the prophetic and epic traditions I am not suggesting influence but drawing an analogy. Like the Old Testament prophets, the great poets of literary epic have always shown in various ways both a dedication to the past and a desire to reject or transcend it. No great poet has ever written an epic without radically transforming it or giving to it new dimensions, and often that intention is explicitly declared. The pattern begins with Virgil himself, who is the key figure in

the evolution of the epic, though the specifically *critical* tradition
dominated by Aristotle's analysis of Homer has tended to obscure
the fact.[15] Despite his imitativeness, Virgil created something really new in the *Aeneid:* into meticulously careful reproductions
of the Homeric molds he poured moral and political messages
which are simply incompatible with the Homeric objectivity. Compared to the Homeric poems the *Aeneid* is individualistic—not,
of course, through eccentricity, but through suggesting at almost
every moment the presence of its author and his attitudes. And we
must remember that, in view of Aristotle's insistence that epic
poets efface themselves, and his praise for Homer as the only poet
who understood the importance of doing so, Virgil's relatively
personal manner is an important new departure. Virgil also departed from Homer through adopting a consciously ceremonial
verse style and through the high imaginative achievement by which
he made the action of his poem part of a vast and purposeful
rhythm of history.[16] Most important, in the light of later literary
epics, is Virgil's remarkable accomplishment in synthesizing the
two radically different works which he used as models. It was this
feat of virtuosity that launched the epic as a *tradition,* for the Virgilian synthesis enabled later ages to see the three great ancient
epics as a complex and not simply as a group of discrete, only
vaguely related works.

   All the Renaissance epic poets are like Virgil in rejecting or trying to transcend the themes and heroic ideals sanctioned by earlier
epic practice, including, of course, Virgil's own. They are at one
in believing that Christian themes surpass in dignity those of antiquity, and each poet flaunts the special advantages and general
superiority of his own subject. Camoëns, building on the tradition
of epic as a national poem, goes beyond his own Portugese theme
to a religious ideal and the celebration of a rapidly expanding
world. He claims to be describing a new kind of valor loftier than
that of the ancients; what, he asks aggressively, are the chimerical
dangers of Scylla and Charybdis compared with the real dangers
of rounding the Cape? The very geography of the modern world

was unknown to the ancients, he insists; the Atlantic and Indian oceans sailed by Vasco da Gama make the Mediterranean of epic legend seem like a mere pond.[17] Tasso, though he looks backward to proclaim the value of chivalry, advocates a united Christian Europe, an ideal that transcends the narrower nationalism of tradition. He also speaks condescendingly of the merely literary part of his task as the superficial means used to make his lofty theme more palatable.[18] Milton further swells the theme by treating, not a part of history or the vicissitudes of a culture, but the very origin and turning point of history, "things unattempted yet in prose or rhyme." His argument, he claims, is not less but more heroic than those of the *Iliad,* the *Odyssey,* the *Aeneid,* and the chivalric poems, despite the fact that he has rejected the themes of romance and war, "hitherto the onely Argument heroic deemd." Not for him the more paltry epic devices—games, shield, feast, "fabl'd Knights in Battels feignd."[19]

Yet, despite such bold departures from the sanctions of the past, the Renaissance epic poems are, like the *Aeneid,* full of textural similarities to their epic predecessors; indeed, some of these similarities go beyond even the strictest of rules. The poets observe the fine print in the letter of the law as markedly as they vaunt their independence in the larger matters of subject and heroic theme. One might argue that the descent into the underworld, far from being simply an imitation of earlier models, is a valuable aid in achieving the cosmic picture that the epic often attempts to create, and that the recurrent minor convention (let us call it the Dido-and-Aeneas convention) which sees woman as an obstacle to duty, a device that appears with varying emphases in all the great literary epics from Virgil on, is part of the pattern of heroic renunciation recognized by any culture whose values have risen above purely martial ones. Similarly, the standard epic view of futurity, whether in the underworld or on top of a mountain, can be explained by the tendency of epic to be etiological. And undoubtedly the flashback narrative which has its prototype in the *Odyssey* has certain technical advantages for the narrative poet.[20] But epic imi-

tativeness goes much farther than the adoption of large devices
and episodes like these, and much farther than in any other literary type. Imitation often seems to be an end in itself. Why else
should the hero almost invariably introduce his long flashback tale
with the rigid formula "What you ask me to relate is difficult to
tell, but I will do my best," or words to that effect? And so with
the other, almost comically familiar store of props and scenes:
bleeding trees, heavenly tempered shields and armor, challenges
to single combat, councils, nocturnal scouting expeditions, ship-
wrecks, games, scale images, hunting images, and a whole host of
minutely detailed verbal echoes often applied to contexts utterly
unlike the original settings. To read the great epics in succession
is like walking through a hall of mirrors. Imitative devices like
these, and not more general or formal traits, are the most dependable signs that a work is a candidate for the epic category, although
at least some of the larger patterns and traits will almost certainly
be present too. It is this seemingly compulsive imitativeness, of
course, that makes epic so vulnerable to parody, a fact which has
significance, as I shall presently try to show.

What we have, then, is the paradox of authors who are aggressively independent in their general purposes and imitative in details, large and small; this pattern prevails from Virgil on. But
the paradox is in fact not difficult to explain. For one thing, the
controversy and confusion which have reigned in epic theory, even
in the relatively orthodox neoclassic period, make imitativeness
the only dependable way to label a poem as epic. More important,
though, is the fact that epic is a tradition rather than a genre; it
operates through propagated family resemblances rather than in
obedience to more abstract laws. A boy conscious of his family
heritage will not try to isolate the essential and defining qualities
of his lineage, he will try to grow a mustache like his grandfather's.
And in much the same way the epic poet is conscious of the idio-
syncrasies of his lineage rather than, primarily, of formal criteria.
An epic is not so much a species as the offspring of a certain family line and is therefore best approached not through the generalizing principles of comparative anatomy but through its peculiar

genetic traits. Finally (if I may be permitted one more seeming paradox), the epic must imitate exactly because progressivism is part of its tradition. The new code which it promulgates is to be seen as moving into the same central position formerly occupied by the older and now superseded code. A fort has been taken, and the fact that it has changed hands will be more dramatically clear if the new banner is run up on the intact old flagstaff.

In the essays which follow this one an attempt is made to relate certain key Romantic poems to the epic tradition and to use this approach as a way of understanding the poems. My criteria for identifying an epic are clear by now, I hope, but perhaps it is advisable to sum them up, bearing in mind that we are discussing entries in the race, so to speak; in one key sense no work is an epic unless it is generally acknowledged to be one. But the epic tradition has usually been enlarged in retrospect rather than by immediate acclamation of new legitimate heirs, so that the seeming logical contradiction need not be a real one.

The most obvious requirement is a significant degree of imitativeness, the echoing of small epic details and of some of the larger patterns such as the ordeal-journey, the purposefulness of the action, the presence of supernatural agencies, and others which I have mentioned. In addition, we shall almost certainly expect to find illustrated a code of human behavior, of heroism. The more markedly such details and emphases are present in the poem, the truer its alignment with the epic tradition. Thus some works are more epic than others, a fact which is illustrated by the marginal status generally awarded *The Divine Comedy* and *The Faerie Queene*. This criterion also works negatively: the more numerous the patterns other than epic that are present in a poem, the less epic it is. For example, strict, elaborate allegory dilutes the epic effect; Dante and Spenser are again the obvious cases in point, and some formalist critics were uneasy about Milton's Sin and Death.[21] Apart from its brevity, one could make a case for *The Ancient Mariner* as an epic if there were not many other sources for the poem and several patterns in it which are far more assertive and make whatever epic impulse it may contain seem very minor. I hope to show that the poems discussed in this book have more serious claims to epic standing, though of course they are not all equally or exclusively indebted to the epic tradition.

III

The present study is not the first to acknowledge at least incidentally an epic strain in English Romanticism; nevertheless, the very idea of Romantic epic usually provokes skepticism.[22] The skepticism arises from three widely held beliefs about the eighteenth and nineteenth centuries. I should like to consider each of these beliefs and try to answer or at least neutralize them.

a) The first is simply the familiar caricature of the Romantics as conscious rebels against the literary forms consecrated by the past and therefore, *a fortiori*, rebels against the epic, that most venerable of forms. Admittedly the caricature has been refined and no longer passes current in the childishly simple guises of fifty years ago. There has even been a time when scholarship threatened to obscure the element of commonsense truth in the caricature by tracing one "Romantic" trait after another to the preceding age, in much the same way that modern Renaissance scholars have tended to incorporate that period into the Middle Ages. (The tendency is perhaps inherent in literary scholarship, since one can sometimes prove that a work is derivative but never that it is original.) But the old-fashioned caricature expresses some important if elementary truths and it therefore ought not to be allowed to die out completely. Fortunately, in very recent years there have been a number of books, such as Robert Langbaum's *The Poetry of Experience*, which have stressed once more the radical originality of the Romantic vision.[23]

That the Romantics were literary and extraliterary radicals need not mean that they disqualified themselves as epic poets. A number of points are relevant.

For one thing, the rejection of the past, as we have seen, is a serious convention in literary epic, both as a rhetorical device used to underscore the central importance of the poet's message and as a sincere expression of some form of progressivism. It remains true, however, that the Romantic poems most influenced by the epic often represent the more traditional and responsible pole of their authors' views. (Southey's *Joan of Arc* and Landor's *Gebir* are special cases.) It is a subtle and complex form of traditionalism, one which, like that of the Prophets, simultaneously appeals to traditional standards and provides a platform for what is new, but it is still traditionalism.[24] *Hyperion* is in all ways a more measured and deliberate statement than *Endymion; Don Juan* is less "romantic" (in a superficial sense) than *Manfred* or *The Corsair. The Revolt of Islam* cannot be called a moderate poem, but it is much closer to Shelley's later, intellectually disciplined poems than the extravagant *Queen Mab,* and more tolerant of the past. *The Prelude* is another special case, mainly because of its textual complications, but even in its earliest version it regards the values of the past with respect and often with awe.

As for the allegedly diminished prestige of epic in the early nineteenth century, the evidence is confusing. H. T. Swedenberg and Donald Foerster in their books on English epic theory compile a great deal of evidence that in the hundred years or so after 1750 critics became more and more tolerant in their definitions of *epic,* until the term had become almost meaningless and lost much of its former prestige.[25] But if we turn from criticism and epic theory to the poems actually written, we find that the first half of the nineteenth century saw the publication of a great many attempts by obscure poets at fairly traditional epic;[26] in practice if not in theory, and at the level of second- or third-rate literature at least, the age was one of epic revival. If the major Romantic poets were idol-smashers, there seem still to have been many worshipers at one old shrine.

There is nothing unusual about this kind of discrepancy between criticism and contemporary poetic practice. Poetry and criticism are seldom in phase with each other, since critics habitually enshrine as a new orthodoxy the strategic exaggerations which the criticism written by poets themselves had originally promulgated decades earlier with the half-conscious intention of fostering a new kind of poetry. But poets are seldom so truly antipathetic to the past as their own tendentious criticism suggests. (T. S. Eliot has made a similar point in his essay "The Music of Poetry.") Such a pattern is clear in the early nineteenth century. Long after Wordsworth's poetry had re-assimilated much of what he had condemned in the eighteenth-century style and Keats had learned from Dryden how to write a couplet, critics were still rejoicing in their liberation, making a point of throwing off neoclassical fetters which had long since ceased to bind most poets or to inspire their opposition.

But if this discrepancy between poetic practice and critical theory is perennial in literature as a whole, it is especially marked where epic is concerned. For neoclassic epic theory, which is sometimes assumed rather vaguely to have been an accurate reflection of a contemporary great age of epic, was surprisingly self-sustaining and independent of the works it purported to describe. In this area as in so many others, modern critics who mourn the traditions allegedly undermined by the Romantics ought to distinguish between traditions that had been alive continuously for five, ten, or fifteen hundred years and those that dated back a century and a half. Compared with the history of epic poetry itself, neoclassic epic theory was in 1800 an achievement of relatively recent years. In England, at least, it had never been more than a loose consensus springing largely from Le Bossu's treatise and flourishing for a century or so after the first translation of that work into English in the last quarter of the seventeenth century. Shortly before that event Milton called the Book of Job an epic, and Romantic permissiveness could hardly go further than that. This is embarrassingly elementary literary history, but to repeat such facts seems useful in view of the tendency even among broadminded epic theorists to think half-guiltily of the last century or two as having introduced an unprecedented looseness into thinking about the

epic. There are tenable arguments for preferring neoclassic literature and literary theory to Romantic art and thought, but to make
that decision on the general grounds of "traditionalism" is at best
an equivocation.

It is true that the Augustans leaned heavily on Aristotle, a hoary
enough authority, and on Horace. But neither of these two presents a really coherent epic theory or even says very much about
the epic at all. Aristotle repeatedly establishes criteria for the epic
which by his own admission he bases exclusively on the two Homeric epics, choosing to regard the usual practice of poets as aber-
ration. At least once he prescribes practice that is apparently
founded on no precedent at all, when he recommends that the
epic "be shorter than the old epics, and about as long as the series
of tragedies offered for one hearing."[27] (The split between epic
theory and epic practice is this old.) In addition, Aristotle's attitude toward the epic is at times almost petulant; although he admits the unique greatness of Homer, he seems to think of epic in
general as an old-fashioned form whose main achievement was to
prepare the way for the greater art form of tragedy.[28] Aristotle's
own theory bristles with contradictions or at least contradictory
emphases, a fact that is borne out by the many disagreements
among nominally Aristotelian neoclassic critics. Thus the "traditional" definitions of epic prevalent in the neoclassic period did
not represent a live tradition so much as a revival of a long-lapsed
doctrine which even in its own day had been inconsistent and out
of touch with epic practice. Furthermore, although the age of Dryden and Pope produced great translations by those poets of the
classical epics, the consensus which existed about the epic did not
produce any actual epics of more than passing interest.

It therefore seems illogical to deny the possibility of Romantic
epics on such grounds as we have been considering. The definitive
epics being as few, varied, and individual as they are, the poet
who aims to write a new epic tends not to generalize about form
or to be affected by the generalizations of his contemporaries; he
is more likely to be thinking (with the mixed feelings previ-

ously noted) of those particular poets who for him represent his
epic ancestry. Milton described his plans for an epic not so much
in terms of theory as of models: the *Iliad,* the *Odyssey,* the
Aeneid, Jerusalem Delivered, the Book of Job, and the Spenserian
chivalric poem, leaving open the question of whether to follow
the "rules of Aristotle" or "nature" as tactfully as Raphael leaves
open the question of heavenly motions.[29] In the same way, Spenser, who in view of his ethical Aristotelianism might be expected
to have made a gesture toward Aristotle's epic theory, defines his
literary context for the *Faerie Queene* by simply citing Homer,
Virgil, Ariosto, and Tasso.[30]

   b) A second reason alleged for the supposed disappearance of
epic in the Romantic age is the decline of the old heroic ideal.
Certainly heroism is crucial to any discussion of the epic; it is one
of the very few subjects central in both epic theory and practice.
Indeed, if we did not have to consider the *Odyssey,* which is
anomalous in this respect as in so many others, we could say that
no poem can be an epic unless it presents a portrait, either com-
posite or individual, express or implied, of the perfect man.
(Odysseus is admirable, of course, but it is hard today to see him
as what many neoclassic theorists considered him, an ideal portrait.) But when we examine the fortunes of heroism in the Romantic age we become aware of another problem in definition.
For *heroism,* like the word *man* itself, can mean more than one
thing. One meaning stresses virility; by this criterion the hero
need not be moral but must be bold, strong, extroverted.[31] The
Romantics are often accused of weakening or destroying this tradition of heroism through their concern with introversion and
with men in humble or bourgeois stations. The other meaning is
almost the exact opposite; here heroism is the quality of high and
essential humanity—in the etymological sense, "kindness." Morality is obviously relevant to this definition. But here too the Romantics are charged with betraying their past, either through an
amoral championing of experience as a good in itself or through

the substitution of a relativistic inner light for the older view of conduct and conscience based on right reason.[32]

As generalizations the two charges of antiheroism brought against the Romantics tend to cancel each other out. But this summary answer is not enough, for it is possible that the age was inconsistent and further possible for the heroic tradition to have been destroyed, like a man being quartered, by forces pulling in different directions. In any case, the charges of antiheroism are not capricious; some of the greatest Romantic poems are clearly cognizant of these two dangers to the heroic ideal and concerned with circumventing them. In fact, it is primarily because they saw the problem as their detractors do that the Romantics used the epic form or epic elements so seriously, for the relationship of modern heroism to older versions of it could best be shown by pouring the new wine into old bottles.

Since this essay is intended to clear ground and not primarily to advance a general thesis about Romanticism, detailed discussion or defense of the various Romantic codes of heroism must await the later essays which deal with individual poems. But a few preliminary points can be made.

The objection that the Romantics sentimentalized heroism by idealizing the cozy and the bourgeois or by turning it inward makes two assumptions: that traditional heroism had always been a fairly simple code of active extroversion, and that heroic magnanimity is inconsistent with a humble or outwardly unadventurous life. These assumptions are different, but in practice they tend to be found together and to blend into each other. The Romantics themselves did not confuse the two; indeed, they made important distinctions between them and differed among themselves in the conclusions drawn. Byron, for example, though he often attacked the very concept itself of heroism, identified it more readily than Wordsworth with the code of aristocratic virility and was therefore skeptical about the possibility of heroism in his own unheroic age. But both men agreed that, whatever heroism may be, it must connote energy and expansiveness; Wordsworth believed that the inner life of the imagination was the field of true heroism, but no more than Byron or anyone else did he equate heroic qualities with drab quietism or the life of the marketplace. Except in relatively minor poets like Southey, the heroic code illustrated in the Romantic epics and near-epics is never simple sentimentalism.

In addition, none of the great Romantics interpreted the history of heroism so simply as do certain of their critics. In *Don Juan* Byron asserts that heroism was almost as much a sham in the past as it is in the age of Castlereagh. Moreover, the history of literary epic from Virgil on shows a clear trend toward the softening of the epic hero. The main obstacle in the way of Aeneas is Turnus, but almost as dangerous to his imperial enterprise is the love which he indulges for Dido. And, while Adam's sin is essentially disobedience, at the crucial moment it takes the form of uxoriousness. (One of the most interesting things about the Romantic epics is their obsession with the Dido-and-Aeneas convention; even in earlier epics, however, the theme of temptation by woman had been very important.) In general, the Romantics were able to use the epic and many of its conventions, despite distrust of literary conventionalism, because their forerunners had made the criticism and refinement of earlier heroic values an integral part of the epic formula. The Romantics, like Milton, saw themselves as having inherited a tradition of sporadic moral progress.

The other objection to the Romantic versions of heroism, that they reject older moral standards for more personal or relative ones, carries us to the limits of literary criticism and perhaps beyond them, but the criticism is relevant, since the epic has never been simply a literary form. Perhaps the only general answer that can be made to the charge is that in most of the great Romantic poems molded significantly by epic pressures the religious or moral emphasis is central; the poets recognized the relevance of theology, ethics, and spiritual ideals, often choosing explicitly religious settings, subjects, or guiding metaphors. Whatever may be true of their thought in general, in their epic attempts the Romantics were seldom simply naturalists or psychologists in the sense that would justify the charge I am trying to prove false. It is true that these poems present visions that are, in a sense, highly personal, but the values preached are not primarily relativistic. (Byron is an exception.) On the contrary, the Romantics usually preach values or assert standards which are meant to be applicable to man in general or in the lives of their contemporaries and immediate followers. Most of them thought, like Milton, that the epic should be doctrinal and exemplary to a nation. That their religious messages were to at least some extent heterodox can scarcely be doubted (though the same can be said of Milton and Pope), yet none of the major writers thought of his epic message as an entire break with the past. They generally tried to diagnose and cure moral or spiritual diseases of their time, and this urgent sense that something needs to be done is one of the things that connect the Romantics most clearly with the epic poets of earlier ages.

c) There remains to be considered one other source of resistance to the notion of Romantic epic: the belief that the increasing popularity of the novel drove epic from the field. To some extent this argument is simply historical, factual: one surveys the last two centuries, finds a paucity of epics and an abundance of novels, and draws the appropriate *propter hoc* conclusion. Seen in this light, the argument can be answered best by adducing contrary facts, and that is one aim of the following chapters in this book. One general fact needs emphasizing, however: there has never been a time when epics were written in great numbers. No age has thought of the epic casually, as part of its familiar literary furniture; even unsuccessful epics have been in some way attempts at the extraordinary. (Interestingly enough, in *English Bards and Scotch Reviewers* Byron charges the writers of his day with having violated this sacred tradition; formerly "An Epic scarce ten centuries could claim" and was "The single wonder of a thousand years," but "Not so with us" —ll. 189–99.) Certainly epics have never been as common as novels have been in the last two cen-

turies. In short, the decline in the number of epics is at least partly
an illusion.

Often, though, the argument goes deeper; it assumes that both
epic and the novel are genres and that, while they are dissimilar
in a few crucial matters such as the use of verse and prose, the
two forms are closely enough related so that the creative energies
once expended on epic have come to flow more naturally into the
novel, as a stream is diverted by being directed into a more acces-
sible, lower-lying channel.

A fairly obvious answer can be made to this argument: it is entirely possible for one art form to encroach on another without
making the older one completely and immediately obsolete, just
as photography has largely but far from completely displaced portrait painting. A more subtle weakness in the argument is its false
assumption that the epic impulse is primarily a formal one and not
the response to an ancestry. (That the novel itself is a genre is, of
course, highly debatable.[33]) The argument assumes that the author
of epic defines his task in terms of epic rules or the static characteristics of the form. This is true only in a very limited way. For
example, both the epic and the novel are long works, and it has
not been uncommon for authors contemplating either form to
start with the generalized desire, independent of a particular
theme, to do something big. But for the standard epic poets this
aspiration has always involved much more than length, more even
than supreme literary quality. Besides these the great poets of literary epic have aimed at grandeur of theme and subject; they have
tried to be doctrinal and exemplary to a nation, to mark milestones
in the progress of human values and ideals, and usually to locate
human life in a cosmic continuum. At the same time the epic poets
have tried to assert their continuity with the past and the connection of new values with old ones by copying with some fidelity
the traditional settings of earlier works.

There is no theoretical reason why a long prose work should be
incapable of aligning itself with the epic tradition in just these
ways, though in fact novelists have been far more preoccupied

with formal innovation than with imitativeness. Perhaps a good case could be made for *Ulysses* as a work in the true epic tradition. I do not think a good case can be made for *Joseph Andrews* or *Tom Jones* or the other novels which derive from the realistic tradition of the eighteenth century.

The definitive argument for the novel as epic is, of course, Fielding's own theory as outlined in the Preface to *Joseph Andrews* and in *Tom Jones*. If it were not for these theoretical statements I doubt that critics or other readers would ever have labeled either novel as epic except occasionally, briefly, and whimsically. Only on technical grounds does either assert its place in epic history. And apart from the explicit theories they propound, the whole tenor of the two novels is that the traditional epic is dead and that in its place a new form is necessary. *Joseph Andrews* is intended to illustrate an existent form, but a rare and almost unprecedented one, one "hitherto unattempted in our language."[34] This claim is fundamentally different from the traditional claim of epic poets to novelty, for example Milton's boast that he will deal with "things unattempted yet in prose or rhyme"; Milton, like the other true epic poets, is declaring the superiority of his subject, not claiming in effect to usher in a new genre. The epic poet seldom states generic rules or delimits formal critical categories as Fielding does, for the epic poet must use or implicitly claim to use an old form, a tradition that everyone already understands, so that the new values he preaches will stand out the more boldly. Like Milton and Spenser, he typically appeals not to rules but to living precedents.

The most notable precedent cited by Fielding is a work whose status is entirely theoretical—Homer's *Margites,* a lost work and therefore not part of any live tradition except that of critical theory, in which it enjoys an abstract and honorific place because of Aristotle's citation of it as a comic epic. No bit of evidence could better illustrate the independence of the traditions of epic practice and epic theory and the fact that Fielding's novels take their departure not from the practical tradition but from the theoretical.

Tom Jones is indeed a serious work, but it is not serious in the way that traditional epic usually is. The reminiscences of epic in *Tom Jones* are not used to place the book in a long and honorable tradition, but rather to reject the tradition as outmoded. They are part of the pleasantry, "similes, descriptions, . . . and poetical embellishments," which Fielding sweeps away when the approach of his ending dictates that he become "plain and serious" (IV, i; XVIII, i). They are virtually never used by him except in a jesting tone which sometimes becomes a sneer. When Milton derides such trappings he does so in order to assert the superiority of his own *theme* to the superseded ones of romance and war, but in fact he uses many of the devices he sneers at, and uses them seriously. Fielding is rejecting the epic form itself, along with the whole approach to human conduct which the epic and especially its theory have consecrated.

Tom Jones, when it is not dealing directly with its serious theme of moral education, sets off that theme by the use of a mock-epic technique whose purpose is not to exalt our imaginations but to bring us down to earth. The main action of the book has virtually nothing to do with epic, although for the sake of emphasis Fielding creates a mock-epic framework.

The epic cannot be parodied simply through the exaggerated use of its recurrent devices, for one can hardly go farther than the serious epics have themselves gone in the way of imitation. Parody of epic can arise only from the substitution of an incongruous version of heroism for the usual lofty one; once this substitution is made the epic devices begin to appear ludicrous and the joke becomes one (usually playful) at the expense of the epic itself. True epic does the opposite; it imitates (though it sometimes claims not to) in order to show that the old values have yielded to even loftier ones through legitimate succession. Fielding's purpose is to deflate false idealism, to attack unrealistic standards of conduct which have been divorced from the gritty facts of human nature. Thus his clear-eyed concern with the earthly realities is emphasized by his undermining of the lofty heroic ideal, and more especially of the oversimplified versions of heroism encouraged by idealizing epic theoreticians. Hence Fielding's delight in giving naturalistic explanations where, he hints, the reader may be expecting the supernatural, his habit of translating inflated epic phrases into commonplace prose, his explicit attack on supernatural machinery and his suggestion that Homer was burlesquing the superstitions current in his day (VIII, i). Hence too Fielding's assertion in the Preface to *Joseph Andrews* that the comic prose epic should avoid concentrating on serious vice and take as its subject the comic, the ridiculous, the affected. The authority for *Tom Jones* is the "vast authentic Doomsday-Book of Nature" (IX, i). In short, Fielding's novels are moral rather than spiritual; they deal with life in the world, with man seen in the framework of society and not, as in the true epic, man seen through the long vistas which lead to numinous mystery or the dim recesses of time. Fielding's attack on epic machinery is central to an understanding of his naturalistic view of literature and morality. When Tom and Partridge encounter the gypsies in the barn Fielding alludes to the incident in the *Aeneid* where Aeneas gazes with awe at the pictures in Dido's temple and broods tearfully over the mystery of universal human mortality.[35] This sense of mystery is parodied in the trembling cowardice of Partridge, and the gypsies, whose natural humanity has been emphasized by his mistake, become the occasion for a treatise on practical government and natural virtue.

The novel has almost always gone this naturalist way rather than the supernaturalist one familiar in epic. There is no reason why this must be so, at least no formal reason, and indeed not all novels are naturalistic or content with social reality as the ultimate and unquestioned framework for the action. But surely it is true that the novels in the main stream of literature over the last two centuries have limited their horizons in just this way and have avoided the supernatural and the final spiritual questions. Like Fielding himself, novelists may be obsessed with morality, but that is an entirely different thing. And what we are concerned with here is not what the novel must be or has always been, but rather what it has generally been in historical fact, for the argument that novels have replaced epics rests largely on assumptions about the general effect the novel has had. A few novels, like *Moby Dick,* have been centrally concerned with spiritual values and the place of human life in the cosmos. But such works are exceptions, and to use them to show where the epic impulse has gone is to equivocate, since some of them, like *Moby Dick,* have been described as epics. The more dominant, naturalistic approach in the novel is well illustrated in *War and Peace;* there Tolstoy, after giving us what is perhaps the most naturalistically convincing picture of life ever achieved, treats the more mysterious question of individual man's relationship to forces beyond his control in the well-insulated "Second Epilogue," an essay in which Tolstoy makes it clear that he has abandoned the novelist's proper role for that of philosopher and historical theoretician. It is difficult, then, to see most novels as organically nourished by that complex of prophetic impulses and conventions that we call the epic tradition. If the epic line is analogous to that of the Prophets, the novel is loosely analogous to the levelheaded Biblical wisdom books.

IV

I repeat that, except for parts of the chapter on Southey and Landor, what follows in this book is not primarily intended to provide evidence for the generalizations hazarded in this introductory chapter. I am mainly interested in the individual works themselves. But I have thought it advisable to describe my general approach to epic so that the reader may understand my assumptions and be spared in later chapters long and digressive essays in epic theory. Although my approach to epic is different from that of most critics and theorists, I have tried to be faithful to readers' unrationalized sense of what the epic is and of the way it works. In this respect, it seems to me, the present approach is conservative and traditional.

A similar assumption—that readers know what an epic is without necessarily having tried to define it—has been made by the authors of the standard literary epics and by those Romantic poets who wrote epics or poems strongly conditioned by epic patterns. And because of the curious mechanics of the epic tradition the Romantics were able to express their deeply personal views and at the same time generalize about human life and the place of their own age in the continuum of history. This paradox, of extreme individualism in combination with extreme group-consciousness, has long been recognized as symptomatic of Romanticism and of nineteenth-century attitudes in general. But the same paradox is an important part of the epic tradition, which generates one of the most flexible and at the same time one of the most rigidly patterned of literary types. In its adaptability to a wide variety of cultural climates and circumstances the epic is one of the marvels of literary history, a fact that may cheer somewhat those critics who, like Aristotle himself, are inclined to regard it as an obsolescent or superseded form.

Two: "EPOMANIA"
SOUTHEY AND LANDOR

ROBERT Southey is representative of a long line of literary professionals which includes such men as Michael Drayton among the Elizabethans and Edmund Wilson in our own day. Such men are typically both creators and, on a high level, literary journeymen, both artists and trade professionals. As a result, they are in unusually close touch with the literary currents of their respective ages and are sensitive indicators of the details of changing tastes and ideas, which at the same time they reflect, influence, and propagate. Southey, in particular, is a valuable barometer because he reflects not only the literary movements of his day but political changes as well. Sometimes both areas are mirrored in the same work, and this is especially true of his three epics. *Madoc* (published in 1805), the second of the three, is symptomatic of contemporary interest in the Americas and of Southey's own preoccupation with the Pantisocratic experiment. *Roderick* (1814), the last, is relevant to the Peninsular campaign. The most striking example is Southey's earliest epic, *Joan of Arc* (1796), which, like Walter Savage Landor's nearly contemporary and startlingly similar poem *Gebir,* typifies an important strain of political radicalism in the 1790's.

My concern here is with *Gebir* and *Joan,* especially the latter, for they illuminate with unusual clarity, both positively and in their limitations, the approach to epic which is typical of greater, standard epic poets. *Gebir* and *Joan* go the way of the epic, but not all the way, and to see how and why they renounce the path is instructive. Especially interesting is the shrill rebelliousness the two poems express toward the past and the epic-heroic tradition. Though not necessarily the better poem, *Joan* is the longer, more clearly epic, more historically important of the two, and it there-

30

fore deserves to be seen against the background of Southey's epic approach in general. Moreover, a general glance at Southey's epics and other long narrative poems can be justified by the merit of the poems themselves. Southey's poetry is not great, but neither is it the unreadable stuff that a sketchy critical tradition has labeled it. Furthermore, Southey's approach to narrative and epic poetry is in many ways the ground bass on which his greater contemporaries were to build their modern harmonies.

To write epics was Southey's chief ambition during the first, more poetically prolific, half of his life. This zealously cherished goal, combined with his tendencies toward literary libertarianism, make Southey a good exemplar of the paradox mentioned earlier as common to almost all poets seriously interested in the epic, especially those greater ones whose works have served to define the tradition. In Southey's rough notes for *Madoc* we find the following typical comment: "The religious rites before their embarkation described. On such a departure both V. Flaccus and Camoens have written. That, however, matters not."[1] In this note Southey makes clear what is almost always obvious in his epic poems and in his discussions of them: that he is highly conscious of the minutiae of epic tradition even when he is not deliberately following it. With regard to literary traditionalism in general Southey sometimes tried to assume an air of Olympian superiority to the whole issue, as in an important letter he wrote to Landor a few weeks after Landor had offered to be Southey's financial patron in his epic and narrative efforts. Referring to his romance *The Curse of Kehama*, Southey writes, with his characteristic inflatedness:

I will use such materials as have stood the test; those materials are the same in all languages, and we know what they are. With respect to meter it is otherwise: there we must look to English only. . . . The mass of mankind hate innovation: they hate to unlearn what they have learned wrong, and they hate to confess their ignorance by submitting to learn anything right. I would tread in the beaten road rather than get among thorns by turning out of it; but the beaten road will not take me where I want to go.[2]

This kind of measured acceptance of the claims of both past and present is also evident in certain statements by Southey wherein he tries to solve the problem by appealing to a standard of great poetry which is applicable in any age and based on immutable esthetic principles. Like several of the greater Romantic poets, he insists that his literary radicalism is a re-affirmation of a traditional standard older and more genuine than neoclassic convention and critical fiat. "As for my contempt of the received rules of poetry, I hold the same rules which Shakespeare, Spencer [sic], and Milton held before me, and desire to be judged by those rules; nor have I proceeded upon any principle of taste which is not to be found in all the great masters of the art of every age and country wherein the art has been understood."[3] Here Southey comes close to the position that rules are not isolable from past literature, that they inhere in the individual works which comprise tradition.

But this judicious balance, and the attempt to reconcile the old and the new by resorting to a *ratio aeternitatis,* are the exception rather than the rule in Southey's discussions of literary conservatism. He was an energetic, outspoken man, and, although he is not thoroughly consistent or predictable in his opinions, he is usually on one side of the fence. Except in his youth, in such upstart manifestoes as the Preface to *Joan of Arc,* his literary theorizing is generally moderate, but also distinctly progressive. He continued to believe, though somewhat equivocally, in the general progress of the world, even after he had become in politics and religion a pillar of the reactionary Establishment,[4] and although Byron was in a sense right when he indirectly sneered at the laureate who "praised the present, and abused the past, / Reversing the good custom of old days,"[5] the implication of insincerity is not entirely justified; homely proto-Victorian idealist that he was, Southey could see the world as going to the dogs and at the same time really believe that God and history were in beneficent league with each other. Certainly Southey's confidence in the present carried

over into the realm of literature. He once rebuked his good friend
Grosvenor Bedford vigorously for Bedford's low estimate of modern poetry, and originality in language was a cardinal principle
in Southey's literary program: "A writer of original genius must
wield language at his will. The syntax must bend to him. He must
sometimes create—who else are the makers of language?"[6]

He was also vigorous in defending the originality of his own
poetry. He claimed, for instance, to have added notes to *Thalaba*
in order to distinguish clearly, for the benefit of the *Edinburgh*
reviewers, between his source material and the original parts of
his story, which he insisted were the best and most striking parts.[7]
While writing this poem, a romance, he had pointed out that by its
use of "machinery" the work would demonstrate that his rejection
of machinery in *epic* poems was not due to lack of ability.[8] And
a series of entries in his *Common-Place Book* shows Southey as first
planning to use in *Madoc* an episode in which ships are burned and
then deciding to eliminate the incident because it "would be too
like other poems."[9]

But Southey's conscious modernism in literature and his desire
to be original are considerably tempered by his dedication to the
epic. The classical epic and the Renaissance epics and romances
molded his literary ambitions and indeed his convictions about the
nature of literary fame. Almost from the time, early in life, when
he first read the great epics, his impulse to compose such poems
himself continued to exist as an abstract ideal independent of his
changing ideas and the merit of particular subjects. The traditional
associations which have accumulated to form the myth of the epic
poet made a strong appeal to Southey. At the outset of his career
as a serious epic poet he expressed in a letter to his friend H. W.
Bedford a fairly orthodox though unusually permissive canon
of epic poets and also the feeling for the idealized glories of the
past which is common to virtually all the great epic poets. Milton
stands first, "as much from the singularity of the subject as the excellence of the diction." The ancient epic poets are Homer, Virgil,
Lucan, Statius, S. Italicus, and V. Flaccus. The modern poets men-

tioned are (besides Milton) Ariosto, Tasso, Camoëns, Voltaire, and "our own immortal Spenser"; at this stage of his life Southey confesses ignorance of "the other Italian authors in this line, and the Spanish ones." (Once more a tradition is identified with its exemplars rather than with rules.) He becomes rhapsodic over the heroic age of ancient Greece celebrated in Glover's *Leonidas* and mourns the contemptible state to which modern Greece has fallen.[10]

Southey's literary ambitiousness is usually expressed in a bravura tone which may be attributable to his worship of Milton. "Pour out your mind in a great poem," he counsels Landor, for (Southey continues) the reputation of kings and conquerors is perishable, while the greatness of the poet will endure as long as the language in which he writes.[11] On the other hand, poetic greatness is not to be measured by popularity. Late in life he was to declare in Miltonic phrasing that in composing *Madoc* he had been bent "upon following my own sense of propriety, and thereby obtaining the approbation of that fit audience, which, being contented that it should be few, I was sure to find."[12] Southey prided himself on what he wrongly considered his superiority to temporary fashions in literature, and the fewness of a poet's admirers he made a positive criterion of greatness. It is this criterion which explains Southey's unshakable confidence in the ultimate triumph of his long poems, even in the face of public indifference, a bit of presumption for which Byron ridiculed him mercilessly.[13]

When he came to write epic poems Southey accepted much of the epic tradition, and in a spirit of conservatism. Except in one work, where as we shall see he deliberately chose to see epic as symptomatic of a benighted old regime and its values, he never thought of epic as having been rendered obsolete or irrelevant by the new preoccupations of his own era; apart from a certain sentimental tone and a few "modern" mannerisms of style and diction, Southey's epics might well have been written a hundred years earlier. Characteristically, he was angered by the habit of lumping the classics together as a standard—like many men of his age, he preferred Greek to Roman literature and the simplicity of Homer to Virgilian artifice—but more than once he described his taste as essentially classical.[14] He also liked to invite critical comparison of his poetry with that of his great epic predecessors.[15]

It is clear from Southey's letters and notebooks that he had an epic formula, one based on both a familiarity with older epics and critical theory. One of the most debated questions in neoclassic epic theory concerned the function of supernatural agencies in the epic; generally they were considered essential, but some critics rejected them.[16] Southey's views on the subject show the same interest in the question and the same inconsistency. Though he somewhat rebelliously claimed to spurn the use of machinery in his first epic, *Joan of Arc,* he made use of it in *Madoc,* though even here, he said, it was not the foundation of the poem, "but, as usual in what are called epic poems, only incidentally connected with it."[17] That he thought of machinery as being only incidental in the epic lends greater significance to his discussion of it; clearly it was not for him essential to the spirit, message, or structure of the poem, but was one of several devices whose function was to identify the poem as an epic. Other evidence that Southey worked in terms of an epic stereotype is provided by the poet's early sketch for *Roderick* in which he mentions that the machinery of the poem will be Catholicism and that the cave of Toledo will be useful for an enchantment scene, Cavadonga for "the battle."[18] It is also revealing that, although the essential heroism in Southey's epics is not simply martial, they all focus on scenes of war.

Southey also accepted fairly unself-consciously certain more general marks of epic both illustrated in the models and emphasized in critical theory. One is the national emphasis. *Joan, Madoc,* and *Roderick* are all stories involving the effort of a people to establish itself in freedom or to rid itself of tyranny.[19] The collective nature of the effort is always heavily underlined. And, although Southey never wrote an epic glorifying the English, he believed that such a subject, if a good one could be found, would be the most proper one for epic treatment by him.[20] That an epic should have local roots was for Southey another mark against Virgil, in whose work, Southey claimed, manners "are of no time and no country."[21] On the other hand, Southey was Virgilian enough in his insistence that the action of an epic be, in the literal sense, consequential; he declared that the "indispensable requisite . . . in a subject for me is, that the end—the ultimate end—must be worthy of the means."[22] Moreover, though all three of Southey's epics are topically relevant to contemporary events or ideas, all conform to critical prescript by being set in the relatively distant past.[23]

Southey's epic conscience, his solemn belief that the epic ought to have high seriousness and observe an old-fashioned and stately decorum, is reflected in the careful distinction he generally made between his three genuine epics and his romances—*Thalaba* and *The Curse of Kehama.* To lump all these poems together under the general heading of epics, as is sometimes done,[24] is to lose sight of the more conservative approach which Southey generally adopts in his true epics. At times he used the word *epic* in a rather loose way,[25] and, as we have seen, he could place Ariosto in the same category with Tasso and Camoëns. But almost always Southey distinguished scrupulously between his own epics and romances. Most neoclassical epic theorists had granted fabulous material a place in the epic, though often uneasily; they had, after all, Aristotle's sanction for admitting probable impossibilities.[26] But on this score Southey is often more royalist than the king, for his epics, unlike his romances, are basically naturalistic, despite their exoticism. The romance, Southey claimed, might dispense with "epic laws." Furthermore, romance had the prerogative of digression, and loose construction he seems to have accepted as almost the definitive mark of the form.[27] In such attitudes Southey shows himself to be the heir of countless critical discussions of epic unity and the function of "episode."[28]

Another important mark of the distinction Southey made between his epics and his romances was their versification. The epics were to be written in blank verse, the romances in a less pure, more bizarre strain. He seems to have thought of blank verse as a perspicuous medium to be used when the inherent grandeur of a subject was to be allowed to shine through the verse without distortion—in other words, when the poet was attempting the sublime, a quality which critics of the preceding age had often linked with simplicity.[29] On the other hand, the irregular meters of *Thalaba* and *Kehama* were respectively designated "the *Arabesque* ornament of an Arabian tale" and "French cookery, which pleases . . . diseased and pampered palates, when they are not healthy enough to relish the flavour of beef & mutton."[30] *Roderick,* for example, was to be written in blank verse, since "where the whole interest is to be derived from human character and the inherent dignity of the story, I will not run the hazard of enfeebling the finer parts for the sake of embellishing the weaker ones."[31] Southey's avoidance of blank verse in *Thalaba* and *Kehama* was, in fact, a kind of protection for the true epics; the distinction between blank verse and the meters used in his romances was to mark outwardly the superior dignity and loftier intentions of the epics.[32]

Southey considered his epics more important than his romances,[33] but the distinction between the two forms is not the simple distinction between the serious and the frivolous. The romances belong to a comprehensive plan whose value is independent of the individual subjects of the poems, the plan which Southey conceived during his school days of illustrating the various mythologies of the world in a series of narrative poems.[34] The plan is primarily educational and has something of the quality of a tour de force, like playing a number of themes in the same musical style. The greater importance of the epics is a literary rather than a moral distinction. The romances, in fact, are more forthrightly didactic; they are closer to Spenser than to Ariosto, and Southey sometimes thought of them in allegorical terms. Recorded in the *Common-Place Book* is the note "Cannot the Dom Danael [in *Thalaba*] be made to allegorize those systems that make the misery of mankind?" and in one of his letters he wrote, "My next mythological poem, should I ever write another, would be founded upon the system of Zoroaster. I should represent the chief personage as persecuted by the evil powers, and make every calamity they brought

upon him the means of evolving some virtue, which would never
else have been called into action." The aim of this projected poem
was "that the fables of false religion may be made subservient to
the true, by exalting and strengthening Christian feelings."[35] The
grand plan of a series of didactic tales is another link between
Spenser and Southey.

The importance of *Thalaba* and *Kehama* is qualified by their being installments in a plan whose general documentary value meant
more to Southey than any of the component parts; individually
the romances are in many ways virtuoso entertainments. Yet their
strong moral emphasis is an important link between them and
Southey's epics. All of Southey's long poems contain the same
central moral idea—the confidence in Faith, the self-reliance
which scorns external events as by their nature foreign to the soul
and unable to affect it in any important way. The romances differ
from the epics, however, in the way they express this moral. To
the extent that the epics are moral (a large extent), they are so in
an exemplary way; their purpose is to present, not lessons, but
images, of heroism. This fact probably explains their more naturalistic approach. The romances, though not true allegories, have
something of the artificial, masquelike quality of allegory. The
actions of the heroes—Thalaba's destruction of the evil Domdan-
iel, the overthrow of Kehama and his enchantments—are projec-
tions on a thoroughly fanciful supernatural plane of the values
which Southey believes in. The immediate application of these values is not spelled out; they are abstract, like the cardinal virtues.[36]
The romances do not sound rallying-cries; they preach sermons.
Their values are meant to be relevant to life, but the reader must
generalize an abstract moral from the exotic tale and then re-in-
terpret and apply the moral in familiar human terms. Like typical
allegory, Southey's romances operate on two levels, that of narrative action and that of ideals. But Southey inverts the usual relationship of these levels; the narrative vehicle is a supernatural,
wildly fabulous tale, while the underlying message is moral—usually, in fact, domestic. The emphasis on domestic values is one of

the most characteristic strains in Southey, and it can be illustrated by comparing his didactic method with, say, Spenser's. For Spenser, didactic allegory provided imaginative release, enabling him to explore the delights of this world and thereby to dramatize through the theme of carnal temptation the conflict between good and evil. But Southey seldom mentions the delights of the flesh without something like a shudder. "Upon amatory poems," he once wrote, "a general condemnation may be past."[37] In his romances, at least, there is no such sense of the power of sensuality as Tasso and Spenser use to dramatize the heroism of virtue. In Southey vice is conquered with regularity and supreme ease.

There is an important statement by Southey which indicates his basic moral intention in *Thalaba* and points toward his more sentimental notion of heroism, both in his romances and his epics. "It would be well," he writes, "to make Thamama's [that is, Thalaba's] most painful obstacles arise from those domestic feelings which in another would be virtue."[38] Here, as he does in *Joan* and as Landor does in *Gebir,* Southey introduces the kind of conflict which runs back through all the definitive literary epics—the conflict between duty and happiness. But, as both his statement and his poems indicate, he substitutes domestic contentment for voluptuous pleasure as the alternative to duty, instead of posing the problem in the familiar form of duty versus carnality. In *Joan* this modification of the traditional conflict serves a functional purpose, since there the peace of domesticity contrasts with the horror of war and therefore emphasizes that horror. But in *Thalaba* the new version of the old struggle is less useful; here the conflict is a typically puritan one, a conflict between two kinds of righteousness, one easy and pleasant, the other stern and bitter. Southey's abhorrence of sensuality prevents him from posing the problem in the traditional way, even in a semi-allegorical romance where the pleasures of the flesh could be used to best symbolic advantage.

In one way or another almost every important Romantic poet attempts to invert or otherwise modify the Dido-and-Aeneas convention—Wordsworth, in *The Prelude,* by using a metaphor of

enchantment and seduction to dramatize the threat to his imaginative growth posed by revolutionary rationalism; Shelley, in *The
Revolt of Islam,* by pointedly interrupting a description of the pu-
trefaction following a battle with a defiant scene of idealized eroti-
cism which dramatizes the evil of war; Byron, in *Don Juan,* by
casting his unheroic hero as a willingly passive dallier, an Odysseus repeatedly content with his Calypso of the moment.

Returning to Southey, we find that in *Thalaba* he does include
an episode describing the destruction of a bower of bliss. There is
even a formalized little scene in which the attractions of the place
are described in detail, with separate sections for various senses
(VI.241–330). But here Thalaba never hesitates or shows the
least susceptibility to any feeling other than disgust. The only time
he falters is when he tries to abandon his divinely appointed mission for a happy married life with his love, Oneiza. It is significant, too, that in *The Curse of Kehama* the worst peril endured by
the heroine, Kailyal, is an indefatigable campaign waged by Ar-
valan (Kehama's son) against her virtue. These attempts on her
are repulsed and punished with vehemence and almost comic regularity.

Apart from these general similarities—the moral emphasis and
sentimentalism—Southey's romances occasionally resemble his
epics in using elements copied in some detail from traditional
epic.[39] Some of these elements are among the recurrent accessories
of older romances as well as of the epic or romantic epic—one recalls Southey's somewhat permissive epic canon and the unself-
conscious inclusion of Ariosto in it—but they do add something
of epic dimension and atmosphere. To put it another way, epic
and romance were different forms for Southey, but they were not
in every way mutually exclusive.

In Southey's general attitude toward literature of the past, and
especially in his attitude toward epic, one finds not only the inconsistencies which are, after all, to be expected from a person as outspoken as he was, but also the sharply ambivalent attitude toward
tradition which is typical of epic poets. Southey is atypical of them,

however—apart from his obvious inferiority as a poet—in his serious preoccupation with the legalisms of epic *theory*. Sometimes Southey scornfully rejects the theory, but by and large he observes it, and sometimes he pretends to reject it while in fact following it. In any event, he uses epic *theory* as a point of departure much more systematically than the great epic poets or his own contemporaries usually did. His well-known rejection of "the degraded title of Epic"[40] for *Madoc* almost certainly originates in the scorn he felt for the critical principles of the eighteenth century and his sense of immediate pressure from them. Greater epic poets have imitated their models but have not generally felt so much conditioned, one way or the other, by rules, since their main concern has been with the values preached by their poetic predecessors and not with prescriptive formulas. This distinction between Southey and other epic poets is significant, and I shall return to it in evaluating the achievements of *Joan of Arc* and *Gebir*, two poems in which a curious blend of traditionalism and rebelliousness is used with extraordinary ingenuity.

II

The last decade of the eighteenth century saw a new awakening of interest in the epic. Southey used the term "epomania" to describe this new trend, and although it ought not to be honored by being called a "movement," the trend reflected a mood of excitement which was widespread and strong. The revolution in France, by showing the relevance of heroism to modern life, had brought a new and practical urgency to the old debate about the nature of heroism in literature. And if the 1790's brought forth no first-rate epics, it was not because the epic impulse was lacking.

The most memorable expression of this revived interest in epic is to be found in a poem only partly motivated by the epic intention and not completed until the middle of the next decade—*The Prelude*. But more typical in many ways are *Joan of Arc* and

Gebir, lesser poems which had a narrower propagandistic aim.

When *Joan of Arc* appeared in 1796 no epic poem worth mentioning had been published in England for almost sixty years—
since Glover's *Leonidas* in 1737—and blank verse epics had been
especially uncommon and uninspiring.[41] *Leonidas* had enjoyed
great success and Southey had admired it in certain respects.[42] By
1800 Southey was boasting, in rather ambiguous language, that
"my Joan of Arc has revived the epomania that Boileau cured the
French of 120 years ago; but it is not every one who can shoot
with the bow of Ulysses, and the gentlemen who think they can
bend the bow because I made the string twang, will find themselves somewhat disappointed."[43] Apart from its blatant egotism,
this curious boast seems to imply an uneasy mixture of attitudes;
reverence for the grand stature of the true, bow-bending epic poets
and for the tradition they comprise; contempt for epic poetasters;
anger toward the deadening letter of critical orthodoxy; perhaps,
through the irreverent word "epomania," even a hint of disdain
for the true epic tradition. Mutually contradictory as these emphases
are, their co-existence is not unusual in poets with a feeling for the
paradoxical dialectic of epic. During the preceding year Southey
mentioned in a letter to his wife that John Thelwall and Samuel
Rogers were writing epic poems, that George Dyer was contemplating writing one, and that William Taylor was trying to persuade Southey himself to undertake an epic on the subject of Noah
and, as Southey put it, "take my seat with Milton and Klopstock."
Clearly, the epomania had not brought forth much, though there is
reason to believe that Coleridge too had been at least contemplating an epic, the subject of which was to be the origin of evil.[44] But
in September, 1799, we find Southey waxing enthusiastic over a
new poem by an anonymous author. "There is a poem called
'*Gebir*,' of which I know not whether my review be yet printed
(in the Critical), but in that review you will find some of the
most exquisite poetry in the language. . . . I would go an hundred
miles to see the anonymous author."[45]

There are close parallels and connections between the careers of Southey and Landor, the author of the anonymous *Gebir*. Born in successive years, Southey in 1774, Landor a year later, the two young men attended Oxford at the same time and were both fanatical republicans and French sympathizers. When in 1800 Southey departed on his second trip to Portugal, *Gebir* was one of the few books he kept near him for reading on board ship.[46] But they did not meet, despite Southey's review of *Gebir* and his enthusiastic admiration of it, until 1808. At that time Southey's high expectations of finding a kindred spirit were more than fulfilled, and he remarked that he had never seen "any one who so cordially and instinctively agreed with me on so many of the most important subjects."[47] It was during this meeting that Landor offered to pay for the printing of *The Curse of Kehama* if Southey would finish it—an offer which, although it was refused, spurred Southey to the completion of this poem and eventually, perhaps, to the composition of *Roderick*.

Not the least striking of the parallels between Landor and Southey is the fact that during the stormy 1790's both of them wrote epic or near-epic poems with similar political purposes: the discrediting of English policies and the championing of the French in their struggle for freedom. There is little reason to believe that *Gebir*, which appeared in 1798, was influenced by *Joan;* no clear evidence of such influence emerges from the texts of the poems, despite their similarity in purpose, and Landor himself once testified that most of *Gebir* had been written in his "twentieth year"— that is, in about the same year as *Joan*.[48] That two men should, within such a short period, write heroic poems with so similar political intentions is, more probably, symptomatic of the political temper of the decade. And the coincidence is even more symptomatic of a renewed respect for the epic's utility as a vehicle for propaganda.

Neither *Joan of Arc* nor *Gebir* could conceivably have been read, when it was first published, as an example of innocent literary archaism or as an attempt to work in a traditional medium for purely artistic reasons. The epic, in the hands of its masters, had always been highly propagandistic, and both poems take advantage of this traditional privilege. Both are attacks on political reaction, foreign wars, and imperialism in general. Nor is there any reticence on the part of the authors about their political motives. Citing the accepted rule that an epic should be national, Southey writes: "To this rule I have acted in direct opposition, and chosen for the subject of my poem the defeat of my country. If among my readers there be one who can wish success to injustice, because his countrymen supported it, I desire not that man's approbation."[49] Landor is similarly explicit. Though his faith in France and in Bonaparte ebbed away in the five years following the poem's publication, the 1803 Preface to *Gebir* declares roundly the poem's purpose (which had been obvious enough in 1798): "In the moral are exhibited the folly, the injustice, and the punishment of Invasion, with the calamities which must ever attend the superfluous colonization of a peopled country."[50]

To express his antipatriotism and the quasi-religious values that were his in 1795 Southey could hardly have chosen a better vehicle than the story of Joan, especially in view of his tendentious interpretation of her character. The fifteenth-century English wars in France are associated with the names of great English heroes, and for Southey to depict these wars as adventures in greedy imperialism fought against a pastoral people led by a sweet-tempered young girl was a brilliant tour de force of propaganda. As Haller has mentioned, Southey was when he wrote the poem a tenderly chivalric feminist, and while he makes Joan courageous, he never forgets that she is a woman. Moreover, in 1795 Joan had not yet acquired the halo of awesome heroic sanctity which she was to assume through the work of nineteenth-century historians,[51] and it was therefore easy for Southey and his readers to see her career as an entirely human study in pathos.

Through Joan the young Southey expresses not only his views on English opposition to the French Revolution but also a system of religious values which are at times Wordsworthian in their emphasis on natural piety. This religious note, perhaps accidentally, also serves Southey's propagandistic purpose, for Joan is like the revolutionary French patriots in being opposed both by the English and by the religionists of the Old Regime. Examined for suspected witchcraft by the learned theologians, Joan tells them that she knows nothing of religious ritual and that her faith in God has been learned amid the natural surroundings of earth and sky (III.354–91, 436–51). In fact, though, the religious message is not mere occasional propaganda. The entire scheme of religious and moral values in the poem hints at the general ethical concept which is to remain fairly constant through Southey's later long narrative poems, whether they be epics or romances—the confident belief in the ultimate triumph of the righteous cause. In these later poems Southey is to emphasize continually that righteousness will prevail by virtue of its own invincible force, whatever merely external obstacles it encounters. In *Joan* this confidence is more directly connected with divine aid, but the heroine's serene rejection of merely circumstantial obstacles is as great as it is ever to be for Southey's later heroes. One of her officers once suggests that some English soldiers, helplessly at bay, be slaughtered because the French cannot spare the necessary guards. Joan scornfully rejects the base counsel:

> "Foul fall such evil policy!"
> The indignant Maid exclaim'd. "I tell thee, chief,
> GOD is with us! but GOD shall hide his face
> From him who sheds one drop of human blood
> In calm cold-hearted wisdom—him who weighs
> The *right* and the *expedient*, and resolves,
> Just as the well-pois'd scale shall rise or fall."
>
> (VIII.507–13)

Joan's trust is soon vindicated by the miraculous collapse of an English tower and bridge (VIII.652–54). Because of such simple resolutions of conflicts, *Joan* loses something in dramatic effectiveness; the young peasant girl, like all of Southey's heroes, conquers too easily for her victories to have anything more than a mechanically exemplary value, as in pious cautionary tales.[52] *Joan of Arc,* like *Gebir,* challenges the conventional idea of heroism. The sophisticated, literary epic had made heroism more than mere martial prowess, but it had always included and (sometimes grudgingly) praised such prowess; even in Milton the angels are great warriors. In *Joan* the whole value of fighting is questioned, and the grim necessity of war for the freedom of one's homeland is established only after the issue has been explored at some length. The most important discussion of the question is a debate between Theodore, Joan's sweetheart, who defends the pacifist position, and Conrade, a firm believer in his mission of military liberation (I.359–434). As is to be true in Landor's *Gebir,* the main conflict is between the ideals of retirement and involvement. Eventually both Theodore and Conrade go to war, along with Joan, but the debate, together with Southey's circumstantial description of the horrors of war, emphasizes the pathos of the situation: the French people must go to war, but in doing so they violate their better, peaceful nature. Southey himself found the battles "detestable" to write.[53]

During the time when Southey was writing and publishing *Joan of Arc,* his attitude toward traditional epic seems to have been inconsistent and fluctuating. The Preface which accompanies the 1796 edition treats the standard epics and their heroes with cavalier independence, but many years later he acknowledged some kind of debt to them; his intention, he stated, had been not to imitate but to follow.[54] This statement may well be an old man's pious rationalization in retrospect; it would be more accurate to say that the poem *does* imitate but does *not* follow. It is true, though, that some of Southey's choicest youthful invective was directed at what he considered epic poetasters and their servile imitations. The following passage is from an early preface to *Joan:*

> The multitude of obscure epic writers copy with the most gross servility their ancient models. If a tempest occurs, some envious spirit procures it from the god of the winds or the god of the sea. Is there a town besieged? the eyes of the hero are opened, and he beholds the

powers of heaven assisting in the attack; an angel is at hand to heal his wounds; and the leader of the enemy, in his last combat, is seized with the sudden cowardice of Hector. Even Tasso is too often an imitator. . . .

I have avoided what seems useless and wearying in other poems; and my readers will find no descriptions of armor; no muster-rolls; no geographical catalogues; lion, tiger, bull, bear, and boar similes; Phoebuses or Auroras. And, where in battle I have particularized the death of an individual, it is not, I hope, like the common lists of killed and wounded.[55]

Southey is also inclined to domesticate the epic hero. He prefers the *Odyssey* before either the *Iliad* or the *Aeneid* because "its personages inspire love rather than command admiration. The good herdsman Eumaeus is worth a thousand heroes."[56]

Yet Southey wanted *Joan of Arc* to be, in an important and publicly recognizable way, an epic. Looking back much later on his early life, he wrote that to compose an epic had been, during his youth, the highest ambition possible, and that it had been the earliest of his own daydreams.[57] It was not simply that he had certain ideas which seemed to demand the epic framework for their expression; his attraction was partly to the form for its own sake. But, as we have seen, an epic is not really identifiable by a lofty tone or certain general literary objectives or the poet's reverential attitude toward his subject. For an epic to be recognizable as such, it must have some of the devices which mark it as a lineal descendant of other epics, superficial as these devices may seem in isolation. Consequently, despite his alleged independence of rules and refusal to imitate, Southey does what Milton, despite a similar declaration of disdainful independence, does in *Paradise Lost:* he imitates.

Most of the imitations in *Joan* are obvious. The central situation in the poem is the siege of Orleans, a familiar enough setting. The poem begins in the middle of things: the war between France and England has been going on for some years. There are scenes of a minstrel's singing (IV.1–3, 165–75), there is a brief catalogue of the French chieftains under Joan (VII.75–117), there are councils

48 *Southey and Landor*

(VI.57–95; VIII.728–54). The poem begins with the conventional "I sing" formula (I.1–6), and the flashback technique is used more than once (II.483–709; V.102–498). Battle scenes are prominent and slaughter is described in anatomical detail. A description of an elaborate storming tower used by the French against the English walled garrison (VIII.280–85, 298 ff.) is reminiscent of similar towers used in Tasso.[58] There are obvious attempts at Miltonic style.

But *Joan of Arc* uses the epic associations most ingeniously through deliberate or pointed departures from standard epic devices or by occasional adoption of such devices with a twist which alters them for Southey's own purpose, usually political propaganda. Thus, *Joan* is in a very real sense a national poem, as many neoclassic theorists believed an epic should be, for although Southey aggressively chooses not to glorify his own country, the message of the poem is directed at the English and concerns English ideals. Southey tries to reveal to his countrymen, for their edification, a heroic standard which is defined negatively—that is, by English departures from it.[59]

By having Joan reject a proffered glimpse into the book of Futurity Southey once more underlines Joan's and his own pious quietism:

> "All-gracious Heaven!
> Benignant in withholding, hath denied
> To man that knowledge. I, in faith assur'd,
> That he, my heavenly Father, for the best
> Ordaineth all things, in that faith remain
> Contented." (IX.787–92)

Here Southey expresses a favorite attitude through the aggressive inversion of an epic convention. In fact, though, Southey does not entirely dispense with the convention; he brings it in through another door by means of an incident in the underworld which glances at the historical future, which for Southey's generation is the present and the recent past. In the underworld Henry the Fifth is introduced; here he is portrayed not as the heart-stirring hero of Agincourt but as a ruthless oppressor. He is suffering and is to suffer for his wrongdoing until the world shall have repaired through benevolence the harm done by his aggressive imperialism (IX.714–44). The incident is another obvious attack on British policy toward the French patriots.

Southey denounces war through another free adaptation of an epic device: the thumbnail sketch of a warrior during a scene describing his fight and death; the author uses this Homeric technique, but for his own ends. He takes an unknown soldier and tries to give him individuality by describing his background (VII. 320–31). More specifically, he takes a single soldier and sketches his life before the war, a life of peaceful domestic bliss (VIII.219–22) or of rustic cheer (VIII.236–50) or of convivial hospitality (VIII.464–76) or of peaceful enjoyment of the comforts of life (VIII.269–76). The effect is to underline the pathos of war and to disparage the false glory of heroic exploits. Southey does not preach peace at any price, but he does stress the suffering and disorder caused by war. And again a traditional epic device is used, somewhat ironically, to drive home the point.

Perhaps the most striking way in which Southey uses the epic tradition as a springboard is in his choice of a woman as hero. As I have remarked earlier, this departure from precedent has powerful propaganda value. It is true that Southey had a number of epic precedents for Joan in the warrior maidens who figure in almost every important model. Camilla in the *Aeneid*, Clorinda in *Jerusalem Delivered*, Bradamant in *Orlando Furioso*, Britomart in *The Faerie Queene*. But in Southey's poem the warrior maiden is the central figure. It is also true that the question of a woman as hero had come up earlier in connection with a seventeenth-century epic, also about Joan of Arc, by Chapelain.[60] Nevertheless, Southey's substitution of heroine for epic hero would have seemed a blatant repudiation of the tradition of epic virility, a pointed request that the reader compare basic human values with merely martial or brutal ones. Here it is the critical clichés which make Southey's propaganda point possible; the reader is asked to accept the much

oversimplified view (shared by some falsely nostalgic people today) in which earlier epic heroism consists in mere strength and
derring-do; if the reader thinks of epic so simple-mindedly, the
shock value of Southey's reversal of precedent is obviously
heightened. In preferring the "good herdsman Eumaeus" to "a
thousand heroes" Southey is expressing both his sentimentalism
and his dismay at the epic's thirst for blood; his choice of a woman
as hero of his first epic expresses the same two feelings. In his
later epics the quasi-pacifist leanings first weaken and then (in
Roderick) completely disappear, but in *Joan* Southey is still an
extreme liberal.

Joan, as epic heroine, is faced with the same problem as are
many epic heroes—the problem of the conflicting demands of her
love and her vocation. Of course, there is never any possibility
that she will neglect her mission; Southey's protagonists are almost as superior to temptation as they are to sin. She may regret
her stern duty and the renunciation it demands, but she does not
waver. Still, we are given some sense of Joan's sacrifice, as well
as her lover's, and thus the pathos of war is again emphasized.
But her temptation does not involve unruly passions, as, say, Rinaldo's does in Tasso. For Joan heroism in war is a hard alternative to something which is good in itself—namely, a retired life
of domestic happiness. There is no moral question involved, only
the question of the heroine's having sufficient heroic stature. Rinaldo leaves Armida's bower, something evil and destructive of
sound values, for the performance of heroic deeds in war, and
these deeds are good. Joan has to give up the truly good life for
war, which is not good in Southey's scheme, but simply necessary:

> "Hours of delight, ye are for ever gone!
> I shall no more with chearful toil prepare
> The rural cates for high solemnity
> At holy hour. . . .
> The cot's calm quiet and the village sports
> These leave I willingly, those do I change
> For the camp's din, the clangor of the war,
> The pomp of slaughter: such the high command
> Of Duty: that command I shall obey."   (I.335–44)

The tone here, as in much of the poem, is a curious blend of sentimentalism and puritan zeal.

Like *Joan of Arc,* Landor's *Gebir* (published 1798) attempts to put down the mighty and exalt the humble, and more particularly to attack by implication the reactionary attitude of England toward the French Revolution. In addition, the poem springs from a view of literature very similar to Southey's youthful rebelliousness.

The story of the poem is as follows: Gebir, the monarch of Gibraltar, in order to fulfill a vow that he will prosecute a hereditary enmity with Egypt, leads his forces to that country and invades it. Charoba, the Egyptian queen, is fearful at first, but when she and Gebir meet each falls in love with the other; Charoba, however, tragically conceals this love from her nurse and counselor Dalica. Gebir's brother Tamar, who, incongruously but significantly for the message of the poem, is shepherd over the invaders' flocks, falls in love with a sea-nymph who wrestles with and defeats him. Gebir, after learning of his brother's encounter with the nymph, disguises himself as Tamar and wrestles with her himself; this time he is the victor. He takes advantage of his victory to obtain from her information about magic rites which must be performed before he can complete a project he has undertaken, the rebuilding of an Egyptian city; these rites include a descent into the underworld. Gebir in return promises the nymph that Tamar shall marry her. The monarch then goes to the underworld, where he meets his ancestors. The poem ends with two marriage ceremonies, one happy and one abortive. In the first Tamar joyfully marries his nymph, who warns him of approaching danger and carries her passive and completely unheroic husband away with her. Gebir is not so fortunate. His ceremony ends in tragedy when Dalica, who thinks that the queen's willingness to marry the invader is a politic ruse, gives Gebir a poisoned robe which causes him to die in agony. Here the poem concludes.

Many of Landor's comments on *Gebir*, like Southey's in his shrill Preface to *Joan*, assert petulantly the author's independence of old literary rules and models and the basic originality of his poem. *"Gebir,"* he writes in an 1800 Post-Script to the poem (an appendage which he decided not to publish), "in different quarters has been differently received. I allude not to those loyal critics, who . . . are foremost to oppose the return of that traitor, whom, while he was amongst them, Englishmen called Freedom, but now they have expelled him, Anarchy."[61] Or he expresses a lordly contempt for the whole question of influence: "I have followed no man closely; nor have I turned from my road because another stood in it; though perhaps I have momentarily, in passing, caught the object that attracted him."[62] Although he acknowledges using a source for the basic story, he rather aggressively insists that "every line of appropriate description, and every shade of peculiar manners, is originally and entirely my own."[63]

Sometimes this eagerness to defend his independence puts Landor in a curious position. For example, a note he inserted in the 1803 edition reads in part: "Let not this [line] be considered as an imitation of the verse *'Diis aliter visum.'* There is no great merit in quoting old quotations, however apposite."[64] The note then proceeds to argue that the famous line from the *Aeneid* has generally been badly understood and applied. Here the defense certainly protests too much and too elaborately; one can hardly help concluding that Landor indeed had had his mind riveted on Virgil when he wrote his own line. In any case, the Virgilian and Miltonic flavor of *Gebir* is absolutely unmistakable, both in style and in particular reminiscences of the devices of epic tradition.[65]

Many of the epic devices which Landor takes over from traditional epic models are used without any more justification than the fact that he too is writing in an epic vein, however colored it may also be by the conventions of the heroic romance and heroic idyl. For example, the "I sing" formula which comes near the beginning of the poem is almost perfectly conventional:

> I sing the fates of Gebir! how he dwelt
> Among those mountain-caverns, which retain
> His labours yet, vast halls, and flowing wells,

Nor have forgotten their old master's name,
Though sever'd from his people: how, incens'd
By meditating on primeval wrongs,
He blew his battle-horn, at which uprose
Whole nations: how, ten thousand, mightiest men,
He call'd aloud; and soon Charoba saw
His dark helm hover o'er the land of Nile.
What should the damsel do?   (I.12–22)

The athletic games celebrating the prospective marriage of the queen and Gebir are described in some detail in the seventh book, although Landor, possibly in accordance with his pacifist sentiments in the poem, makes all the sports noncombative.[66] Landor said himself that he considered the poem "classical," though without defining very clearly his understanding of the word.[67]

But much more important than these casual epic parallels are the passages in which Landor, like Southey in *Joan,* takes a theme or device which is recognizably familiar in traditional epic and adapts it, sometimes through deliberate reversal or inversion, to his own purposes. For example, Landor too makes extensive use of the Dido-and-Aeneas convention by which woman is shown as an obstacle to duty. But he reverses the traditional values of the convention.[68] Pacifism, the renunciation of ambition, withdrawal from the world of action—these are the values endorsed in the poem, and the contrast between them and the martial ambition which brings Gebir to Egypt is neatly reflected in the allegory of Gebir and his brother Tamar, with their very different nuptials. Gebir, the soldier, and Tamar, the shepherd, represent the two opposite sets of values; Tamar's marriage to his water-nymph and their withdrawal from the world are a picture of bliss reinforced by the sensuousness which in the traditional epics usually stands for dereliction of duty. This marriage is described in the sixth book, Gebir's tragic wedding day in the next, the last, book. The "sweet and honest avarice of love" (VI.110) as Landor calls it, the gratification of the senses, is the reward for Tamar's having chosen the better part. That Landor meant this incident to derive force from the pattern of the older epics is made more probable by the fact that almost all the parallels which illustrate this moral are the result of changes which Landor made in the Clara Reeves story from which he got the basic plot. Landor, not his source, makes Tamar Gebir's brother; Landor contributes the matter of Books Four and Six, the latter being concerned with Tamar's marriage, the defense of retirement, and the most important political allusions of the poem.[69]

Another important link between *Gebir* and the traditional epics, a link which Landor exploits for the purpose of his political message, is the episode of the descent into the underworld. Like Odysseus and Aeneas, Gebir is first told by a woman of a long ritual which he must perform before certain supernatural secrets can be revealed to him (II.203–24).[70] He then descends into an underworld which in certain schematic details resembles those of Homer and Virgil.[71] Like Aeneas and Odysseus, Gebir is allowed to see his ancestors, and in this incident Landor neatly converts the traditional underworld scene to his own purposes. For the ancestors are thinly disguised representatives of the kings of modern European history. By representing them allegorically as Gebir's ancestors Landor can show them as being punished for their monarchal crimes and thus underline his political moral. The sinner must be dead, of course, if he is to be shown as suffering divine retribution for his misdeeds, and therefore Landor shows us Gebir's ancestors instead of the equally traditional vision of the future and of the hero's progeny. The whole scene in Hell was added by Landor.

While Gebir, who represents an old regime and is finally killed through its techniques of violence and intrigue, is given only the vision of the past, his brother Tamar, who represents the gentler virtues which are to fill the earth, is granted a view of futurity. This vision comes in Book Six, when his new bride takes him around the Mediterranean in a panoramic voyage which resembles that described in Tasso's *Jerusalem Delivered*.[72] The nymph predicts the political future and prophesies the emergence of Napoleon, who in 1798 seemed to Landor to have brought hope for the cause of French freedom. In this political prediction we have the link between present and past which we expect in the literary epic, with its function of explaining the present in terms of what has gone before.

III

In *Joan of Arc* Southey preaches radical political values and reinforces them with an iconoclastic attitude toward the epic and its tradition. In his later epics, *Madoc* and *Roderick,* the political radicalism largely disappears, and in general the approach to epic mellows toward conservatism; that is, the epic devices are generally used in a straightforward way, without irony or restiveness—this despite Southey's continuing progressivism about literature as a whole. There are exceptions, however, especially in *Madoc,* the composition of which spans both the years of Southey's youthful radicalism and the first years of his retreat from that position. *Madoc* is thus a transitional work in Southey's career as an author of epics. It is filled with self-conscious reminiscences of the standard epics. On the other hand, the 1805 Preface Southey wrote for it rejects vehemently the "degraded title of Epic"; thus, it claims, the real question is "not whether the story is formed upon the rules of Aristotle, but whether it be adapted to the purposes of poetry."[73] And there is one revealing incident in the poem wherein Southey strategically reverses epic precedent. Just as Joan had rejected the vision of the future, so Madoc rejects heroic precedent by declining a challenge to decisive single combat. The reason, apparently, is that Southey wants to distinguish Madoc's noble, quasi-religious cause from the less elevated ones celebrated in earlier epics. The fight between Menelaus and Paris in the *Iliad* concerns a merely personal grudge, and when Tasso's Argantes and Tancred fight, valor is largely an end in itself. But Madoc's cause is that of Christianity against paganism, and in this cause Madoc and his people cannot afford the luxury of large, swaggering gestures. Even general war they use with great reluctance and only as a last resort. In their struggle the result transcends personality and cannot be trusted to the hazardous outcome of single combat.

Through the third and last of his epics Southey preaches this somewhat impersonal, highly idealized kind of heroism. In *Roderick* it takes a strange and very repellent form, one that seems in some ways to depart from the older heroic values but in even more emphatic ways is old-fashioned enough—certainly that if blood is the criterion. In the poem Southey manages to combine exactly the kind of operatically mawkish heroism which by some lights typifies the Romantic betrayal of earlier epic with a militaristic zeal that seems the more appallingly fierce and cruel for its merger with high-sounding, suprapersonal values. The reconciliation is accomplished in much the same way as in the "Battle Hymn of the Republic." But, putting aside this ambiguous idea of heroism, Southey's approach to epic in the two later poems is fairly conservative; if we refuse the title of conventional epic to *Madoc* and *Roderick,* we do so mainly on the score of quality, for the poems have many of the traditional features of epic, used in fairly conventional ways. Both as polemic and as a document in the history of epic *Joan of Arc* is much the most interesting of the three works. It is not squarely in the epic tradition, but the reasons that ultimately disqualify it tell us more about the way epic works than do the more pallid efforts with which Southey followed it up.

Joan of Arc fails of genuine epic status not only because, like *Madoc* and *Roderick,* it is not good enough, but also because its targets include the epic tradition itself and not merely earlier, inadequate visions now to be superseded. Through his career as a whole, Southey generally felt veneration for the epic; he might sense and occasionally resent the pressure of neoclassic rules, but he also felt a reverent sense of guidance by the organic continuum represented in the great epics themselves. The Preface to *Madoc,* a poem that tries, however unsuccessfully, to carry forward the epic tradition, attacks indignantly the *rules* of Aristotle; the Preface to *Joan,* a truly anti-epic poem, claims to repudiate the very texture, the recurrent devices, of the epic tradition. Not that this disclaimer is conclusive in itself, for epic poets tend to indulge in exactly such rhetoric; what matters is that in *Joan* Southey really does what he threatens, he tries to undermine what epic has stood for, to cut the lifeline of the tradition. The poem, however, is a youthful outburst eccentric to his epic career. In *Joan*—and Landor does the same thing in *Gebir*—Southey chooses for deliberate and temporary reasons to take the oversimplified, inflexible view of epic by which, for all their actual flatness at times, he tries not to be rigidly bound in his later epics. In *Joan* and *Gebir* the two poets invite the reader to see not only earlier heroism but the epic vehicle itself as part of the dead letter of the past, political and literary; from this oversimple platform of expectations and associations, this calculatedly naïve view of what epic and epic heroism have been, the authors' ironic distortions of epic precedent in the direction of quietism derive much of their force.

If it is necessary to classify *Joan of Arc* and *Gebir,* we may call them noncomic mock-epics. It is certainly more than coincidence that the eighteenth century, the age of relative critical consensus about the epic, is also the great age of mock-epic. All mock-epic depends on the widespread acceptance of a rigid traditional pattern, whether the pattern has been absorbed through the kind of desperate simplifications fed to schoolboys or through critical theory at large. The true epic imitates in order to dramatize through the familiarity of the setting a new and loftier heroic ideal that has allegedly surpassed the old ideals by way of growing out of them; mock-epic takes as at least one of its targets the epic vehicle itself, which it ridicules, often gently, by substituting for an oversimplified traditional heroism an absurdly incongruous version of it. *Comic* mock-epic depends on an inflexible view of epic because the more inflexible and narrow-minded the reader's stereotype, the funnier the joke at the epic's expense. The joke depends on a stereotype just as do jokes about Jews or Irishmen or mothers-in-law. This comic technique is, very often, exactly what Southey and Lan-

dor use in their two idol-smashing epics, except that their aim is
not comic but serious; the incongruity they dramatize is the difference between the specious honor of the warrior, which for propaganda purposes the poets are willing to equate with the traditional idea of the epic in general, and the true virtues of quietism.
As in comic mock-epic, the reader must oversimplify; along with
the poets, he must choose to forget the spiritual depth of many
earlier epics, their frequent emphasis on the poignant brevity of
life and the tragedy of death. He is permitted to remember the
bravado of Turnus, but not Sarpedon's ruefulness about the fearful price of being a hero.

Admittedly, in the last analysis it is difficult to draw a clear line
between the true epic and the kind of serious mock-epic we have
been considering. The great standard epics and also the major Romantic attempts at epic statement often convey the same sense of
repudiating the past that we observe in the lesser though more
stridently revolutionary poems *Joan* and *Gebir*. But somehow most
of these greater poems, even such a work as Shelley's idol-smashing *Revolt of Islam,* can attack as inadequate the earlier values
preached in epic and at the same time pay homage to the tradition as something organic and beneficent. These more truly epic
works stand on the shoulders of their predecessors, but along with
Newton they acknowledge with awe and courtesy that they are
standing on the shoulders of giants.

Three: WORDSWORTH

THE WAY OF THE HERO

COMPARED with Wordsworth, both Southey and Landor are essentially conservative in their epic practice. Yet in many ways the opposite would seem to be true. In 1796, at a time when Wordsworth's political radicalism was still strong, he called Southey's iconoclastic Preface to *Joan of Arc* "a very conceited performance."[1] At about the same time Wordsworth was himself uttering political protest by means of a favorite eighteenth-century neoclassic medium, the "imitation of Juvenal"; no gesture could be more Augustan. *The Prelude, Wordsworth's great attempt at epic* expression, points toward the past on almost every page, as Miss Abbie Potts has shown in a book which has furnished some important points of departure for the present study.[2]

It remains true that *The Prelude* is a poem of its age (and even of later ages) in a way that is clearly not true of *Joan of Arc, Gebir, Madoc,* or *Roderick.* Despite the topical references in *Madoc* and *Roderick,* their relevance to contemporary utopian egalitarianism and to the Iberian campaigns, it is impossible to think of these poems as being doctrinal and exemplary to a nation which had seen the disruption of the Old Regime and the emergence of modern liberalism. Timely as they were in a journalistic way, *Madoc* and *Roderick* were primarily antiquarian documents neither of which had deep spiritual relevance to its age. The diffused but powerful epic impulse which dominated Southey's youthful imagination did not result in his finding a theme peculiarly his own yet meaningful to his contemporaries. We get the impression (an impression verified by a reading of Southey's letters and *Common-Place Book*) that the subjects of both *Madoc* and *Roderick* were preferred to others for casual reasons, and that Southey's energies would have been expended on any other of his

possible themes with approximately similar results. *Joan of Arc,*
like Landor's *Gebir,* illustrates certain progressive tendencies
which are to work powerfully upon other, greater poets. Yet, despite its defiance of tradition, *Joan* does not contribute essentially
to the growth of epic; in some ways it actually impedes such
growth by recognizing *de facto* a rigid and specious epic orthodoxy, albeit with a sneer. Neither *Joan* nor *Gebir* produces any important mutation which adapts the epic tradition to a new spiritual
or historic environment. And this is precisely what Wordsworth
does accomplish in *The Prelude,* despite a traditionalism which
habitually impels him to link his own intentions and achievements
with those of the great elder poets.

The Wordsworth's most significant critical statement on the epic is to
be found in a letter to Southey written about 1815: "My opinion
in respect to epic poetry is much the same as that of the critic
whom Lucien Bonaparte has quoted in his preface. Epic poetry, of
the highest class, requires in the first place an action eminently influential, an action with a grand or sublime train of consequences;
it next requires the intervention and guidance of beings superior
to man, what the critics, I believe, call machinery; and lastly, I
think with Dennis that no subject but a religious one can answer
the demand of the soul in the highest class of this species of poetry." Wordsworth then goes on to discuss the limitations of a
stanzaic movement in epic writing (a subject much debated in neoclassic theory), and in the course of this discussion he gives us the
nearest approximation to his own epic canon. He names Tasso,
Spenser, Homer, Virgil, and Milton, an almost perfectly orthodox
list.[3]

The applicability of this epic formula to *The Prelude* is the general subject we are concerned with, but a few points require immediate notice. The words "what the critics, I believe, call machinery" are astonishing; it seems almost incredible that this term,
one of the most hackneyed in neoclassic theory, should have been
only vaguely familiar to Wordsworth. The implication is that he
knew at first hand almost none of the standard treatises, and it is

true that references to the Augustan critics are very few in Words-worth's writings. On the other hand, Wordsworth's phrase may have an element of pose about it, like the similar "Aristotle, I have been told" of the Preface to *Lyrical Ballads;* that is, Words-worth may have wanted to strike a superior attitude by affecting ignorance of musty laws. If so, the affectation would be entirely in keeping with the role often assumed by the epic poet.

Also worth scrutiny is Wordsworth's third requirement for epic poetry, that the subject be religious. The word "religious" is almost certainly not to be taken in the common, relatively narrow sense in which Wordsworth understands the term when, late in his life, he points out with regret how many people read *Paradise Lost* "not as a poem, but a religious Book."[4] Wordsworth is not likely to have condemned readers for applying to the work which for him most nearly represented the epic law and the prophets the very criterion he had himself declared to be essential. It is much more likely, as Miss Potts indicates, that in his definition of the epic he is using "religious" in the sense which he assigns to the word in a letter to Landor written in 1824. Here he identifies religious poe-try with imaginative sublimity: "even in poetry it is the imagina-tive only, viz., that which is conversant [with], or turns upon in-finity, that powerfully affects me,—perhaps I ought to explain: I mean to say that, unless in those passages where things are lost in each other, and limits vanish, and aspirations are raised, I read with something too much like indifference—but all great poets are in this view powerful Religionists."[5]

Finally, the reference to "the critic whom Lucien Bonaparte has quoted" is of some importance. The brother of Napoleon had pub-lished in 1814 an epic poem entitled *Charlemagne, ou L'Eglise Délivrée,* which was translated a year later into English.[6] The only piece of criticism quoted in the Preface is Clement's seventh letter to Voltaire. The entire passage follows:

Without doubt, the intervention of God, of angels, and saints, ought not to be employed to enliven our poetry, as Homer employed Mars, Juno, Vulcan, Venus and her cestus. The marvellous of our religion, which tends only to grandeur and sublimity, ought not to be prodigally introduced, and indeed cannot be employed with too much caution and judgment; but in our system, as in that of the ancients, the marvellous ought to animate the whole poem: the poet who calls himself inspired, and who ought to be so, should be seized, if I may so express it, with a divine spirit like the ancient prophets; so that he may read in Heaven the decrees of Providence; may see the chain which links the events of this world to the divine will, and the supernatural agents which direct and influence mankind. The entire action of the poem ought to be connected with the marvellous: so that Heaven should decree, and mankind conduct themselves accordingly. From the beginning to the end we should see the supernatural agents give an impulse to the actors, and man every where under the direction of God.[7]

The view of machinery expressed here is a fairly sophisticated one. It should manifest itself not in isolated, magical events, but rather in an air of inspired prophecy and supernatural wonder diffused throughout the entire poem, a spiritual atmosphere which shows the mysterious link between man and an order more powerful than and superior to man. Now, it is in very nearly this manner that Wordsworth, half metaphorically, describes in *The Prelude* the interaction between himself and his own "machinery." But of this more later.

The extent of Wordsworth's epic traditionalism and of his traditionalism in general is both conditioned by and reflected in his reading. His frankness in confessing the gaps in his literary background (rather surprising when we consider how vain Wordsworth often was), his self-criticism for scholarly indolence at Cambridge, the magnitude of his intellectual debt to Coleridge, the anti-intellectualism of certain poems in *Lyrical Ballads,* his vagueness in *The Prelude* about the influence of specific books, and the literary rebelliousness of the 1800 Preface have combined, along with other influences, to create a Wordsworthian equivalent of the "native wood-notes wild" theory. Yet, whatever limitations Wordsworth's general reading may have had, they certainly do not apply to poetry. English poetry he knew thoroughly, especially eighteenth-century poetry and that of the great masters he acknowledged: Chaucer, Shakespeare, Spenser, and Milton.[8] He discusses knowingly the poetry of Ovid, Juvenal, Virgil, Homer, Horace, Lucretius, and Catullus.[9] Italian poetry was one of his passionate loves, and references to Tasso and Ariosto are frequent in his correspondence.[10] The authors he knew best, such as Milton and Virgil, he knew with a particular, microscopic intimacy. His taste gravitated sincerely toward the literary giants of the past, so that he seldom needed to apply that distinction between the personal and objective estimates which Matthew Arnold prescribes as necessary for good criticism. Nor did Wordsworth simply feel a vague awe for the monuments of the past, the kind of feeling he attributes to himself upon his first arrival in London:[11]

> A weight of ages did at once descend
> Upon my heart; no thought embodied, no
> Distinct remembrances, but weight and power,—
> Power growing under weight.   (*Prelude,* VIII.552–55)

His comments on the great writers often have a kind of sincere casualness which rings very true, and he was capable of finding fault with even the greatest of poets. Though he admired Dante's style early in his life, he later confessed a dislike for Dante's "grotesque and fantastic fictions," and he admitted finding *The Divine Comedy* tedious for various reasons. He expressed varying estimates of Homer's poetry, generally rating it high. Yet he was frank in acknowledging his distaste for Homeric "manners."[12]

From three of Wordsworth's letters, two written in early 1804 and one, to Sir George Beaumont, in June, 1805 (most of the original *Prelude* was written between these two dates), we know that at this important period Wordsworth contemplated writing a narrative or epic poem and not simply the philosophic poem which was later partially realized in *The Excursion*.[13] His failure to write the epic, like his failure to complete *The Recluse,* has been explained by his having achieved both aims earlier than he immediately recognized, that is, in *The Prelude*.[14] If this is true, the references to epic in the letters, especially the 1805 letter to Beaumont, do not describe a definite project which Wordsworth had in mind so much as they reflect the pattern which, perhaps half-

consciously, was emerging in *The Prelude* itself. Stated as un-
subtly as I have put it, this explanation might seem to deny Wordsworth's conscious artistry, but the inference would not be valid;
in the psychology of the creative process it is not at all uncommon
for one's notion of what he has accomplished to lag far behind
what has actually been done, even though quite specific decisions
have been made at every stage in accordance with a distinct if in-
completely formulated pattern. This is especially likely to be true
when the subject, like that of *The Prelude,* is profoundly personal
and when the poet's mind, like Wordsworth's, is so seamless. As
further evidence we might consider Wordsworth's tendency to
write poems over periods of years, in snippets and segments whose
final use was unforeseen. Yet the resulting poems are usually coherent. That such unity was achieved indicates that the organizing
power of Wordsworth's mind often operated at a deeper psychological level than is usual, a level less schematic than is implied by
deliberate planning for *a* philosophic poem and *an* epic poem.

Perhaps the best evidence that in *The Prelude* Wordsworth was
building more heroically than he completely recognized is that his
later revisions of the poem almost consistently point up the epic
pattern, strong as that pattern already is in the 1805 version; I
shall try to illustrate this fact along my way. Because I am interested chiefly in the epics of the high Romantic age, and because
I am mainly though not exclusively concerned with the early
Wordsworth rather than with the Wordsworth of later years, I
have chosen the 1805 text as the basis of my analysis, but to compare the earliest and latest versions of the poems is to be convinced
that the relatively latent epic form of the 1805 *Prelude* came to be
ever more markedly the dominant one.

There is little need to establish once more the fact, recognized
by several critics in recent years, that Wordsworth's epic theme is
meant deliberately to compete with those of earlier epics.[15] Wordsworth in *The Prelude* was following the precedent of earlier epic
poets by which they claim to herald a higher and more spiritual
ideal than had prevailed in the past and in epics before them. The

time has come, Wordsworth declares explicitly in the poem, to celebrate the loftiest subject of all, the mind of man. The poet is to explore this theme through tracing the growth of the only mind whose vicissitudes he knows at first hand, his own. But this almost exclusive emphasis by critics on thematic innovation has its dangers, for to call *The Prelude* an epic in some loose sense or to imply that it is an epic because of its lofty subject, as though that alone (or mere ambitiousness of intent or tone) could make a poem an epic, is to reinforce, perhaps unintentionally, the mistaken idea that the "true" epic was dead in the Romantic age.

I should therefore like to concentrate on the epic *pattern* of *The Prelude*, a matter which has been much less adequately treated. Nevertheless, some discussion of the poem's theme is in order, if only to make my discussion of the pattern more coherent. A more important reason for retracing part of this familiar territory is that Wordsworth's definitive statements about his heroic theme are grounded in the details of epic tradition in much more specific ways than has been generally appreciated.

II

The best key to Wordsworth's epic creed is the passage from Book I of *The Prelude* (157–271) in which he draws up a poetic balance sheet and measures the demands of various heroic subjects against his literary powers. The many Miltonic allusions in this passage and the similarity between the problems it raises and those that Milton felt in his own search for a noble theme indicate beyond much doubt that Wordsworth was placing himself in the heroic tradition exemplified by his great mentor. What Wordsworth tells us here seems to furnish both an index to his own ideas on epic and his version of the history of epic. He begins with a general analysis of the personal endowments required of a poet with such lofty aims as his. They include "that first great gift . . . the vital soul," "general truths," "external things," including

forms and images, and other aids of "less regard" but needful for
the poet. (The priority of the mind and general truths to techniques, images, and other aids of "less regard" is important in
Wordsworth's theory of poetry as a whole.) But all these are essentially prerequisites, even the "external" images stored in the
mind and soul; the poet must objectify his inner endowments by
finding "Time, place, and manners"—in short, a theme. His aim
is to "summon back from lonesome banishment" some "little
Band of yet remember'd names" and "make them inmates in the
hearts of men / Now living, or to live in times to come." The subject, then, should be taken from the past, but not the utterly obscure past—a compromise perfectly consonant with much neoclassic theory. (Wordsworth seems most conscious of epic theory
when, as here, he is still groping toward a theme.) A further implication is that the past must be linked with the present or the
future in some meaningful way.

Wordsworth then lists a series of contemplated subjects for
heroic treatment. The first is "some British theme, some old / Romantic tale, by Milton left unsung." Next he considers a pastoral-
chivalric tale. Or, "more sternly mov'd," he would tell of Mithridates, who "became / That Odin, Father of a Race, by whom /
Perish'd the Roman Empire," or of Sertorius' friends and followers, who settled in the Fortunate Isles and left there a tradition of
liberty which fifteen hundred years later inspired a gallant struggle against the Europeans. Or he would tell how

> in tyrannic times some unknown Man,
> Unheard of in the Chronicles of Kings,
> Suffer'd in silence for the love of truth,

or narrate the avenging expedition of Dominique de Gourges to
Florida in the sixteenth century, or Gustavus I's liberation of Swe-
den from Danish oppression, or Wallace's fight for Scotland and
his bequeathal of his name and deeds as ghostly tokens of "independence and stern liberty" in his country.

Abandoning his list of martial themes, Wordsworth considers
as another possibility "Some Tale from my own heart, more near

akin / To my own passions and habitual thoughts," lofty but "with interchange of gentler things." The heroic subject, he admits, puts an unnatural strain on his powers. Lastly he mentions his favorite aspiration, a

> philosophic Song
> Of Truth that cherishes our daily life;
> With meditations passionate from deep
> Recesses in man's heart, immortal verse
> Thoughtfully fitted to the Orphean lyre.

But he draws back in fear and self-distrust before the "awful burthen" he envisages, and the passage ends with a thick cluster of Miltonic reminiscences, two of "Lycidas" and one of the sonnet "On His Blindness." Like the mourning shepherd shrinking from premature effort, Wordsworth takes refuge in the timorous hope "That mellower years will bring a riper mind / And clearer insight," and, again like the shepherd, he thinks longingly of the "vacant musing, unreprov'd neglect / Of all things, and deliberate holiday" which are the tempting alternative to stern ambition. The whole passage ends with the allusion to the "Blindness" sonnet when Wordsworth compares himself to "a false Steward who hath much received / And renders nothing back," though doubtless the Biblical influence was also direct.[16]

Several important facts emerge from this passage. First, the epic impulse which Wordsworth feels is in part the same kind of generalized ambition to do something great that Milton expresses in much of his literary autobiography before *Paradise Lost*—in the *Vacation Exercise*, in "Elegy VI," in the *Apology for Smectymnuus*, in *The Reason of Church-Government*.[17] Wordsworth chides himself for having

> no skill to part
> Vague longing that is bred by want of power
> From paramount impulse not to be withstood. (I.240–42)

This generalized ambition is related to Wordsworth's great capacity, often illustrated in *The Prelude*, for expectations whose intensity depends in part on their vagueness; such were his expectations of Mount Blanc before its "soulless image" had "usurp'd upon a living thought / That never more could be" (VI.454–56). A more important implication of this vague longing for a great theme is the personal nature of the search. Wordsworth's problem is not merely to find an adequate theme, but, more important, to find the theme best for him. Epic, according to this view, exists first in the mind of the poet, as an undirected, potential force which must then be channeled into a particular theme, as electric power is stored in a battery before it is used to run a motor or heat an element. Yet the theme is by no means accidental, and herein Wordsworth's approach differs from Southey's, for the theme must be peculiarly right for the poet as an individual; it must be an appropriate fulfillment of his own aspirations. In any event, the search for a theme becomes an occasion for introspection and solemn self-analysis.

Secondly, Wordsworth's list of possible subjects is a catalogue of the various traditional epic subjects. He mentions the "romantic tale," the vehicle used by Spenser and Tasso and ultimately rejected by Milton. In the Mithridates story he has a tale of empire suggestive of Virgil, though Wordsworth's story would tell of the destruction of an empire rather than its origin. Some of the themes (Gustavus, Wallace) are primarily national, as much neoclassic theory believed epic subjects should be, and possibly Wordsworth is considering Biblical material in his reference to "the Chronicles of Kings," though probably the phrase means something different.[18] The stories of Mithridates and Sertorius are tales of wandering, like the *Odyssey* and the first half of the *Aeneid*. Even the "Tale from my own heart" and the "philosophic Song" are to be treated in a lofty way.

Thirdly, all the subjects have a spiritual significance and often they are "influential" in the light of later history, the apparent exceptions being the personal and philosophic subjects. (They are, in fact, only apparent exceptions.) Many of them have for their theme liberty, certainly a spiritual ideal for Wordsworth. Like his master Milton, Wordsworth rejects the purely martial idea of a hero. It is interesting that the only theme listed which in the early version is not moral by statement or implication is the chivalric tale, and this is expanded in later revision from the simple pastoral theme of the 1805 version to a conception of

> a song that winds
> Through ever changing scenes of votive quest
> Wrongs to redress, harmonious tribute paid
> To patient courage and unblemished truth,
> To firm devotion, zeal unquenchable,
> And Christian meekness hallowing faithful loves.
>
> (I.180–85)

Fourthly, there is a fairly definite progression in Wordsworth's list from subjects which most strictly confine themselves to things, manners, and other externals (like the romantic tale as briefly described in the 1805 version), through expressions of political idealism, to the most universal theme, the "philosophic Song / Of Truth." There is also a movement from those subjects most remote from modern man's experience through those, remote in time but morally or politically relevant, to those most directly bearing on contemporary life or of greatest personal significance to the poet himself. Unless the order in which the themes are mentioned is an accident, Wordsworth is implying a conception of epic as a growing rather than a static form.

Finally, the position of the pastoral theme at the head of Wordsworth's list is probably important. Renaissance convention held that the interest in pastoral poetry was an early stage in the development of the epic poet. Virgil had furnished the precedent; Spenser and Milton conformed to it. And in view of the echoes of "Lycidas" in the passage we are examining and Wordsworth's insistence later in the poem on the difference between his version of pastoral and the older, idyllic one, it is a reasonable inference that Wordsworth was recalling the pastoral-to-epic tradition.[19] In fact, the place of pastoralism in *The Prelude* has great significance, for it symbolizes the general direction of the poet-hero's developing mind—from love of Nature to love of Man. Pastoralism is one example of Wordsworth's belief that his literary forms are not replicas of older models but rather developments of them. *The Prelude* is in part a modern pastoral, and Wordsworth, though he apparently discards the themes listed in Book I, actually uses nearly all the types there represented in his poem. There is a coloring of romance and the supernatural, description of a war for liberty, a philosophic song. A national theme is prominent—"national" in the sense which is applicable to *Joan of Arc,* where England is not glorified but English ideals are closely scrutinized. And, of course, the autobiographical nature of the poem fulfills the promise of the "Tale from my own heart." But all these elements are finally subordinated to his main epic theme, the mind of man.

Like the great epic poets of the Renaissance, Wordsworth felt the need for a new heroic ideal. Milton, Tasso, and Camoëns had all exalted their heroes' exploits above those of antiquity. All three had made the heroic ideal Christian, and Milton in particular had pointed the way for Wordsworth by making the essential heroic attribute not deeds but a state of mind. The deepest hell is within Satan, and to Adam is revealed a "paradise within thee, happier farr." The triumphant Christ in *Paradise Regained* wins victory through the maintenance of inner integrity rather than through action.

Thus Wordsworth had ample precedent for making the heroic ideal an interior one. Yet he believed he was making a new departure, and he was right. For one thing, his method is basically different from Milton's and those of the other writers of literary epic. Wordsworth does not simply depict the heroic ideal in action; he is even more concerned with its genesis and growth in the individual hero, namely—and embarrassingly for Wordsworth—himself. The "action" of *The Prelude,* the story of Wordsworth's mental growth, is justified by the final product—the poet's mature mind.[20] The action is purposeful and "influential," as the wanderings and struggles of Aeneas influence the growth of Rome and as the fall of Adam influences the whole later history of the world. (The analogy is not merely fanciful, nor on the other hand should it convict Wordsworth of being a megalomaniac, since his sub-

ject—the human mind—is indeed a grand one, and since Wordsworth's personal history is mainly an *exemplum* of the mind's development.) In Virgil and Milton heroism is a given quality, a
means toward an end, the end being action or the adoption of a
moral stance or both. But in Wordsworth heroism is the *product*
of the influences and actions described in the poem. Aeneas's
pietas helps to build the Roman Empire, and Adam, exemplifying
heroism in a negative way, acts to bring "Death into the World,
and all our woe," but in *The Prelude* the heroic ideal—mental
equipoise, the harmony between man and his environment—is primarily an end and not a means, at least within the boundaries defined by the story of Wordsworth's early life. This last qualifica-
tion is important; I shall argue presently that *The Prelude* too
points toward action beyond the acquisition itself of Wordsworth's
version of heroism, that the poem is not content to state an ideal
of *being*. But that action is not part of the pattern of development
traced in the *events* of the poem.

The emphasis on origins and development permeates much of
The Prelude, and not merely in a narrow autobiographical sense.
Wordsworth's attempt to define heroism is itself rooted in the
epic poems and heroic ideal of the past. This way of thinking is
probably best illustrated in Wordsworth's description of his native
region as lovelier than all the beautiful paradises of fable (VIII.
119–58). As De Selincourt observes, the passage is based on Milton's description of Eden as surpassing all other delectable gardens.[21] But Wordsworth's passage is not a mere echo. The allusion is to a passage in *Paradise Lost* which, like many other passages in that poem, vaunts the superiority of its subject matter over
fables and traditionally heroic tales. The implication of Wordsworth's allusion, in connection with other such comparisons in *The
Prelude,* is the still greater loftiness of his own theme; in other
words, Wordsworth implies a kind of growth and progress in earlier epics toward his own subject, "the mind of man." Another example of this technique is the thorough discussion of the difference between the ancient pastoral life and the more vital pastoral-

ism of the shepherds Wordsworth knew (see, for example, VIII.
182–428).

But it is not only in the function he assigns to heroism that
Wordsworth differs from the traditional epic poets; the heroic
ideal itself is new. Its concentration on the inner man has precedents, as we have seen, but the degree of emphasis is far greater
than in previous epic writers. And there are still other innova-
tions. Wordsworth's climactic statement of his great theme, the
theme toward which Book I shows him as groping, suggests the
main new elements in his heroic code:[22]

>   Of Genius, Power,
> Creation and Divinity itself
> I have been speaking, for my theme has been
> What pass'd within me. Not of outward things
> Done visibly for other minds, words, signs,
> Symbols or actions; but of my own heart
> Have I been speaking, and my youthful mind.
> O Heavens! how awful is the might of Souls,
> And what they do within themselves, while yet
> The yoke of earth is new to them, the world
> Nothing but a wide field where they were sown.
> This is, in truth, heroic argument,
> And genuine prowess . . .
> Points have we all of us within our souls,
> Where all stand single; this I feel, and make
> Breathings for incommunicable powers.
> Yet each man is a memory to himself,
> And, therefore, now that I must quit this theme,
> I am not heartless; for there's not a man
> That lives who hath not had his godlike hours,
> And knows not what majestic sway we have,
> As natural beings in the strength of nature.　　(III.171–94)

There are three basic elements in the heroic ideal offered here:
an emphasis on spiritual and psychological qualities ("my theme
has been / What pass'd within me"), a form of egalitarianism
("there's not a man / That lives who hath not had his godlike
hours"), and individualism ("Points have we all of us within our
souls, / Where all stand single"). All these are fairly novel in the

light of the traditional heroic pattern, especially as it exists in epic
"orthodoxy"—the inner emphasis because of the enormous importance which Wordsworth gives it, the egalitarianism because it
goes so far out of the way to deny that the hero is unique, the individualism because Wordsworth makes it a universal and
markedly philosophical ideal.

The main emphasis in the quoted passage is on the spiritual and
psychological nature of the theme. Despite the lengthy treatment
of the French Revolution, the poem's values are antimartial
(though, as in Southey, not strictly pacifist), and the older concept
of a hero as a great warrior is nowhere in evidence, not even in
Beaupuy, who is glorified mainly as a thinker. Wordsworth's anti-
militarism leads him to confess with some sense of guilt that he
once was led by French military victories to confound them with
another victory "far higher and more difficult, / Triumphs of un-
ambitious peace at home / And noiseless fortitude" (X.591–93).
Later he rejoices that the "wiser mood" has been re-established
which sees "little worthy or sublime / In what we blazon with the
pompous names / Of power and action" (XII.45–49). His description of the pathetic separations and the domestic havoc
wrought by war (IX.273–79) is very much like Southey's in *Joan
of Arc*. Southey too might, with slight modifications, have written
what Wordsworth wrote in 1794: "I am a determined enemy to
every species of violence. I see no connection, but what the ob-
stinacy of pride and ignorance renders necessary, between justice
and the sword, between reason and bonds."[23] By 1802 Wordsworth
had modified his views somewhat, but he still believed that "ex-
cessive admiration was paid in former times to personal prowess
and military success; it is so with the latter even at the present day,
but surely not nearly so much as heretofore."[24] It is one of the
more striking bits of evidence for the "lost leader" theory that in
1816 Wordsworth's views had been so transformed that he believed that "martial qualities are the natural efflorescence of a
healthy state of society," and that he cites in support of this thesis
the authority of Milton, among others.[25] But it is equally signifi-

cant that Wordsworth never deleted from *The Prelude* the passages I have just mentioned, for the poem always retained for him
an integrity of pattern independent of his self-revelation. Even the
brief temptation to join forces with the revolutionists is mainly a
reaction to the French need for guidance and moral authority (X.
129–58).[26] And, significantly, one of Dorothy's great restorative
services is to "soften down" her brother's "over-sternness" (XIII.
226–27).

When in announcing his theme Wordsworth states that he rejects "outward things," "Symbols or actions," in favor of "What
pass'd within me," he is not describing his poem with complete
exactness, for *The Prelude* contains many pictures of the great
world and of momentous events. But this passage was almost certainly written at a time when the whole poem was still intended
to be only five books long and more limited in scope than it
turned out to be.[27] In the full poem Wordsworth takes pains to
show the reality, indeed the practicality, of his theme. This insistence on the reality and truth of his subject is one of the things
that place Wordsworth most directly in the tradition of literary
epic. "What pass'd within me" is not the stuff of dreams; the "godlike hours" are part of our empire "As natural beings in the
strength of nature." In his early days of revolutionary zeal he had
rejoiced that his efforts and the efforts of men like him would be
exercised "Not in Utopia," but "in the very world which is the
world / Of all of us" (X.724–27), and on regaining his emotional health after his moral crisis he seeks "good in the familiar
face of life," and not in "sanguine schemes" (XII.65–67).

No statements could illustrate better than these the difference
between Wordsworth's heroic standard and the standards expressed by Southey and Landor. All three poets define heroism
idealistically, but Wordsworth's brand of idealism is at the more
utilitarian end of the idealist's spectrum, whereas Southey and
Landor preach a much simpler doctrine, bordering on escapism.
The utopian ideal which helps to inform *Madoc* and the political
quietism of *Gebir* are both foreign to Wordsworth's intentions in

The Prelude, for in emphasizing psychology at the expense of martial heroism Wordsworth is not retreating from the field of human action except in what he would consider a superficial sense of the word *action,* despite his frequent praises of rural and domestic retirement. On the contrary, in exploring the mind of man he claims to be focusing on the area of human life where the most truly significant action occurs, the area which is most "substantial." It is Wordsworth's concern with the real applicability of his message which explains why *The Prelude,* if it had been published in 1805, might have been doctrinal to an age and nation in a way that was not possible for the contemporary epics of Southey and Landor. When Wordsworth, having reviewed his past life near the end of the poem, confirms his dedication to a newer, more truly heroic program, he ponders "How oft high service is perform'd within" (XII.226). But, although one terminus of the events narrated in *The Prelude* is the poet's decision to write verse which will celebrate the inner nature of men in humble life, he declares that in this enterprise he will "Deal boldly with substantial things, in truth / And sanctity of passion" (XII.234–35);

> it shall be my pride
> That I have dared to tread this holy ground,
> Speaking no dream but things oracular,
> Matter not lightly to be heard by those
> Who to the letter of the outward promise
> Do read the invisible soul.   (XII.250–55)

Wordsworth does not preach subjectivism; he simply believes that mental experience is entirely real and, furthermore, that the greatest practical problem of his own age is not material or institutional, but spiritual.[28] One can readily surmise the effect this creed must have had on one of Wordsworth's disciples, the author of *Culture and Anarchy.*

Far from being neglected, external narrative has a special importance in Wordsworth's poem. It is through the action of the poem that ideas and ideals are made concrete—the ideal of true liberty, for example, through the poet's experiences with the

French Revolution. Furthermore, as in Virgil, the action traces the origin, growth, and cause of the resultant—which, in *The Prelude*, is a man's mature mind. But Wordsworth's special emphasis on psychology needs external narrative not only as symbolic explanation (as in the Snowdon episode) but also as factual example. In the Wordsworthian hero, as typified by the author himself, the inner and outer worlds are in equipoise and thus interact with each other. Hence external contingencies and action in the world are important as specific proof of the part played by the experience of external things in shaping the imagination and thought of the developing man.

The other chief ingredients in Wordsworth's heroic ideal, democratic egalitarianism and individualism, are closely dependent on each other. It had been at least half-assumed by most earlier epic poets that the hero was a great leader enjoying special gifts of Nature and Fortune. He relied on himself in all that was within human power and is distinctly contrasted with his less gifted fellows. Though Wordsworth sometimes speaks in such terms, it is in a different context, which I shall examine later; in general, Wordsworth's individualism has a more philosophic cast than in older versions of heroism. And since it is democratic, it applies to all men ("Points have we all of us within our souls, / Where all stand single"). We "stand single"—the individual is unique. But this is true of "all of us," and therefore individualism is formulated as a universal, democratic ideal.

This democratic note pervades *The Prelude;* Wordsworth denies, for example, that love requires "Retirement, leisure, language purified / By manners thoughtful and elaborate" (XII.189–90). Yet he cannot deny the differences between men or the rarity of individuals who satisfy his heroic ideal, and the problem troubles him. The dignity of individual man—"no composition of the thought," but "the man whom we behold / With our own eyes"— is a fact of experience, but

> Why is this glorious Creature to be found
> One only in ten thousand? What one is,
> Why may not many be? (XII.83–92)

Wordsworth's heroic ideal postulates, not a great individual hero, but a great race of individualists. The message of serious literary epic is usually a collective one in some sense, and Wordsworth's justification in turning his personal memoirs into heroic argument is his belief that, as Shelley was to put it, we have one human heart.

III

To be epic a poem needs more than an appropriately great subject; it must have an epic pattern as well. Although the theme of *The Excursion*—Despondency and Its Correction—has negative overtones, it is not really very different from the theme of mental discipline celebrated in *The Prelude*. But the method of *The Excursion* is discursive rather than narrative and therefore the poem could never be considered epic unless the term were unreasonably broadened, narrative method being one of the few things which epic theorists have agreed to demand of epic. *The Prelude*, however, has a standard form of epic development, a unity that is more than conceptual. The progress of the hero is essentially a mental progress, for the theme is not empire or Christian action but the mind of man. But, as much as Aeneas or Godfrey or da Gama, Wordsworth's representative hero has a mission, a vocation. The mission is a lofty one, and its way is mined with perils and surrounded by tempting and fallacious mental bypaths. Wordsworth's progress toward the goal set for him is a task requiring heroic powers. *The Prelude* has other patterns, of course, but this standard pattern of literary epic, that of progress toward a goal, is the dominant one in the poem. Without it *The Prelude* would seriously lack unity; through it the poem becomes structurally intelligible.

Most students of Wordsworth will recognize that I am indebted to Abbie Potts for her remarks on the epic and ordeal patterns in *The Prelude*, as well as for smaller points which have been useful to me even when I have not agreed with them. I should make it clear, however, as much in fairness to her as to myself, that in connecting the epic and ordeal patterns as closely as I do and especially in treating the ordeal as the predominant structural metaphor of the poem I am making claims which are narrower than and at the same time perhaps more far-reaching than hers.

In a way, I believe, Miss Potts's study suffers from its greatest virtue: its almost awesome comprehensiveness. She traces so many patterns in *The Prelude* that one begins to see the poem as a kind of random diary and workbook. But, though all or nearly all these patterns are present, some are more important than others. Of all the patterns, it seems to me, the governing one is that of epic mission and ordeal; indeed, one of the most impressive things about *The Prelude* is the way in which the epic-ordeal reduces these heterogeneous emphases to a satisfying artistic unity. Granted, the subordination is not perfect (though it is much more nearly so than most readers have recognized). Book VII, for example, "Residence in London," remains something of an anomaly. In the narrative structure its function is to show Wordsworth's introduction to the real world of man, as distinguished from the real but egocentric world of childhood and the human but mostly artificial world of Cambridge. We learn that the poet, during his first residence in the great city, was not yet ready for the genuine experience of love for humanity. But for the most part Book VII concerns the city itself rather than the author's experiences in it, and thus the place of the London section in the whole poem seems only vaguely articulated. The length of the description is entirely out of proportion to the importance of the poet's London experience, at least as that is revealed in *The Prelude*. Yet the patterns of mission, ordeal, and progress do account for almost every important incident in the poem and the order in which they are recounted. Without these interrelated patterns *The Prelude* would have virtually no structure, for even the autobiographical unity is defective, as has long been recognized.[29]

Wordsworth's mission is that of poet, and a poet's function is, in the broadest sense, to "teach, / Inspire, through unadulterated ears / Pour rapture, tenderness, and hope" (XII.237–39). He and his friend Coleridge are to be, Providence willing, "joint-labourers" in the work of man's "redemption," "Prophets of Nature" (XIII.439–42). But just as (on the level of the poem's composition) Wordsworth's true epic theme becomes manifest only after experience and a gradual revelation, so (on the level of the poem's action) with the nature of his service. The moment when Wordsworth becomes fully conscious of where his duty toward the world lies is preceded by a vague sense of dedication to a great but still undefined duty. At Cambridge, he tells us in messianic language, he had been disturbed by a strange sense that "I was not for that hour, / Nor for that place." But he was a "chosen Son . . . with holy powers / And faculties" both to apprehend the workings of the visible world and to change it, a man who "to majestic ends was strong" (III.80–90). As Milton had "in the privat academies of *Italy*" felt confident for the first time that he "might perhaps leave something so written to aftertimes, as they should not willingly let it die" (a passage that Wordsworth liked to quote),[30] so it was at Cambridge, likewise an academic setting, that Wordsworth was first encouraged to trust "that I might leave / Some monument behind me which pure hearts / Should reverence" (VI.67–69). Describing elsewhere his life at Cambridge, the poet distinguishes characteristically between his own responsibilities and those of good but less inspired men; there for a time he forgot "the pledges interchanged / With our own inner being" and associated with a "shoal / Of more unthinking Natures; easy Minds / And pillowy" (III.518–23). The climactic though unconscious moment of poetic dedication is one when

> I made no vows, but vows
> Were then made for me; bond unknown to me
> Was given, that I should be, else sinning greatly,
> A dedicated spirit. (IV.341–44)

This is messianic language; it is also language applicable to the charismatic epic hero.

During the period of vague dedication Wordsworth (regarded as the hero of his poem rather than as its author) considers several vocations. The Arab of his symbolic dream in Book V, trying to preserve science and art from threatened oblivion, has often tempted the poet to forsake domestic ties and to "go / Upon like errand" (V.160–61). In France he almost devotes his life to the Revolutionary cause, but he returns to England, as he tells us in an early addition to the original text, "Forc'd by the gracious Providence of Heaven." Had he become a partisan in France he might have perished, "A poor mistaken and bewilder'd offering," all his resolutions and hopes wasted, "A Poet only to myself, to Men / Useless" (X.190–201). The pattern by which the hero must be guided into his true path of achievement—here, significantly, achievement useful to men—is part of the pattern of the traditional literary epic. Aeneas, Adam, Tasso's Rinaldo—all have to be made aware of their vocations through supernatural visions of the future and of their own relationship to it. In the last book of the poem Wordsworth too is to solemnize such a moment of climactic insight, of confirmation in an almost sacramental sense; throughout the poem, though, he has his autobiographical hero grope toward illumination tentatively and with dim recognitions.

The agencies by which the young Wordsworth is guided, half-consciously, toward his true mission in life constitute the epic "machinery" of the poem. But this basic term needs explanation, especially as it applies to *The Prelude*. Sometimes the word refers simply to fanciful departures from naturalism. In this sense Southey uses "machinery" in Book IX of the original version of *Joan*, where he introduces personifications of Despair, Superstition, Credulity, and similar qualities having allegorical but little narrative importance. More usually epic machinery describes a real interplay between two motivating impulses: the hero's own will and the outside forces, usually spiritual, which partly control him.

Wordsworth uses machinery in this more meaningful sense. The agencies of his machinery are, first of all, Nature, and, in a lesser degree, Books.[31] It goes without saying that their function as machinery is mainly metaphorical. The poet's description of Books as machinery is entirely so, as to a large extent is his description of Nature, though here we encounter one of the oldest and knottiest problems in reading Wordsworth. Except in a few passages, Nature is not described as acting on the poet primarily as the instrument of a personal God. Nor, of course, did Wordsworth believe literally that Nature had a conscious plan for him; that is, he was not a pagan. But he was intensely aware of forces which guided his life independently of his conscious will. The reader may prefer to explain these forces as subconscious ones rather than as impulses from a vernal wood, but we cannot legitimately ascribe that simply naturalistic view to Wordsworth himself. We cannot strip Wordsworth's metaphor of Nature as machinery too bare unless we are willing to oversimplify his message. Like the Platonic myth in the "Immortality" Ode, the symbolism of machinery in *The Prelude* cannot be taken literally. But, in a way that cannot be very clearly defined, Wordsworth felt it to be real.

The most striking thing about Wordsworth's relationship to Nature is its personal quality on both sides.[32] Not only does the poet love Nature; Nature herself is pictured as having conscious intentions. She exerts an active, deliberate force on the growing poet, leading him in her own paths. This personification of Nature is partly a literary device, but what is any epic machinery but a literary device, used to emphasize man's involvement with a higher order of reality and to dramatize the limitations of his human power? One reason why *The Prelude* is such a great poem is that the idea of nature's influence, which in some of Wordsworth's lesser poems can appear banal and naïve, is here reinforced and dignified by its association with a metaphor that is not simply Wordsworth's own: the epic metaphor which shows the supernatural powers manipulating human beings in the service of a divine cause.

The metaphor which endows Nature and Books with conscious purpose is thoroughly consistent and explicit in *The Prelude*. Nature operates with a "dark / Invisible workmanship," uses "means" to an "end":

> Nature, oftentimes, when she would frame
> A favor'd Being, from his earliest dawn
> Of infancy doth open out the clouds,

> As at the touch of lightning, seeking him
> With gentlest visitation;

or she can use "Severer interventions, ministry / More palpable"
(I.351–71). The incidents of the theft of birds from a neighbor's
trap and of the borrowed boat illustrate the same metaphor. After
the birds were stolen the young boy hears "Low breathings coming after me, . . . steps / Almost as silent as the turf they trod"
(I.330–32). After taking the boat, he sees the menacing cliff appear "As if with voluntary power instinct," and it strides after
him "like a living thing" (I.407–12). Here Wordsworth tells us
directly that he is using a metaphor and thus emphasizes the deliberateness of his choice to portray Nature as a conscious guide.
But normally he uses the figure more unself-consciously, a fact
that indicates how pervasively the metaphor governed and reflected his view of his life. Fleeting illustrations in the texture of
the poem are almost innumerable. "Was it for this," he asks,
"That one, the fairest of all Rivers, lov'd / To blend his murmurs
with my Nurse's song . . . ?" (I.271–73); "not in vain" did the
Spirit of the universe "intertwine for me / The passions that build
up our human Soul" (I.428–34). The influence of Nature helps
the poet to weather "this time / Of dereliction and dismay" without losing his confidence in humanity;

> the gift is yours,
> Ye mountains! thine, O Nature! Thou hast fed
> My lofty speculations.   (II.456–63)

Life in London turns his thoughts more and more toward concern
for his fellow man, but Nature is still at work: "Nature had led
me on," he insists, though he often seemed "To travel independent of her help" (VIII.864–65).

   To regard Books as part of the epic machinery may seem whimsical, but although their shaping effect on Wordsworth's mind does
not equal Nature's the two influences are of the same order. His
mission, gradually revealed through the experience the poem relates, is a literary one, and therefore it is not surprising that litera-

ture should be an agent parallel to, if less powerful than, Nature. Only by recognizing this parallelism can one fully understand Wordsworth's hope that a work of his may "become / A power like one of Nature's" (XII.311–12). Like Nature, Books are personified as a conscious agent, and the poet repeatedly links the two forces in a way which shows the pairing to be more than casual. He marvels at the mighty "power / Of living Nature" which could for a time keep him from books, "the best of other thoughts," so that he asks how he could even in infancy have played "an ingrate's part" (V.166–72). (The 1850 version further points up the metaphor and the pairing with Nature by calling Books "the best of other guides / And dearest helpers"—V. 168–69.) Books are "Powers / For ever to be hallowed; only less, / For what we may become . . . Than Nature's self . . ." (V.219–22). Books of romance represent a "gracious Spirit" presiding over the earth and the human heart, one that comes "invisibly," "directing those to works of love / Who care not, know not, think not what they do"; they are "Friends" who in our childhood reconcile us to the limitations of our new human life (V.516–47). Among the conditions of his life which led the poet to sympathize with the ideals of human equality and liberty were his lifelong tutelage to "God and Nature's single sovereignty . . . And fellowship with venerable books" (IX.237–39). And near the end of the poem, in describing his plan to write of men in humble stations, he defines his theme as "the very heart of man" as found among those who are not "uninformed by books, good books though few, / In Nature's presence" (XII.240–44).

Since Wordsworth's theme is (in the broadest sense) psychological, his emphasis on the debt he owes to powers outside himself—to the "machinery" of Nature and Books—is valuable in giving something of epic objectivity to what might have been the most fanciful and subjective of themes. But to stress external influence so heavily is to court another danger, that of depicting a heroic ideal which is entirely passive and therefore, of course, not heroic at all. From this danger Wordsworth saves himself by his familiar and basic belief in the reciprocating power of Imagination. The mind does not only perceive; it forms and creates. The poet seems to be distinctly aware that his emphasis on machinery, related though it is to the heroic tradition, poses a threat to the heroic pattern he is tracing in the poem, for several times he caps a passage describing his responsiveness to natural scenes with an emphatic assertion that man's greatness ultimately comes from himself, that the mind itself has an "auxiliar light" and a "plastic power" (XI.332–34; II.377–95), the text in both these instances emphasizing the reversal with a monitory *but*. The climactic statement of the necessity for self-reliance comes in the final book, where after naming once more the faculty of Imagination as his theme and identifying it with "intellectual Love," Wordsworth declaims in the repetitive style of the orator:

> Here must thou be, O Man!
> Strength to thyself; no Helper hast thou here;
> Here keepest thou thy individual state:
> No other can divide with thee this work,
> No secondary hand can intervene
> To fashion this ability; 'tis thine,
> The prime and vital principle is thine
> In the recesses of thy nature, far
> From any reach of outward fellowship,
> Else 'tis not thine at all.   (XIII.186–97)

Here the words "Helper" and "fellowship" do more than describe a division of powers between self and environment; they draw on the epic metaphor which sees this interplay of forces as dynamic and personal on both sides.

Thus Wordsworth's hero-self, like the hero of traditional literary epic, engages in a dialogue of action with the powers that rule his world, sometimes being impelled by his own will, sometimes by influence from above or without. But there is no question of being suspended between two conflicting forces. Wordsworth is no naturalist in the sense of the word that describes writers like Zola; in Wordsworth's universe harmony between self and environment is a realizable aspiration. His dialogue with Nature might more justly be called a dialectic; the effect of the interplay between inner and outer worlds is not hopeless conflict but synthesis. The ideal of harmonious resolution is precisely expressed in the imagery of the passage wherein Wordsworth, summing up his Alpine tour, interrupts a description of the external scene in order to extol the importance of the observer and the role played by his imagination. Here the mind is no "mean pensioner / On outward forms"; what the poet perceived with his senses "was but a stream / That flow'd into a kindred stream, a gale / That help'd me forwards," directly toward a responsiveness to grandeur, more circuitously toward "tender thoughts" (VI.667–80). The harmonious imagery of merging streams and assisting wind is significant; Wordsworth is to re-evoke it later in the poem to illustrate the greatest threat to his imaginative progress. Incidentally, the 1850 version adds to the statement of circuitous progress the words "but not less sure / Duly to reach the point marked out by Heaven" (VI.752–53). It is easy to interpret this elaboration as symptomatic of Wordsworth's much-discussed (and, I think, much-exaggerated) tendency to bring the poem in line with Christian orthodoxy. But "to reach the point marked out by Heaven" is exactly the destined role of every hero in literary epic; Wordsworth may have been refining his epic metaphor rather than his doctrine.

The ideal of balanced harmony is stated more explicitly later in the poem, where Wordsworth describes his having come to the conviction that "outward circumstance and visible form" are subject to inner passion while meanwhile

> the forms
> Of Nature have a passion in themselves
> That intermingles with those works of man
> To which she summons him,

and that therefore the poet may go boldly among mankind "Wherever Nature leads" (XII.287–96). Nature issues the call; the poet himself must respond with the resources of his own nature. In this harmonious dualism we have something very like the great theological dualism of grace and merit. Wordsworth seems to have thought occasionally in such terms, even in 1805, as when he ascribes such traits as his liking for geometry to "grace of Heaven and inborn tenderness" (VI.189).[33]

In following the pattern of literary epic which sees progress through life as mysteriously purposeful, even in its apparently trivial events, Wordsworth turns to advantage one of his most characteristic traits: optimism. In "Tintern Abbey," the "Immortality" Ode, "Elegiac Stanzas," the "Ode to Duty," and other poems Wordsworth shows his tendency to extract profit from all situations and experiences, even those involving painful loss. This is one reason why he is considered a poet of joy, yet at times the habit is irritating, since it seems to cut him off from any real appreciation of the tragic view of life. In *The Prelude,* however, with its epic pattern of purposefulness, the optimistic sense of a great guiding force and consequent belief that all is "gratulant if rightly understood" (XIII.385) are not only sanctioned but demanded by the traditional pattern.

In every great literary epic a harmonious resolution issues from the complex trials to which the hero and his ideals are subjected. But the resolution is not an easy achievement; it is attained only after agony, tears, and suffering, after an intense experience of evil and a hard-fought battle with it. Wordsworth differs from his epic predecessors by describing evil chiefly in mental terms (though he does not take the viewpoint of naturalistic psychology). Once this re-interpretation is accepted, the pattern of epic "ordeal" becomes clearer. As Miss Potts points out, *The Prelude* has a pattern of fall and redemption analogous to those of *Paradise Lost* and its sequel, except that Wordsworth's fall is not from "celestial comity" but "imaginative integrity." "How had the eighteenth-century mind, his own, deviated from the ways of poetic health? How could the nineteenth-century mind, also his own, better maintain or successfully restore its proper loyalties?"[34]

Wordsworth is not thinking only of the Miltonic pattern, and for Wordsworth too a complex kind of morality is in issue, but the question as Miss Potts puts it is essentially the one he sets out to answer, both as an individual and as a spokesman for his time.

He is constantly reminding us that his life as the poem presents it was a halting advance through temptation and peril. During a summer vacation from Cambridge he had become conscious of life as a heroic endurance test which he describes in heroic language:

> Man, if he do but live within the light
> Of high endeavours, daily spreads abroad
> His being with a [1850: armed with] strength that cannot fail,

and he had envisioned "amplest projects; and a peaceful end / At last, or glorious, by endurance won" (IV.159–66). The final version of the poem contains a passage near the end where the poet retrospectively reminds us of the ordeal pattern; Wordsworth contrasts his own history, "of lapse and hesitating choice, / And backward wanderings along thorny ways" with that of an ideal hero who should have held his course "unchecked, unerring, and untired, / In one perpetual progress smooth and bright" (1850, XIV.133–38). Yet (to return to the 1805 version) the author defends himself too, and in so doing glances at the diction of romantic chivalry; he reminds us that, however "misled" in his "quest" of right and wrong, he had never meanly tampered with conscience or been the "dupe" of "selfish passions" or yielded willfully to "mean cares and low pursuits" (XIII.130–35).

The Wordsworthian ordeal differs from those in traditional literary epic in one especially interesting way. The heroes of earlier epics had generally had to undergo in one form or another the temptation of sensuality.[35] Sometimes the flesh is used as a symbol, sometimes as a more literal temptation; in all cases it is both lovely and, at least potentially, evil. The heroes of literary epic had been entrusted with high spiritual or political missions that as a prerequisite for their accomplishment had demanded proof of moral stature, and it is therefore fitting that these heroes should be faced with moral tests and obstacles. But Wordsworth avoids almost entirely any suggestion of sensual temptation. Undoubtedly this is due partly to a strain of prudishness in Wordsworth and also to the autobiographical nature of his subject. Yet he was certainly aware of the tradition of luxurious temptation, and he makes some use of it in *The Prelude.*

We have seen that Southey substituted for sensual temptation a longing for domestic contentment. Joan and Thalaba are briefly tempted by the possibility of abandoning heroic action for the quietude of a happy family life. For them this is the alternative to stern duty, just as more lurid attractions are the alternative to duty for such heroes as Aeneas, Tasso's Rinaldo, and Spenser's Sir Guyon. For Wordsworth the domestic ideal has the same charm it has for Southey, a fact that is apparent not only throughout *The Prelude* but also in many of the minor poems. The curious thing about Wordsworth's ideal of domesticity is that in no sense does it conflict with the poet's duty. The whole of *The Prelude* makes it clear that Wordsworth's heroic ideal far transcends mere domesticity, but it remains true that the farther Wordsworth strays from the joys of humble life, the more he departs from his true path, both as a man and as a poet. It is true that once we see him contemplating a quixotic mission like that of the Arab in his dream, ready to leave behind personal ties of affection in favor of the large, rather vaguely defined task of preserving for posterity the elements of literary and scientific truth: "Enow there are on earth to take in charge / Their Wives, their Children, and their virgin Loves"; contemplating the Arab's mission, Wordsworth is tempted to "share that Maniac's anxiousness" and go "Upon like errand" (V.153–61). But, despite the superficially heroic tone used to describe the Arab, to share his mission would have carried Wordsworth away from his true path. The word "Maniac" gives us the key to Wordsworth's emphasis; the Arab has a kind of heroism, but it is that of a fanatic and not the kind, rooted in the norm of reality, that is Wordsworth's own vocation. The point is clinched in the next line, where the word "entrancement" places this temptation in the context of others in Renaissance epic and romance. And, as happens so often, the 1850 text points up the effect still more clearly, by substituting for "anxiousness" the words "fond anxiety."

The traditional hero of literary epic has to choose between personal happiness and the performance of a suprapersonal duty. For Wordsworth there is no such conflict. The cause to which he must adhere is that of personal and poetic integrity, with which domestic joy is closely linked. As a result, happiness and duty, though they are not identical, coincide. Wordsworth's departures from his high mission either bring him unhappiness and despair or, like his abortive career as Revolutionary patriot, would have done so in the long run. For Wordsworth the heroic ideal does not consist in self-sacrifice, but in self-fulfillment. In his universe the ultimate goal is harmony, equipoise between self and environment. He reconciles all difficulties and explains away pain and suffering as ultimately of small importance; everything is "gratulant if rightly understood."

There is one obvious exception to Wordsworth's rejection of sex as subject matter in *The Prelude:* the Vaudracour and Julia episode, included in the 1805 version, excerpted and printed separately in 1820, and merely hinted at in 1850. It would be idle to deny that Wordsworth's reasons for suppressing the passage were largely personal; no formal pattern, one feels, could have superseded the poet's timidity about such intimate revelations, even in the camouflaged dress he gave them. But the passage has been treated too exclusively from the autobiographical standpoint. The episode has clear possibilities as supplying one of the traditional elements of literary epic; it involves sensuality and it is set in France, a country traditionally hostile to England and a halfway house for the hero which, Aeneas-like, he temporarily considers as the goal of his wanderings and the arena of his action.

Considered in this light, the suppression of the episode could still be attributed to chivalrous motives: Wordsworth might well have been reluctant to cast Annette Vallon in the role of temptress and mere obstacle. But aesthetic grounds may be relevant too, and this apart from the wretchedly bad verse in which the passage is written. Once more we find the 1850 version refining and pointing up the pattern of mental and aesthetic ordeal; the final version eliminates an episode which, because it deals with the conventional kind of moral lapse, might obscure Wordsworth's transformation of the traditional ordeal into an ordeal of imagination. The climactic *apologia* near the end of the poem, wherein Wordsworth distinguishes emphatically between his own lapses and moral ones, has little meaning except as an affirmation by Wordsworth that he is using an old epic metaphor for a new kind of ordeal. The author has violated not conventional morality but his own better self. This emphasis on an integrity which is not primarily moral, or at least not so in the traditional sense, has become familiar in later literature—in Joyce, for example. And, though he would have rejected entirely Joyce's separation between art and public affairs, it remains true that all the lapses Wordsworth experiences in *The Prelude* are deviations from *imaginative* soundness. True, he attaches a real moral urgency to these aesthetic and mental issues (as Joyce does, for that matter), but that is different from treating traditional moral issues primarily for their own sakes.

This conversion of traditional values into a more personal and more aesthetic code accounts for Wordsworth's stern self-recriminations over matters which seem morally trivial and, from the heroic standpoint, pedestrian. The Cambridge sections are especially full of these remorseful confessions. But Wordsworth repeatedly insists that the failings were not moral ones, and to ignore the epic metaphor from which such disclaimers arise is to see him as not only priggish but repetitiously so. He tells us that the "deeper passions" of his fellow-students such as envy, jealousy, and pride, and those of "dissolute pleasure" were unshared, scarcely observed, by him, "So little was their hold upon my being"; the real failing is revealed in the following lines: "Hush'd, meanwhile, / Was the under soul," so that "not a leaf of the great nature stirr'd" (III.532–41).[36] Such explicit distinctions are rendered necessary by the pervasive metaphor through which the poem identifies imaginative soundness with morality. By his laziness and mental inertia the poet is neglecting his mission as Aeneas does in Carthage and as Rinaldo does when he abandons himself to the luxury of Armida's island retreat. Thus, in contrasting "deeper pleasures," "better things," with the "weekday works of youth," he identifies the latter with "leafy arbours";[37] Imagination "slept" while the poet wasted his time on "Companionships, / Friendships, acquaintances," casual play, "Unprofitable talk," "lazy books," "senseless horsemanship" (III.237–56). The hallowed rooms and the even more hallowed memory of Milton, the "temperate Bard," are desecrated, it would seem, through what after all is only slight inebriation caused by toasts to him, and also through the slight vanity occasioned afterwards by Wordsworth's ostentatious attendance at chapel in his privileged surplice. Exceedingly slight trespasses like these are labeled by the poet "weakness," "unworthy vanities," "Empty thoughts" of which he is "ashamed."

> In this mix'd sort
> The months pass'd on, remissly, not given up
> To wilful alienation from the right,
> Or walks of open scandal; but in vague
> And loose indifference, easy likings, aims
> Of a low pitch; duty and zeal dismiss'd,
> Yet nature, or a happy course of things
> Not doing in their stead the needful work.

The violation of "duty" and "the needful work" consists in the fact that "the inner pulse / Of contemplation almost fail'd to beat." (III.299–338.)

In a similar vein Wordsworth chastises himself for the seemingly harmless revelry of his summer vacation, when there was "an inner falling-off" caused by "heady thoughts . . . , gawds, / And feast, and dance, and public revelry, . . . sports and games." The effect was to "Seduce me [1850: lure my mind] from the firm habitual quest / Of feeding pleasures," from "eager zeal" (IV.270–79). Such revelry and the poet's stern self-indictment for having indulged in it form the background for the famous passage describing his poetic dedication, which, rather strangely, tends to diminish the poet's contrition for his "heartless chace / Of trivial pleasures," his "poor exchange / For Books and Nature" (IV.304–6). The curious psychology is exactly similar, though in reverse, to the equally curious passage describing the betrayal of Milton. The sense of high achievement associated with Milton had magnified the seriousness of trivial moral lapses; the poetic dedication is conditioned and intensified in its awesome meaning by the nightlong, lighthearted dancing party which had preceded it. The similarity between the two passages arises from Wordsworth's attempt in both to contrast a sense of high mission with the human weakness which threatens its accomplishment. In the dedication scene the finger of God has been laid upon the hero, as it was on Moses and Aeneas and St. Paul.[38] Such charismatic experiences are familiar in the epic tradition as well as in the pattern of religious conversion implied by the baptismal imagery of spiritual dedication through vicarious vows. The summer revelry is equivalent to the *felix culpa,* the evil which makes redemption necessary and possible, a concept acclimated to the epic by Dante, Spenser, and Milton and perhaps foreshadowed in Virgil's treatment of the paradoxical significance of the fall of Troy. The comparison may seem lopsided, but such analogies are part of what Wordsworth commits himself to when he decides that the mind of man as illustrated in his own growth is a truly epic theme.

Perhaps this idea that progress is conditioned by reversal and defeat explains those passages in which Wordsworth modifies his temptation metaphor by implying that his impediments were in fact needful, his trials and ordeals things to be welcomed. This view would explain not only the soothing of his regret for summer revelry, but also such passages as that in which he rejoices in having been left "safe" in his childhood from the oversupervision that might have dried him up by keeping him away from Nature (V.224–45). (The 1850 text calls these early days the "season of unperilous choice" and thus amplifies the original emphasis on the paradoxical safety of freedom.) Here the poet seems to reverse the metaphor of temptation; in fact he is only modifying it so that Nature herself, in the interest of the hero's growth, provides some of the very temptations out of which she is to help deliver her protégé. Biblical heroes are often so tried, as are epic heroes by deceiving visions and ambiguous oracles. Wordsworth is thus for a time misled by the beauty of Nature into infatuation by overwrought Fancy and the "thraldom" of the sense of sight (XI.191–99). But he hints at means which Nature "studiously" uses "to thwart / This tyranny," means by which she summons each of the senses "To counteract the other and themselves," making them "subservient . . . To the great ends of Liberty and Power" (XI. 178–84).

The deliberateness of the poem's structure is illustrated by the existence of a parallel passage in Book VIII, where Wordsworth shows Nature's coadjutor, Books, as a potential danger, which again takes the form of overdomination by that "adulterate Power," Fancy. The faculty of "plain imagination and severe" to "The notions and the images of books / Did knowingly conform itself" (VIII.592, 512–18); the poet becomes addicted to the falsely sentimental graveyard school of poetry, lends the charm of romance to a mysterious gleam of light visible at a distance among the trees, and turns a woodman's prosaic illness into repining caused by unrequited love. Nature once more rescues her favorite, through the "real solid world / Of images" with which she has provided him (VIII.559–623). The 1850 text lessens the conflict thus implied between Nature and Books by insisting that Fancy was acting "in no hurtful mood" and was even "tending towards that point / Of sound humanity to which our Tale / Leads, though by sinuous ways" (VIII.421, 451–53).

The supreme test of the hero's imaginative strength is his experience with the French Revolution and its ideals, which brings him face to face with danger not so easily explained away, a peril that nearly destroys him as it did many of his contemporaries. The age which has succeeded that of liberal optimism is one of "fear,"

"melancholy waste of hopes o'erthrown," "indifference,"
"apathy," "wicked exultation," "selfishness," "sneers / On visionary minds"—in short, "dereliction and dismay" (II.448–57).
This spiritual shipwreck, later definitively represented in the Solitary of *The Excursion,* has been caused less by the failure of the
Revolution than by the error through which men, including Wordsworth, built their hopes for the future on a false interpretation of
human nature.

We see the poet ready at one point to jeopardize his future
by becoming a Revolutionary partisan in France, a temptation to renounce poetry for politics which Miss Potts likens to the ordeal in
Book III of *Paradise Regained.*[39] But the crisis of political action
is, as usual, less important than the inner threat to integrity posed
by extreme rationalism, which is espoused by Wordsworth after
England declares war on France and the cause of liberty as the
young poet understands it. Wordsworth's other temptations had
been relatively minor, usually necessary or even wholesome; but
England's rejection of the liberal cause brings on an unprecedented
crisis. This, he relates, threw him for the first time "out of the
pale of love," corrupted his sentiments; it "was not, as hitherto,
/ A swallowing up of lesser things in great" but rather "change
of them into their opposites," opening a way for dangerous "mistakes / And false conclusions of the intellect" (X.761–69).

> Not in my single self alone I found,
> But in the minds of all ingenuous Youth,
> Change and subversion from this hour. No shock
> Given to my moral nature had I known
> Down to that very moment; neither lapse
> Nor turn of sentiment that might be nam'd
> A revolution, save at this one time,
> All else was progress on the self-same path
> On which with a diversity of pace
> I had been travelling; this a stride at once
> Into another region.   (X.232–42)

(No passage in *The Prelude* outlines the poem's form more
clearly.) The supreme heroic test had arrived, and at this signifi-

cant moment the poet takes even greater pains than usual to universalize his experience ("Not in my single self alone . . .").

This great temptation of rationalism consists in a rejection of man as tradition has known him and the attempt to create through pure reason a new type. The initial attractiveness of this ideal in the earlier, half admirable form it had taken for Wordsworth is expressed in extravagantly glowing terms wherein a reference to Eve's bower in the true paradise is blended with more sinister glances at romantic epic. Political science had taken on "The attraction of a Country in Romance"; Reason was a "prime Enchanter" (1850: "enchantress"), and as in "the bowers of paradise itself" the budding rose of future hopes was valued more than the full-blown rose of future reality. And yet this alluring goal seemed realizable in the world and not simply, as in romance, "in Utopia, subterraneous Fields, / Or some secreted Island, Heaven knows where" (X.694–728). The allusion is partly to such utopias, also rationalist, as those of More and Bacon, but also, through the emphasis on romance, to remote retreats like that of Tasso's Armida and to enchantresses like her, Circe, and Acrasia.

The result of Wordsworth's return after this crisis to his true path of imaginative integrity is the confirmation of human and social principles which prior to the crisis had been "Lodged only at the Sanctuary's door, / Not safe within its bosom" (X.678–79). Yet the heroic achievement represented in this triumph over narrow rationalism is much diminished by the tremendous debt Wordsworth acknowledges owing to Nature and to Dorothy and Coleridge for recalling him to his true mission (X.905–27; XII. 15–26). At this crucial point Wordsworth puts little emphasis on his own will power, a fact that represents a real weakness in his epic pattern. Possibly the exigencies of autobiography overrule here the heroic pattern which generally gives structure to the poem. At any rate, the manner of Wordsworth's return to imaginative health seems arbitrary and inwardly unmotivated; for almost the first time we lose sight of his inner state and see him, as it were, from outside.[40]

The often-remarked water images in *The Prelude*[41] also bear the
stamp of the ordeal and progress patterns. For in this poem it is
flowing water, water with a source, a way, and a destination, that
most interests Wordsworth, and he is impressively consistent in
using it to express his perils and progress.[42] The "smooth enthral-
ment" of his life at Cambridge is reflected in the artificially channeled brook in his garden at home (IV.39–55). More ambitiously,
he uses stream imagery near the end to summarize the entire structure of his poem; Imagination has been traced from the "blind
cavern" of its birth through "open day" and "among the ways of
Nature," through a place where it is lost to sight, to the point
where it reappears strong and triumphant, reflecting the "face of
human life," to its final goal of religious and metaphysical implications (XIII.172–84). The guiding influence of natural machinery is felt in the Derwent's blending of its murmurs with the
nurse's song and thus sending "a voice / That flow'd along my
dreams" (I.271–76) and in the poet's willingness to trust Nature's signposts; "shall a twig or any floating thing / Upon the
river, point me out my course?" (I.31–32). Raisley Calvert,
through his legacy, "clear'd a passage for me, and the stream /
Flow'd in the bent of Nature" (XIII.366–67).

Temptations and impediments to the hero's progress are likewise suggested through stream imagery. While indulging in the
trivial pastimes of his summer vacation, Wordsworth was surrounded by an air of contagion, so that his very garments seemed
to "prey upon my strength, and stopp'd the course / And quiet
stream of self-forgetfulness" (IV.290–94). The grander temptation to become a Revolutionary partisan makes him compare himself to

> a stream
> That gather'd up each petty straggling rill
> And vein of water, glad to be roll'd on
> In safe obedience.   (X.150–53)

The supreme danger, the great crisis of mind which begins with
England's betrayal of liberty, is again represented in a stream im-

age, this time one which carefully and deliberately reverses an earlier, optimistic one. Earlier he had likened his harmonious progress, aided by Nature, to "a stream / That flow'd into a kindred
stream." But now his sentiments are "Sour'd and corrupted up-
wards to the source"; the effect of England's treachery is no longer
"A swallowing up of lesser things in great" but "change of them
into their opposites"; "my likings and my loves / Ran in new
channels, leaving old ones dry" (X.762–71). Finally, his restoration is represented by still another stream image. This time it is
Dorothy who is compared to the stream. She

> like a brook
> That does but cross a lonely road, and now
> Seen, heard and felt, and caught at every turn,
> Companion never lost through many a league,
> Maintain'd for me a saving intercourse
> With my true self.   (X.911–16)

That the stream imagery is used to describe the composition of
The Prelude itself, as MacLean shows, is consistent with the other
stream images, for again the idea of progress, usually against obstacles, is involved. In fact, the progress of the poem and that of
the poem's hero are essentially bound up with each other, for, just
as his life is an attempt to find himself and to become fully aware
of his mission, so *The Prelude* itself shows a groping progress by
its author toward confidence in his theme and form.

IV

Like Milton in his different way, Wordsworth tries to render the
heroic ideal more spiritual, and, again like Milton, he rhetorically
rejects external epic array in favor of what is truly "heroic argument" and "genuine prowess," the inner mind of man. But in fact
both poets do imitate. *The Prelude* contains no set scene or passage
so obviously traditional as Milton's infernal council or war in
Heaven or catalogue of devils. But, leaving aside the pattern of

epic trial and the glances at epic diction we have been discussing, there are enough of the more arbitrary epic imitations to remind us of the poem's ancestry. The effect of these imitations is cumulative rather than particular; in scarcely a single instance can we be certain that Wordsworth was deliberately imitating an epic device. But neither must we accept at face value his claim to reject "outward things / Done visibly, . . . words, signs, / Symbols or actions" (III.174–76), which is in part a rhetorical device of emphasis like Milton's.

Before looking at Wordsworth's more serious use of epic devices, we may note one special technique which he sometimes uses: mock-epic. Much of the description of London in Book VII is in this ironic vein. In *The Prelude* Wordsworth is seldom traditional enough to invoke the Muse in the old-fashioned way; inspiring creative energy is usually identified with a force of Nature like the gentle breeze of the opening lines, which produces within the poet a "corresponding mild creative breeze" (I.43).⁴³ When he does call upon the traditional Muse by name he makes it clear that she is being used for an exceptional, comic purpose not allied to the serious theme: "For once the Muse's help will we implore, / And she shall lodge us . . . Upon some Showman's platform" (VII. 655–58). The whole seventh book is a kind of catalogue, and Wordsworth may have been trying to suggest this fact when, near the end, he says of certain scenes, "But these, I fear, / Are falsely catalogu'd" (VII.641–42).

In describing the political atmosphere of London and Parliament Wordsworth adopts a curious tone halfway between straightforwardness and mock-epic. He gives us here a whimsical equivalent of the epic council, one that finally "Grows tedious even in a young Man's ear" (VII.516–42); this scene parallels the more serious one describing Louvet and Robespierre in the French Tribune (X. 83–103). And Wordsworth invites us to think of the London debates, at least, in terms of antiquity, for his account is sprinkled with references to the past and to great names surviving from ages of British heroism—Bedfords, Glocesters, Salisburys. The later addition of a panegyric to Burke, however true or false its spirit may be to Wordsworth's early political views,[44] reinforces the epic pattern at least through its diction and imagery: Wisdom, like Athene, breaking forth "in armour of resplendent words, / Startling the Synod," "ancient story," "classic eloquence" (1850, VII. 538–42).

It remains true that Book VII, both in its earliest version and in that of 1850, is more in the eighteenth-century manner than any other part of the poem. The glances at traditional epic which reinforce Wordsworth's more serious themes are less heavy-handed. I have mentioned the substitution of the inspiring breeze for the Muse in the invocation of the poem. Another way in which Wordsworth gives the poem epic texture is in his use of the scale image, an epic cliché especially useful for the author because it connotes evaluation, especially self-evaluation. He mentions "Examinations, when the Man was weigh'd / As in the balance" (III.65–66); he attempts to evoke invigorating thoughts from earlier years in order to "fix the wavering balance of my mind" (I.650); after returning home from Cambridge, the poet states, "I took / The balance in my hand and weigh'd myself" (IV.148–49). In the city his thoughts had turned from Nature to man, but

> My Fellow beings still were unto me   5
> Far less than she was, though the scale of love
> Were filling fast, 'twas light, as yet, compared
> With that in which her mighty objects lay.
>
> (VIII.867–70)

One climactic use of the scale image is especially close to those in traditional epics, where it is often used to dramatize the will of the gods or the turn which events take at a crucial moment. The final crisis of Wordsworth's spiritual disease follows the betrayal of liberty by the French themselves when their war of defense turns into an aggressive one. The familiar image reappears: now "mounted up, / Openly, in the view of earth and heaven, / The scale of Liberty" (X.795–97). The very phrasing here recalls several passages in traditional epics.[45]

Another epic device is Wordsworth's equivalent of the omen.
The choir of redbreasts and the glow-worm (VII.20–48) are mysterious signs sent to enlighten him about the task he must pursue.
In the same vein is his willingness to take any wandering cloud as
a "guide" and to have his "course" pointed out by "any floating
thing / Upon the river" when, as he relates at the beginning of
the poem, "The earth is all before me" (I.15–32). "And Providence thir guide," Milton had added, but Wordsworth has his own
form of Providence, Nature. His omens are therefore more than
textural reminders of the epic tradition; it is fitting that he should
look to Nature, his "machinery," for casual but mysterious guidance, since it has much the same relationship to him as the gods
in epic have to their favorites as well as the same relationship that
the Muse has to poets. The apparently awkward way in which
Wordsworth confesses that the opening lines were written on the
very day they describe should be seen in this light. Nature, the inspiring Muse, has vouchsafed him easy unpremeditated verse such
as Milton says was given to him; to Wordsworth "poetic numbers
came / Spontaneously" and thus "singled out" his spirit for "holy
services" (I.55–63).

The most important formal area in which Wordsworth is indebted to the traditional epic is structural and narrative. The ordeal pattern is part of this area, as is the chronological pattern.
Wordsworth's notorious habit of doubling back is partly dictated
by his need to reconcile personal history with universality and by
his method of organization, which is partly chronological and
partly topical. But the habit is also related to the traditional omnis-
cience of the epic poet—the prerogative by which, for example,
Homer can relate at the moment of a hero's death a poignant scene
from his past—and to the *medias res,* or flashback, convention. In
the traditional epics inset narratives usually clear the scene and
the reader's mind for an impending climax by relaxing temporarily the main narrative tension. After Raphael's discourse comes
the Fall; after Odysseus' story comes his return to Ithaca and his
decisive fight with the suitors. Aeneas's narrative precedes his love

affair with Dido, which is his second-greatest trial. Wordsworth's most sustained use of the long flashback is Book VIII, "Retrospect —Love of Nature Leading to Love of Man." Immediately afterward, at the beginning of Book IX, he plunges into the decisive section of his poem and the account of his severest test, involvement with the Revolution and its ideals. Here, much like Milton in his own ninth book, he heralds "the argument which now / Awaits us; Oh! how much unlike the past!" (IX.13–14).[46] And at this point he again evokes a river image, a very elaborate one which promises a more direct, less "retrograde" motion toward the sea, that is, toward the goal of the poem's action. (The image, incidentally, is in the form of a full-scale epic simile, and in the 1850 version it is expanded into the even more elaborate double simile so often used at climactic moments in epic.) Wordsworth's subsequent account of the Revolution itself likewise begins in the middle, if we discount the sketchier glimpses of France in earlier books. And of course the very beginning of the poem shows us the poet at a time when most of the incidents described later in *The Prelude* have already happened.

One of the most impressive passages in *The Prelude* is the description in the final book of the prospect from Mount Snowdon, and in this passage Wordsworth's method is again very close to that of certain older epic poets. In an age which read *The Prelude* almost exclusively as autobiography it was possible to consider the last book, as Harper did, an "anticlimax."[47] It is true that Wordsworth has reached the personal climax in the preceding book, where he describes the final clarification of the principles of human love whose seeds had been sown in childhood. If *The Prelude* were simply autobiography, the last book, or at least the Snowdon episode, would indeed be superfluous.

But, precisely because the poem is more than this, the Snowdon passage is essential. Book XIII (XIV in the 1850 text) projects the import of the poem into Wordsworth's own future and especially into the great world of which as individual he is only a part. He has earlier expressed the hope that his poetry may become, in

his precise term, "A power like one of Nature's" (XII.312),
that is, a force toward spiritual and emotional wholeness, a re-
storer in an age of dereliction and dismay. The medium through
which this is to be accomplished is the Imagination, which is symbolized in the Snowdon passage. The whole vast symbol—the serene moon in the heavens, the sea of mist at the poet's feet, the
rift in the cloudy floor through which rises the sound of the
ocean's waves—illustrates concretely, and independent of Wordsworth's own history, the resemblance between the workings of Nature and the workings of the "mighty Mind" of the poet, which
transforms the dead letter of experience as the moon does the
scene beneath her.[48] Earlier in the poem Wordsworth has several
times asserted the dominance of his own mind over mere sense
impressions; this time he is concerned not directly with himself
but with the universal applications of the symbol he evokes. He
makes it quite clear that the "mighty Mind" whose emblem he be-
holds is not specifically his own, for after his rhapsody in praise
of such a mind he cries out, "who is he that hath his whole life
long / Preserved, enlarged this freedom in himself?" (XIII.120–
21), adding in the 1850 version that the poem has recounted a
"humbler destiny."

The Snowdon episode departs with special pointedness from the
semi-autobiographical pattern of the earlier books; although
Wordsworth describes an actual climbing of Mount Snowdon, he is
not at all concerned with that as an incident but rather, exclusively,
with the resultant symbolic vision which universalizes the theme
in place and time and which affords a larger perspective within
which the poet's personal experience as told in the whole poem
can be understood. The vision illustrates the highest power of the
human mind in general, and thus it returns us to the passage in
Book III where Wordsworth had triumphantly modulated from a
declaration that his theme has been "What pass'd within me" to a
plural emphasis on "the might of Souls" and had gone on to in-
sist that "there's not a man . . . who hath not had his godlike
hours" (III.174–92). In a strikingly similar phrase and again
with a shift to plural emphasis he tells us of the minds symbolized

in the Snowdon scene: "Such minds are truly from the Deity, / For they are Powers" (XIII.106–7). It is true that Wordsworth claims to be describing here certain "higher minds," but he also emphasizes that the ideal exists for every man; imaginative power is something that "even the grossest minds must see and hear / And cannot chuse but feel" (XIII.83–84). (The 1850 version makes the point even more clearly and emphatically.) The poet is a man like other men except in degree. The two passages, in Book III and Book XIII, are closely parallel to each other, and their function of framing between them the new heroic theme of Imagination stands out even more clearly when we remember that Wordsworth introduces the first statement of his theme, in Book III, with the declaration that he has retraced his life "Up to an eminence" (III.169).

The "eminence" of Book XIII is familiar in epic; it is the vantage point for revelatory vision of the world, its true significance, and the hero's place in it. Adam views from his mountain the future of the world as he has shaped it; in the *Lusiad* Vasco da Gama sees a celestial and geographical vision; Dante, too, has a brief panoramic vision of the universe after he has reached the Heaven of Fixed Stars.[49] Adam's vision is moral and religious; da Gama's is imperial and scientific; Dante's is cosmic. Wordsworth's is imaginative. It is also, like the others, universal, for Imagination allows man to transcend time and circumstance. Men of imaginative power, unlike the older type of hero (it is implied), "need not extraordinary calls / To rouze them"; they are not "By sensible impressions . . . enthrall'd" (we recall the poet's own "thraldom" to objects of sight); they can commune with the "invisible world" (XIII.101–5). The 1850 version claims an even wider empire; great minds can hold converse

> with the generations of mankind
> Spread over time, past, present, and to come,
> Age after age, till Time shall be no more.
> (XIV.109–11)

(This addition is perfectly in the spirit of the original version, since it simply elaborates the idea, important from the outset, that poets are "even as Prophets, . . . Connected in a mighty scheme of truth.") The new heroic theme, the human mind, is of infinite dimensions. The same claim to limitless vistas had been made by the great epic poets.

V

In our age it is a commonplace to argue that the creative artist has replaced the saint. It is the artist (the argument runs) who today must renounce the "world"; only he can find meaning in life and point the way to what we still like to call salvation. He does so not by finding answers for us but by exemplifying the arduous task of self-knowledge. Nor is the claim reserved for writers and other professional artists; the same attitude has resulted in a reverence for creativity on all levels, from the kindergarten to the scientist's laboratory.[50] Paradoxically, the canonization of the artist has coincided with a tendency to empty works of art themselves of moral content and to consider them as self-sufficient aesthetic objects. The process, so to speak, is what counts, not the result.

Equally familiar is the argument that all this began with the Romantics. And it is tempting to see *The Prelude* as a milestone in the process by which the artist has become a cultural hero. Is not this the obvious significance of Wordsworth's translation of the traditional moral ordeal into an imaginative one? As we have seen, he belabors his conscience because of the "trivial pleasures" he had indulged in during his youth and in other ways converts morally indifferent errors into major sins, since they led him from the path of imaginative health. In short, he redefines sin and righteousness according to an artistic criterion.

But it would be wrong, I believe, to draw such a conclusion. For one thing, Wordsworth thinks of himself, in his capacity as hero of the poem, as an artist only incidentally. The poem is about the mind of a poet, but that is mainly because every man is a poet. In some ways, of course, this answer supports the argument which

I am denying, for if Wordsworth sees every man as a poet then he anticipates the modern worship of creativity for everyone. But there is another and more important answer: Wordsworth simply accepts as part of the truth what many modern artists take for the whole truth, namely that man's business in life is to find himself, to discover the sources of his own power. The importance of self-discovery for Wordsworth can hardly be exaggerated, and I do not wish to underestimate it; this is precisely what *The Prelude* is most concerned with. But the poem is not a complete exposition of Wordsworth's beliefs; at least, Wordsworth did not think it was when he wrote it (we must remember that it was intended to be an introduction to his definitive philosophical work), and there are many statements near the end of the poem that point beyond the metaphor of imaginative ordeal toward a larger world of objective and usually traditional values. The end of *The Prelude* is both a terminus and a commencement; the serious metaphor of epic ordeal according to which the acquisition of imaginative power is considered a goal in itself comes to an end, but the question then remains, what should a man do with this power, how should he apply it in the world?

The full answer as it relates to man in general was presumably reserved for the philosophical poem which remained largely unwritten. But for Wordsworth himself the answer is fairly simple. As a result of his ordeal, "The workings [1850: perturbations] of a youthful mind, beneath / The breath [1850: storm] of great events" (X.944–45), he becomes fully aware of his mission in life. It is the application of his imaginative power through poetry, and one of the things poetry means for him is teaching. Here, in this emphasis on the teaching function of art, lies the definitive difference between Wordsworth and the modern artist whom one might suspect to be his descendant. It is true that much of what Wordsworth feels he has to teach is the very thing that he has learned through the experiences recounted in *The Prelude:* how to acquire and fortify imaginative power. But beyond that lesson lie more objective ones; the philosophical poem, we must always remember, is supposedly before him. The Imagination is not a new value; rather, it is to provide a new way of apprehending old ones. For one of Wordsworth's goals is to link present and future values to those of the past.

I stressed earlier what is new in Wordsworth's theme, but at least in *The Prelude* the poet finds that he can look with faith to the future only because of the reassurance summoned from the past, not only his personal past but history as well. To appeal thus to history is to adopt implicitly the definitive humanistic stance, for the appeal acknowledges an irreducible human core which subsists in all ages beneath the veneer of change. But circumstances, at least, *do* change, and the human spirit must express itself in the new ways appropriate to those changes. Hence *The Prelude* looks before and after, not by way of finding a balance between future and past, but by asserting an organic continuity which rests on perennial truths about human nature. This is exactly the position taken by the great epic poets, who are typically both iconoclasts and conservatives at the same time—unlike Southey, for example, who, along with most people in every age, took a more myopic view in his epics, an either-or view which caused him first to spurn the past and then to worship it from afar.

"Every great poet," Wordsworth once wrote, "is a Teacher: I wish either to be considered as a Teacher, or as nothing"; and, however the exact meaning of the statement may have changed for him, the basic belief was a lifelong conviction.[51] *The Prelude* itself is distinctly a didactic poem. Like the *Essay on Man,* it is to convey universal and timeless truths; "general truths" are part of the epic poet's equipment mentioned in Book I. But its more vital message is, like that of almost all great epics, an application of these principles to the needs of the time. Like the traditional epic poet, Wordsworth sees the present as giving meaning to the past, but the reverse is also true: the poet must extrapolate the ideals of the past through the crisis of the present into the future.[52] Wordsworth feels he can help the men of his age because he diagnoses its disease as the very one to which he almost succumbed. He himself has maintained "A more than Roman confidence" (again we find a compliment to the past combined with a boast of superiority to it); the age can do so too. During his crisis he had rejected the past, not, as in his early days of Revolutionary optimism, simply because it had outlived its legitimate day, but with a desperation and impatience which cut human nature off from its roots in history. He had hoped and believed that the future would see a new kind of man, "parted as by a gulph, / From him who had been"; he no longer felt his bond with "the great Family . . . scatter'd through the abyss of ages past, / Sage, Patriot, Lover, Hero." Even the poets to whom he turned for a human ideal seemed tainted, for "If Reason be nobility in man," then surely the heroes of literature were ignoble (XI.57–73). Stated in terms of epic tradition, Wordsworth's disease was loss of faith in the possibility of heroism.

This was a great falling-off for Wordsworth, who had been moved deeply by the Chartreuse monastery, awed by the sense of past achievements in London, haunted even in his Revolutionary days by evocations in the French forests of Ariosto's heroines and Francis I as courtly lover. Though when he first lived in France he had prized the historian's tale mainly because it made the heart beat high and filled the "fancy" with fair forms (IX.206–9), he had even thus "carried about me yet / With less alloy to its integrity / The experience of past ages" (IX.340–42). He and Beaupuy had summoned up "the honorable deeds / Of ancient Story," each "bright spot" in "recorded time" which had told of the victory of truth over error (IX.371–74).

The remedy, for both Wordsworth and the age, is a return to the true sources of health as they are enshrined in the past, a renewed dedication to heroism. Wordsworth's attempt to approach the "hiding-places of my [1850: man's] power" and thus to enshrine "the spirit of the Past / For future restoration" (XI.336–43) refers most directly to his personal past but also to history. Like the great epic poets, he has come to see human experience as a continuum, a meaningful sequence. Hence the curious passage

in which Wordsworth implies spiritual kinship with the Druids,
the ancient British seers, hence his claim that poets are linked together like prophets and his hope that he may be one of the band
(XII.301–53). There is a sense in which the poem, like Burke,

> the majesty proclaims
> Of Institutes and Laws, hallowed by time;
> Declares the vital power of social ties
> Endeared by Custom,

insists "Upon the allegiance to which men are born" (1850, VII.
525–30). Thus Wordsworth's decision to write an epic poem becomes an almost inevitable one, for to write a poem that achieves
a viable formulation of heroism is to assert the possibility of spiritual health for all the poet's contemporaries. (A more detailed
prescription was presumably to come later, in the philosophic
poem.) Nor can the mere youthful optimism which looks to the
future for unprecedented glories be realistically sustained; the
nourishment must come from the past, must be part of what man
has always had within him.

To some extent the task of re-establishing a view of human nature on the basis of past experience is a personal problem, one
that each man must work out for himself. But it is also a social
ideal and in this respect traditionally epic. And, like both the
Prophets and the epic poets, Wordsworth denounces as well as
consoles. His admiration for the Druids takes on special meaning
when we recall an earlier passage where he says that the visions he
sometimes enjoyed while at Cambridge were "madness" only

> If prophesy be madness; if things view'd
> By Poets of old time, and higher up
> By the first men, earth's first inhabitants,
> May in these tutor'd days no more be seen
> With undisorder'd sight.   (III.151–55)

In a similar spirit is his condemnation of the intellectual life of his
university and his call for a revival of the medieval and Renaissance zeal for learning in his own "recreant" age (III.407–91,
409). The context of this passage is, significantly, Wordsworth's

regret over his own recreancy at Cambridge. And, in view of his explicit parallel with France, it seems probable that he wished to portray Sicily as a political *memento mori* for the modern world. Far more sorrowful than the fate of France is the spectacle of "a Land / Strew'd with the wreck of loftiest years," "substantially renown'd / Of simple virtue once, and manly praise," now "without one memorial hope" (X.955–64). But, characteristically, the poet soon pulls himself up and returns to his consolatory task:

> But Indignation works where hope is not,
> And thou, O Friend! wilt be refresh'd. There is
> One great Society alone on earth,
> The noble Living and the noble Dead. (X.967–70)

The lines just quoted are addressed, not directly to the men of the time, but to Coleridge, who in a very special way is a representative, even a conventional, figure in the poem. When Wordsworth last revised *The Prelude* thoroughly, Coleridge had been dead for several years, and even before his death the friendship between the two men had long since cooled. Wordsworth eliminated certain of the original biographical references to Coleridge (for example, his role in the author's restoration), but the final text emphatically retains Coleridge as the general addressee. One reason, I believe, is that Coleridge's role in the poem is not merely autobiographical but also formal: he is, in fact, the traditional epic patron-addressee. In this role he corresponds to the Augustus whom Virgil implicitly invokes, to the Duke of Ferrara in Tasso, and to King Sebastiano in Camoëns, each of whom is urged to maintain and project into the future the ideals celebrated in the poem.[53] In the last thirty lines of *The Prelude* Coleridge is exhorted in messianic language to share with Wordsworth the task of spiritual restoration; they are to be "Prophets of Nature," speaking "lasting inspiration," together glorifying "the mind of man."

Like the traditional epic patron, Coleridge is also invoked as an inspirational guide for the composition of the poem itself. He is asked to "Uphold, as heretofore, my fainting steps" (III.201). And, although Wordsworth eliminated from his first version the request that Coleridge "assist me as a Pilgrim gone / In quest of highest truth" (XI.392–93), the deletion is more than compensated for by Wordsworth's elaboration of a relatively casual compliment to his friend into a magniloquent appeal for Coleridge to help the great epic enterprise:

> thou wilt stand
> On Etna's summit, above earth and sea,
> Triumphant, winning from the invaded heavens
> Thoughts without bound, magnificent designs,
> Worthy of poets who attuned their harps
> In wood or echoing cave, for discipline
> Of heroes.   (1850, XI.453–59)

The discipline of heroes—that is Wordsworth's goal and the final goal of *The Prelude*. And the crusade is to be accomplished under the patronage and with the help of Coleridge, who throughout the poem has been addressed with the urgency and hyperbolical courtesy traditionally expressed toward the epic patron.[54]

VI

The difference between Southey and Wordsworth as epic poets is not simply the difference between a mediocre poet and a great one. They illustrate the curious fact that in some ways the poet who takes most liberties with the epic tradition is the one who most deeply understands and respects it. Wordsworth uses epic devices less conventionally than does Southey but seems to take the epic more seriously. For Southey the epic is a fairly strict form, one that he sometimes reveres, sometimes ironically subverts; in either case he treats it as static and a thing of the past, however strongly he may have believed that it was alive. For Wordsworth the epic is more than a literary genre and more than a vehicle to be exploited for transient journalistic purposes. It is a mode of personal statement as well as an expression of definitive human values, which is what it had been for the great epic poets before him. The epic pattern lies deep in *The Prelude*—so deep, in fact, that the traditional imitativeness seems at first to be lacking. Nevertheless, it is there, not as something added but as the symptom of Words-worth's unforced allegiance to the poets of heroism before him. The epic pattern of *The Prelude* is not perfect; the autobiographi-cal emphasis is not completely harmonized with the general epic theme, so that some small distance seems to remain between the poem and full epic status. But then, at one time critics thought of Milton's allegory of Sin and Death as a damaging violation of the epic form. As the passage of time brings better understanding of Wordsworth's message, makes it appear less eccentric and less purely autobiographical, the small distance which today seems to separate *The Prelude* from true epic may, as with *Paradise Lost*, come to seem less important. The more one reads *The Prelude* the clearer it becomes that in its intellectual and emotional grasp of human life and in the central relevance of its message the poem has the inevitability of the great epic visions.

Four: SHELLEY

"HOLY AND HEROIC VERSE"

T HE orphan of Shelley criticism is *The Revolt of Islam*. The
sources of the poem have been diligently sought out, and books
on Shelley's general development usually treat the poem in at least
an incidental way; but, with a few notable exceptions, critics have
shown little interest in *The Revolt* for its own sake. This fact is
hard to explain, if only because the poem is by far Shelley's long-
est—almost twice as long as *Prometheus Unbound* and more than
twice as long as any of the others. Admittedly *The Revolt* does not
represent Shelley's poetry at its best, yet it is a good poem and in
any case much superior to *Queen Mab*, which as a document has
received critical attention far out of proportion to its poetic value.
There is also a tendency among critics to think of *The Revolt* (or
Laon and Cythna, as it was called before Shelley altered and re-
named it) as merely repeating, with slight modifications, the views
expressed in *Queen Mab*. But in 1817, when *The Revolt of Islam*
was written, four years had gone by since *Queen Mab,* and many
of the most important experiences that were to shape Shelley's
thought and aesthetic had already occurred. It is easy to forget that
within a year after the completion of *The Revolt* Shelley had
started to work on *Prometheus Unbound*. In 1817 the "Hymn to
Intellectual Beauty" was a year old. *Queen Mab,* with its doctrin-
aire necessitarianism and its soap-box invective, belongs to Shelley's juvenilia; *The Revolt of Islam* is, though imperfect, a poem
worthy of respect in its own artistic right.

In *The Revolt of Islam,* then, we have not pale foreshadowings
of the essential Shelley who is to come; we have the poet himself.
But although *The Revolt* is not a juvenile poem, it is a transitional
one. Shelley had come a long way from the active radicalism which
had earlier led him to take action as a propagandist in Ireland,

and the poem shows clearly that he no longer believed that only institutions stood between man and his glorious future. But on the other hand Shelley had not yet become the idealist of *Adonais* and *Epipsychidion*,[1] and *The Revolt of Islam* is still Godwinian in some ways. Moreover, as its Preface makes clear, the poem is meant to have an immediate educational impact, to deal in some fashion with problems that were local and immediate in Shelley's own day. The poem is not simply a gospel for the future; like *The Prelude,* it is an attempt to ameliorate the social and intellectual pessimism left in the wake of the French Revolution.

Because *The Revolt of Islam* is a transitional poem, it contains several important ambiguities—for example, Shelley's wavering attitude toward the immortality of the soul and the rather anomalous position which he assigns to Necessity. Perhaps such ambiguities partially account for the critical neglect of the poem, for it defines adequately neither the "early" Shelley nor the "late," somewhat disillusioned one. But for the very reason that it is a turning-post in his career, Shelley's epic has a special interest; in it the dim-pinnacled idealism of the later poetry and the zealous, impatient extravagance of his youth mingle in a kind of explosion-mixture out of which Shelley creates an erratic but powerful kind of art.

The Revolt of Islam expresses a double vision of man; it sees him both close up and from long range. And for the accomplishment of this twofold purpose Shelley uses, with certain important modifications, the epic form, the form ideally suited to such a plan. For the literary epic generally operates on two planes, that of the local, human, and temporal, and that of the universal, superhuman, and timeless. Of the two, however, it is always the human and relatively familiar plane that is in the foreground; Milton subordinates the fall of the angels to the human fall, and the importance of Virgil's deities in the *Aeneid* lies mainly in their involvement with the human actors. Shelley's *Prometheus Unbound* operates very largely as myth, for although on one level it shows human renewal as realizable within time, it is at least equally concerned with the ontological question of man's relationship to non-circumstantial reality.[2] But, although its doctrine sometimes comes very close to that of *Prometheus, The Revolt* is a different kind of poem; it is almost entirely concerned with the dynamics of human history. It does in certain passages use idealized allegory, and its narrative is set within a generalizing framework, but these remote vistas are intended to sharpen by contrast the reader's vision of the world that lies around him. In *The Revolt* eternity is the shadow cast by men and events rather than the white reality refracted prismatically in them. In short, the viewpoint of the poem is the immemorial charismatic viewpoint of epic.

II

Shelley never said in so many words that *The Revolt of Islam* was an epic, but there can be very little doubt that he meant it to be one.[3] The best evidence comes from within the poem itself. But Shelley also indicated fairly clearly what he thought the epic was, and his definition parallels closely his unusually explicit declarations of what he wanted *The Revolt* to be and do. His epic theory is in some ways genuinely unorthodox, but it is not so much so as one might expect. Indeed, its most salient characteristics place Shelley in the main line of epic.

Like all the great Romantics, Shelley regarded the literary past with both reverence and rebelliousness, but his rebelliousness was directed less at poets than at false literary principles. He was, as everyone knows, one of the best-read of English poets, and surely none of them, even Milton, has ever read so seriously or has responded so imaginatively as Shelley did to the blood brothers whom he was continually finding among the elder poets. His knowledge of and, usually, devotion to the great literary epics of the past, both before and after he wrote *The Revolt of Islam*, are abundantly proved in his letters, in Mary's journal,[4] and in his prose works. Indeed, the literature of the past was, in his opinion, a novitiate for the poetic priesthood, as the Preface to *The Revolt* strongly implies (*Works*, I, 243).[5] Moreover, the debt which in the Preface to *Prometheus Unbound* Shelley acknowledges to contemporary authors is so generally expressed that it can easily be extended to the poets of the past as well: "Poetical abstractions are beautiful and new, not because the portions of which they are composed had no previous existence in the mind of man or in nature, but because the whole produced by their combination has some intelligible and beautiful analogy with those sources of emotion and thought, and with the contemporary condition of them: one great poet is a masterpiece of nature which another not only ought to study but must study. . . . Every man's mind is . . . modified by all the objects of nature and art; by every word and every suggestion which he ever admitted to act upon his consciousness" (*Works*, II, 173–74). At one time Shelley suggested that Byron had used Thomas Hope's *Anastasius* as a source for three cantos of *Don Juan;* "That, of course," he hurriedly added, "has nothing to do with the merit of this latter: poetry having nothing to do with the invention of facts."[6]

The modernist position which at least superficially seems more characteristic of Shelley amounts, in general, to a declaration of independence rather than iconoclasm. If lifeless fact is immaterial to poetry, so is lifeless precept. He criticizes Hunt for following "rules" too meticulously in *The Story of Rimini*, praises Byron's "freedom from common rules" in *Manfred, Lara*, and *The Prisoner of Chillon*, and claims to have avoided "system and mannerism" in his own poetry.[7] One notes that the target is not so much the past as "rules" and "system," which Shelley considers irrelevant just as he believes that the invention of facts "has nothing to do with" poetry. (In practice Shelley was not always able to ignore rules so easily.)

No one could deny that Shelley's sense of the epic lineage is sometimes eccentric, as when in *A Defence of Poetry* he denies the title of epic poet to Lucretius for the sole reason that he had "limed the wings of his swift spirit in the dregs of the sensible world" (*Works,* VII, 130). Such a statement suggests that for Shelley the term "epic poet" was a general honorific and no more. Furthermore, Shelley more than once condemned imitativeness, which is a different thing altogether from renouncing rules. In *A Defence,* for example, he argues that Roman poetry was limited in its value because it aped the Greeks, and a few pages later he seems to reject a whole battery of standard epic poets on the same grounds: "Homer was the first and Dante the second epic poet . . . Virgil, with a modesty which ill became his genius, had affected the fame of an imitator, even whilst he created anew all that he copied; and none among the flock of Mock-birds, though their notes were sweet, Apollonius Rhodius, Quintus Calaber Smyrnetheus, Nonnus, Lucan, Statius, or Claudian, have sought even to fulfil a single condition of epic truth. Milton was the third epic poet. For if the title of epic in its highest sense be refused to the Aeneid, still less can it be conceded to the Orlando Furioso, the Gerusalemme Liberata, the Lusiad, or the Fairy Queen." (*Works,* VII, 124–30.)

These apparently straightforward statements are in fact rather complex ones. The first of the two passages explains that the Romans were remiss not so much because they imitated the Greeks as because they failed to create "any thing which might bear a particular relation to their own condition, whilst it might bear a general one to the universal constitution of the world." In other words, the Romans (and Shelley specifies Horace, Catullus, and Ovid) erred by way of misunderstanding their age and nation. Excepted are Lucretius and Virgil, the second of whom Shelley terms "in a very high sense, a creator." In the second passage, though, we learn that Virgil overmodestly "affected the fame of an imitator, even whilst he created anew all that he copied" and is therefore debarred from the epic pantheon. Here it is difficult to understand what charge Shelley is bringing against Virgil, for if Virgil was indeed a creator he ought not to be denied epic credentials just because he was humble or because he created in spite of himself. In fact, though, we ought not to look for sober consistency in the passage, any more than we ought to try to reconcile Milton's rejection of epic paraphernalia with his practice. Shelley's résumé of the history of epic is one more example of the rhetorical device by which the poet preaches progress through denigrating the past. The contemptuous epithet "Mock-birds" is entirely typical of this rhetoric and even more typical of the tendency, common to epic poets and theorists alike, to exclude all but the very greatest works. Thus the Renaissance epics come off better than the sweet notes of the Mock-birds of antiquity but are excluded on the *a fortiori* grounds of inferiority to the *Aeneid*. Shelley is in effect recognizing the epic lineage in the very act of rejecting it, and by the usual method of citing models and precedents rather than formal rules. The rejection and recognition are complementary, mutually dependent gestures; each gives meaning to the other. There is else little point in naming works only to declare them irrelevant. And indeed Shelley does not quite say that, for the Renaissance poems, at least, are denied only the title of epic "in its highest sense." The only way in which the passage is somewhat atypical of epic tradition is in refusing to sweep away impatiently *all* the epics of the past as dead and superseded.

But Shelley also defines the epic in more general terms, and in doing so he consistently emphasizes that epic is an organic tradition, a succession of progeny. His requirements are two: first, an epic must emphasize human action in a setting of universality, and second, an epic must be in spiritual union with its age. These ideas and lesser points in support of them are fugally developed in Shelley's statements on poetry and the epic; sometimes one emphasis is more prominent than the others but generally they blend with and modify one another.

In his "Essay on the Devil and Devils," which seems to have been written two or three years after *The Revolt of Islam*, Shelley makes a brief and polite bow to formal criteria but essentially defines epic "law" as the law of truth, truth that is ethical and centered in man. Of Milton he writes:

He mingled as it were the elements of human nature, as colours upon a single pallet [sic], and arranged them into the composition of his great picture, according to the laws of epic truth; that is, according to

the laws of that principle by which a series of actions of intelligent
and ethical beings, developed in rhythmical language, are calculated to
excite the sympathy and antipathy of succeeding generations of mankind. The writer who would have attributed majesty and beauty to the
character of victorious and vindicative omnipotence, must have been contented with the character of a good Christian; he never could have been
a great epic poet.[8]

Epic must, according to this formulation, depict human nature
through the actions of individuals, but it must also make an appeal across the ages. One notes too the appropriateness of the metaphor from painting, which is a particularly good one for Shelley
since it illustrates his belief that poetry in general should influence
readers affectively rather than cerebrally. The specific function of
epic is to serve truth, not so much abstract truth as the truth that
is relevant to human nature. Nor is it enough that the epic poet
create embodiments of truth; he must also exemplify it in his own
person. It is no great step from this belief to Milton's avowal that
the poet's own life should be a poem and to the incarnations of that
idea in the autobiographical section of *The Reason of Church-
Government,* in Wordsworth's elaborate self-appraisal in Book I
of *The Prelude,* and in Shelley's very similar inventory of his
powers and training in the Preface to *The Revolt of Islam.*

   A Defence of Poetry defines the relationship the epic poet must
have to his own age; the connection is one which, paradoxically,
depends on his ability to transcend the age. Epic, Shelley argues,
must bear "a defined and intelligible relation to the knowledge
and sentiment and religion and political conditions of the age in
which [its author] lived, and of the ages which followed it: developing itself in correspondence with their development." One
thing Shelley is saying is that no one can see truthfully even what
lies directly before him in his own age if he is ignorant of the
larger verities whose repository is the whole history of man. The
poetry of Dante is "the bridge thrown over the stream of time,
which unites the modern and antient World." He and Milton
were true to the "distorted notions of invisible things" prevalent
in their respective ages, but they also had the larger vision which

by its heterodox recognition of perennial truth gave the two poets a paradoxical timeliness (*Works,* VII, 129–30). In other words, the great epic poets are links in a single chain, and just as an isolated link ceases to have a place and function, that is, ceases in a sense to be anything at all, so the poet who mistakes the prejudices of his time for universal human verities ceases to speak as a true representative even of his own age. And Shelley insists that any poet, but especially the epic poet, must so speak.

The same idea, but with the emphasis reversed, underlies Shelley's criticism of those Roman poets who, unlike Virgil creating anew all that he copied, imitated the Greeks in a spirit of alienation from their own Roman way of life. The poet, and especially the epic poet, must speak for his age; he must represent in his work even the weaknesses and errors of his world. He "considers the vices of his contemporaries as the temporary dress in which his creations must be arrayed, and which cover without concealing the eternal proportions of their beauty." An "epic or dramatic personage" wears the manners of his day as he wears its customary dress, and "it is doubtful whether the alloy of costume, habit, &c., be not necessary to temper this planetary music for mortal ears" (*Works,* VII, 116–17).

Even through the coloring of Shelley's idealistic language one can discern clearly in his comments on epic the convention which sees it as charismatic prophecy, as the expression of a unique moment which takes its meaning from an order that far transcends the moment. Nevertheless, the Platonic idealism of certain of the passages we have been looking at is in some ways out of keeping with Shelley's actual approach to epic in *The Revolt of Islam,* where the cosmic background for the narrative is occasionally the one, eternal, and timeless, but much more often the perennial truth of human nature in the continuum of history. Moreover, though Shelley is explicitly writing of epic in most of these theoretical passages, one sometimes wonders whether he is not also talking about poetry in general; "epic" and "dramatic" personages, one notes, blend into each other. In some ways we get a sharper view of Shelley's epic theory from his letters, especially those discussing Byron's *Don Juan*, a poem whose history is closely related to Shelley's own epic.

On September 29, 1816, Shelley wrote to Byron suggesting that Byron at some time undertake an epic poem and tentatively proposing the French Revolution as a subject. Shelley's language is solemn and magisterial. Byron is not to be concerned with fame in any vulgar way; he is to be content with an audience who share his views. One recognizes the "fit audience though few" convention. Byron is not to undertake the poem immediately; he is to approach it through lesser and intermediate steps (another convention of the epic tradition; the "season due" is not to be disturbed), after which, having seen the "truth of things," Byron is to devote all his "studies" to the "greater enterprise" for which he has been "chosen out from all other men" and which is thereafter to carry all his "worldly hopes." The French Revolution is recommended as a subject "qualified to interest and to instruct mankind." It is hard to see how Shelley could have couched his exhortation in more traditional terms. Even the sentence next following, wherein he states that Byron should make use of no understanding but his own, is not an appeal for Byron to avoid imitating earlier epics but rather urbane self-effacement on Shelley's part: he wants Byron to choose his own theme rather than feel bound by Shelley's suggestion.

Byron did not write the particular epic poem that Shelley had in mind, but Shelley himself tried to do so a year later in *The Revolt of Islam*. He continued, however, to hope that Byron would write an epic. On July 16, 1821, Shelley wrote: "I still feel impressed with the persuasion that you *ought*—and if there is prophecy in hope, that you *will* write a great and connected poem, which shall bear the same relation to this age as the 'Iliad,' the 'Divina Commedia,' and 'Paradise Lost' did to theirs." Having named what for him were the three definitive epics, Shelley adds rather self-consciously that Byron is not to imitate the structure or subjects of these poems or otherwise to take them as models. On the other hand, *"disjecti membra poetae,"* as he calls the poems Byron has already written, will never "place your memory on a level with those great poets." Here Shelley repeats in effect his definition of epic as a poem representative of its age, this time mentioning the requirement of universality only implicitly or not at all.

Less than a month later Byron read to Shelley one of the cantos of *Don Juan,* the first canto of which he had heard and admired three years before.[9] Shelley's reaction was ecstatic: the poem, he wrote to Mary, placed its author far above his contemporaries; every word of it was "stamped with immortality." The "most rigid asserter of the dignity of human nature" could object to nothing in the canto, and he added that "it fulfills in a certain degree what I have long preached of producing something wholly new and relative to the age, and yet surpassingly beautiful. It may be vanity, but I think I see the trace of my earnest exhortation to him to create something wholly new."[10]

Through their heavier emphasis on immediate human reality, these letters serve to isolate Shelley's specifically epic theory from his view of all poetry as local manifestation of transcendent truth, but basically they corroborate the more conscious and elaborate theorizing elsewhere. The epic is to be both new and related to the epics of the past; it is also to deal with human nature and be relevant to the concerns of its age. Now, these are almost exactly the aims which, according to its Preface, Shelley professes for *The Revolt of Islam.* The poem is to be an "experiment on the temper of the public mind, as to how far a thirst for a happier condition of moral and political society survives, among the enlightened and refined, the tempests which have shaken the age in which we live." The poem is to serve "the cause of a liberal and comprehensive morality" and to kindle in its readers an enthusiasm for the inextinguishable, perennial virtue "which neither violence, nor misrepresentation, nor prejudice, can ever totally extinguish among mankind." The vehicle is to be, significantly, "a story of human passion in its most universal character, diversified with moving and romantic adventures," and appealing to the "common sympathies of every human breast." Disclaiming systematic argument and emphasizing that his poem will be narrative rather than didactic, Shelley nevertheless describes his aim as in the broad sense educational; he wishes to illustrate "my moral and political creed, and that of some of the sublimest intellects in the world." (*Works,* I, 239.) Not only does this program duplicate in detail Shelley's epic prescripts elsewhere; it comes surprisingly close to the more orthodox epic theories of the preceding century, even to the point of distinguishing consciously in the familiar way between realistic and fabulous elements.

III

Of the four major poets discussed in this book Shelley seems to have been most significantly conditioned, one way or the other, by the conscious awareness of a critical epic orthodoxy. As I have argued earlier, the standard epic position is to ignore rules. Shelley, however, overtly attacks them in the Preface to *The Revolt:* "Nor have I permitted any system relating to mere words, to divert the attention of the reader from whatever interest I may have succeeded in creating, to my own ingenuity in contriving to disgust them according to the rules of criticism. I have simply clothed my thoughts in what appeared to me the most obvious and appropriate language." He also seems to disavow imitation, though on this score the freedom he claims for himself is more stylistic than formal: "I do not presume to enter into competition with our greatest contemporary Poets. Yet I am unwilling to tread in the footsteps of any who have preceded me. I have sought to avoid the imitation of any style of language or versification peculiar to the original minds of which it is the character, designing that even if what I have produced be worthless, it should still be properly my own." That this is not a broadside against tradition in general is made clear in the sentence that almost immediately follows, which restores the typical epic ambiguity toward the past: "A person familiar with nature, and with the most celebrated productions of the human mind, can scarcely err in following the instinct, with respect to selection of language, produced by that familiarity."

Shelley in fact acknowledges explicitly in the Preface a debt to the past, and particularly mentions the nations which had bred epic poets: "The poetry of antient Greece and Rome, and modern Italy, and our own country, has been to me like external nature, a passion and an enjoyment. Such are the sources from which the materials for the imagery of my Poem have been drawn." (*Works*, I, 242–43.) An abundance of documentary evidence supports these statements; Shelley had fairly immersed himself in epic authors during and just before the period when he wrote *The Revolt*.[11] It is interesting that two years later he claimed that *Prometheus Unbound* was "perhaps less an imitation of anything that has gone before it" than any of his earlier poems had been.[12] Doubtless as a result of the poet's recent sojourn in the epic hall of mirrors, one finds a significant number of epic clichés in *The Revolt*. A few of these are so clearly functional that one can hardly believe they are not studied and deliberate; others are more casual. Since this division is difficult to make, I shall simply list those aspects of the poem that I find reminiscent of earlier epics, reserving for later treatment two more important areas where Shelley is indebted to the epic family.

1. *The siege.* This is a key situation in several great epics and in many lesser ones; it recalls Homer's Troy, Latinus's city in Virgil, Tasso's Jerusalem, and Southey's Orleans. Shelley had read and had once admired *Joan of Arc*, as well as most of Southey's poetry.[13] Like Southey and Landor, whose *Gebir* he had also admired,[14] Shelley sometimes takes advantage of his epic precedents in order to depart from them. For in *The Revolt* the besiegers are not waging war but peace; they are keeping the "watch of love" (IV.xxvii), a nonviolent form of combat in which victories are won by the example of virtue rather than by

the sword. Thus Shelley underlines the antimartial ideal which is a central theme in the poem and his belief in love as a practical agency of human improvement.[15]

2. *The woman warrior.* After the rout of Laon's inspired followers, Cythna gallops across the battlefield on a black charger and saves her lover from imminent death (VI.xix–xx). She appears in this scene and occasionally elsewhere as a reincarnation of Camilla, Clorinda, Bradamant, and Britomart. But, as I shall remark later, woman has a special significance in Shelley's epic, and his evocation of the woman warrior is not simply epic trimming. As its original title implies, the poem is unorthodox among epics in having two heroic protagonists, and Shelley's belief in the equality of the sexes gives Cythna's heroic role particular meaning. Moreover, Shelley's nonviolent ideal tolerates men no more than women on the battlefield.

3. *Fabulous elements.* In the Preface Shelley promises to diversify his poem with "moving and romantic adventures." If we except the allegorical framework in the first and last cantos, all the truly fabulous incidents form part of Cythna's flashback narrative in Cantos VII to IX, and in making the fabulous material part of an inset narrative Shelley has the traditional precedents of the *Odyssey* and the *Aeneid.* The fantastic adventures that befall Cythna after her imprisonment in the submarine cave (scenes that evoke strongly Southey's romances) are only sketchily connected to the adjoining narrative; they are apparently intended to be a Platonic allegory of the mind and its development, one of the very few examples of such philosophical idealism in the poem. One recalls, however, that it is in connection with another descent into a fabulous region that Virgil introduces his metaphysical doctrine of the relationship of nature to universal mind. Shelley would have both remembered vividly that part of the *Aeneid* and admired it.

4. *Elements of the chivalric epic-romance.* These contribute a pervasive tone, which is implied in Shelley's choice of the Spenserian stanza. Especially prominent is the hermit who rescues and

nurses Laon; the hermit lives alone amid esoteric tomes and uses remedies which Shelley calls "inchantments" (III.xxvii ff., IV.i–vii). In the first lines of his Dedication to Mary he pictures himself as returning to her after his summer's task of composition "As to his Queen some victor Knight of Faëry, / Earning bright spoils for her inchanted dome" (Ded., i).

5. *The plague.* Shelley's account of the pestilence that afflicts the Golden City after the wholesale carnage of the battle comprises a major section of the poem, and he combines with the plague the evils of famine, drought, and ensuing madness (X. xiv ff.). Similar afflictions are represented in Virgil, Homer, Milton, Tasso, and Camoëns.[16] Shelley attributes the calamities he describes to the disease engendered among the rotting corpses on the battlefield and thus underlines once more his antiwar message.

6. *The epic omen.* The aerial struggle between the eagle and serpent which occurs in Canto I is an echo of a familiar epic incident, as several critics have noticed.[17] As is always true of epic omens, the struggle is a veiled symbol of great events.

7. *The bard.* There are many references to the beauty of Cythna's singing. She sings Laon's songs to Freedom with the inspired rapture often attributed to the bards in epic poems (II.xxviii–xxix). Her voice resembles that of "some minstrel heavenly-gifted" (V.xlvi), and she accompanies herself on the lute (VII. iv). But, since vocal persuasion is another main theme of the poem, it seems likely—and I shall come back to this—that, as Dowden points out, Cythna's singing has a special importance in *The Revolt.*[18]

8. *The catalogue.* In Canto X (iv–viii), Shelley describes the variety of nations which have contributed to the forces marshaled against Laon and the people. Although this passage is brief and does not contain the characteristic long series of proper names, the passage in its context suggests the traditional epic catalogue.

9. *Epic games.* The festival held by the revolutionists in honor of the idea of equality (V.xxxvii ff.) is somewhat reminiscent of the ceremonial games in epic.

10. *Miltonisms.* These are pervasive in *The Revolt* and often merely casual, as in this description of Cythna's daughter: "she trembled like one aspin pale / Among the gloomy pines of a Norwegian vale" (XII.vi), which is clearly an echo of the description of Satan's spear (*PL*, I.292–94), and in the phrase "Earth like an exhalation" (III.xviii). Others are fleeting but functional, sometimes subtly, to Shelley's purposes. The "dubious Battel" that takes place in Book VI of *Paradise Lost* may well have influenced Shelley's decision to locate his battle, to which he once applies the term "doubtful strife" (VI.xii), in his own sixth canto. Here Shelley describes the "deliberate will" (VI.ix) which inspires Laon's retreating, unarmed followers, a significant variation of the "deliberat valour" which Milton describes as a definitive martial mood (*PL*, I.554). At least four times[19] Shelley imitates Milton's

> Thick as Autumnal Leaves that strow the Brooks
> In *Vallombrosa* . . .   (*PL*, I.302–3)

This is largely imitation for its own sake, though it may be significant that in *The Revolt,* as later in the "Ode to the West Wind," Shelley elaborately develops the image pattern of autumn, wind, and leaves to symbolize the destruction of the old order and the advent of the new (IX.xxi–xxvi). The strange allegory of the opening canto describing the struggle between the Serpent (freedom) and the Eagle (tyranny), who are themselves mutations of more primordial antagonists, the red Comet and the Morning Star, is based, as Baker shows, on the Biblical and Miltonic identifications of Satan (for Shelley a type of the struggle against tyranny) with Lucifer, the morning star, and the serpent.[20]

Other, still more functional adaptations include Shelley's many allusions to Sin and Death and to Milton's version of the fall from Eden. The old madwoman whom Laon meets amid the ruins of battle (she calls herself "Pestilence" and Famine is her "paramour") owes much to Milton's Sin: "All lips which I have kissed must surely wither, / But Death's—if thou art he, we'll go to work together!" (VI.xlix–l). The evil Iberian priest has a voice "like a blast that burst the portal / Of fabled hell" (X.xl). In his final speech to the Islamic Senate Laon asserts that "Hate must be / The nurse and parent still of an ill progeny" (XI.xv) and compares England, once the freedom-loving Queen of Nations but now corrupt, to a mother "By inbred monsters outraged and oppressed" (XI.xxii).

Such allusions are thematically dependent on an even broader metaphor which, through evoking the story of the Fall, implies Shelley's belief that evil and oppression are not part of the original order of things; in this respect at least Shelley's philosophy in *The Revolt* is closer to the Judaeo-Christian emphasis on historical act than to nontemporal myth. It is true that he calls the two antagonistic principles "Immortal, . . . equal Gods," but the same stanza resolves the ambiguity of that phrase by explaining that they "burst the womb of inessential Nought" at the time when "life and thought / Sprang forth." Their conflict is symbolic of the conflict between the good and evil powers within man, not between powers anterior to man; the first struggle between Star and Comet is witnessed by the "earliest dweller of the world," whose thoughts during the struggle "within his mind waged mutual war, / In dreadful sympathy." Victorious evil then begins to reign over "a world of woe," whose first overt manifestation is, like the slaying of Abel, the shedding of a brother's blood. The Comet, Good, soon takes the form of a serpent (and here, of course, Shelley reverses the weight of Milton's symbolism as readers other than Shelley generally understand it), "a dire Snake, with man and beast unreconciled"; that is, the "darkness" which now comes over the world makes what is truly good appear to be the opposite: "for none / Knew good from evil." (I.xxv–xxviii.) Later in the poem, the vegetarian feast at which the revolutionists celebrate their innocent victory and ideals (V.lv–lvi) recalls both in its symbolism and in particular phrases the nonalcoholic vegetarianism of Milton's Eden. Adam's final recognition that the true Paradise is within is reflected in Cythna's comforting words assuring Laon that he has himself anticipated the victory which time will one day bring:

> "turn thine eyes
> On thine own heart—it is a paradise
> Which everlasting spring has made its own, . . .
> In their own hearts the earnest of the hope
> Which made them great, the good will ever find." (IX.xxvi–xxvii)

Adam's awakening from his dream to find it fulfilled is later suggested by Cythna's words after her martyrdom with Laon: "Aye,
this is Paradise / And not a dream" (XII.xxii). Though they do
not have the depth and thematic richness with which Keats is to
imbue his Miltonic allusions, Shelley's Miltonisms are often suggestive and helpful in defining the often subtle differences of viewpoint between *The Revolt* and his later poems.

IV

I come now to the two things that Shelley considered crucial in
his epic: the quasi-structural requirement that the action combine
near and remote levels and the requirement of relevance to the
age. Different as they sound, these two requirements mean nearly
the same thing for Shelley, and to treat them separately is in fact
somewhat artificial. It seems useful, however.

A number of critics, including some generally sympathetic toward Shelley, have condemned *The Revolt of Islam* for poor
structure, and the first canto has seemed to them especially objec-
tionable. This section has been called vague, tedious, overelabo-
rate, halting, and obscure.[21] The use of both protagonists as nar-
rators in the body of the poem has been criticized as impairing
continuity.[22] One must recognize, however, that Shelley himself
knew his method had risks and that he nevertheless decided to
run them. Having submitted the first four manuscript sheets to a
publisher, Shelley explained to him that the better plotted and
more human cantos to follow were written "with more energy
and clearness." But the letter describes the poem as "a work of

which unity is one of the qualifications aimed at by the author";
except for the first canto the poem is "a mere human story without the smallest intermixture of supernatural interference." If this
were not true, Shelley admits, the poem would appeal to very few
readers. "The first canto is indeed in some measure a distinct
poem, though very necessary to the wholeness of the work," he
adds, and insists once more that it is directed "to the common
elementary emotions of the human heart." Here we have virtually
all the elements which Shelley is later to formulate as principles
of epic and many that are commonplaces in epic orthodoxies: the
emphasis on human action and human nature; the need for unity
(though of a complex kind); the requirement that the poem be
meaningful to its age; the distinction between human events and
machinery, which is almost certainly what Shelley means by "supernatural interference." (Shelley is being precise in his allusion
to machinery; the story of Cythna's imprisonment in Canto VII
contains fabulous incidents, but they are not examples of "interference" and therefore not machinery.) Perhaps most characteristic is Shelley's statement, in the same letter, that although the setting is Constantinople and modern Greece, he has written "without much attempt at minute delineation of Mahometan manners"
and that the revolution described in his poem is to represent the
"beau ideal" of the French Revolution.[23] This declaration and his
insistence on human focus illustrate once more Shelley's twin concerns: the presentation of human action against a universal background, and spiritual relevance to the age.

As Carlos Baker has pointed out, *The Revolt* consists of two
parts, one within the other. The human action occupies most of
the poem, but this action is framed by universalizing action on a
more remote plane, as in *Paradise Lost*.[24] The text of the poem,
and not only the Preface, shows how deliberately Shelley tried to
observe this distinction. Laon introduces his narrative, which comprises most of the poem, as a "tale of human power" (I.lviii);
denying that Cythna is a phantom, the pilot of the ship which
rescues her from her island declares: "It cannot be—she is a hu-

man Maid" (VIII.ii); subsequently Cythna tells the mariners, "Disguise it not—we have one human heart" (VIII.xix); of Cythna's proselytizing we are told that her "human words found sympathy / In human hearts" (IX.ix).

The machinery of the poem, its universalizing backdrop, consists mainly of the allegorical framework in the first and last cantos, but the allegory there several times directs our attention back to earth and immediate human reality; we observe, for example, that although the woman whom the poet finds on shore watching the aerial struggle is a natural woman ("mine is an human form, / Like what thou wearest"; her hand is "not a ghost's, but warm / With human blood"—I.xxxv), her lover is immortal (I.xl). In addition, imagistic strategy reinforces the distinction between levels, for although in the frame narrative the Eagle and Serpent stand for, respectively, tyranny and resistance to it, the two animal images are used throughout the remainder of the poem with their usual, reverse connotations.[25] I might add that Shelley's decision to introduce the action proper with a supernatural scene has epic precedents in the celestial or Olympian scenes which precede the main action in the *Odyssey,* the *Aeneid, Jerusalem Delivered,* and the *Lusiad;* Shelley may have been thinking of this convention, just as Milton may have been when he called the Book of Job an epic.

To turn from structural matters to Shelley's intention that his poem be timely is not really to change the subject but rather to look at the same problems from another angle. For example, one incidental mark of Shelley's epic structure, his use of the flashback narrative (VII.iii–IX.xix), is relevant to an understanding of his promise in the Preface that he will not be didactic. This section contains Cythna's speech to the mariners, in which she frankly attacks the orthodox Christian doctrines of sin and guilt. Now, the main story is told by Laon, and therefore we should in theory dissociate Shelley from any of the poem's ideas, except possibly for the first-person discourse in Canto I; in fact, however, Laon's narrative is so long that we forget he is telling it,[26] and hence we are likely after all to ignore Shelley's prefatory admonition to distinguish between his sentiments and the characters'. The content of Cythna's speech, however, requires that the authorial distance be re-established, not necessarily because Cythna's speech might seem blasphemous, but rather because it is *argument,* intellectual persuasion. Characteristically, Shelley wanted the poem to appeal through images of virtue rather than by debating points. ("I have made no attempt," he states in the Preface, "to recommend the motives which I would substitute for those at present governing mankind by methodical and systematic argument. I would only awaken the feelings . . .") Thus, though Cythna's arguments are doubtless Shelley's own, they must be objectified. We are to hear them not as personal opinions but as the voice of events.

Nevertheless, we are meant to hear the poem's message unequivocally. Shelley is attempting to ameliorate the pessimism bequeathed by the failure of the French Revolution, and like all the poets of literary epic he attempts to relate his message to the rhythm of history. The most obvious way in which epic does this is through the vision of futurity, a vision specially vouchsafed to the hero which, through prognostication after the fact, links him with the reader's era. Shelley has a problem here, for his hero and heroine are neither historical nor legendary; they are not already surrounded by an aura of associations, so that the reader cannot think of their deeds as having shaped the order he knows or of himself as extrapolating the protagonists' values. Nor are Laon and Cythna, like Wordsworth's hero, blends of real individual and Everyman, though one may argue that this is Shelley's implicit intention, for there are a number of links between Shelley's self-portrait in the Dedication and what we learn of Laon, especially in the scenes which describe their vows to fight tyranny.[27]

Nevertheless, Shelley uses several mutations of the standard epic "vision," each of which reinforces a central idea common to them all while stressing a particular facet of that idea. The general idea is that history is a continuum, partly cyclic and partly progressive. The pattern of time as men experience it—and in *The Revolt* Shelley seldom pushes speculation further than that except in a spirit of agnosticism—shows a recurrent struggle between moral good and moral evil. Both of these are potentials in man and neither of them can exist apart from conscious intelligence (the Morning Star and the Comet were born when "life and thought / Sprang forth"); the elusive rhetoric of *The Revolt* occasionally obscures this human emphasis, and a few passages are difficult to reconcile with it, but it is the normal emphasis of the poem. The problem lies within the human intelligence and will, and not, except slightly and accidentally, in institutions,[28] despite Shelley's frequent attacks on Custom, which in this poem does not mean primarily an Establishment but rather unenlightenment and self-inflicted illusion. On the other hand, some definitive victory for good lies in the future.

The first canto and, to a lesser extent, part of the concluding one express this thought-pattern in general, but within the first canto there is also a special emphasis on past history. While the poet is being carried over the sea with the Woman and the wounded Serpent, she admonishes:

> Speak not to me, but hear! much shalt thou learn,
> Much must remain unthought, and more untold,
> In the dark Future's ever-flowing urn. (I.xxv)

What she relates concerns the past, though this past is, of course, part of the key to the future. The elevated vantage point from which the poet has observed the aerial struggle is an epic convention, but so is the voyage over the sea, as Shelley would have known from reading Tasso and Landor's *Gebir*.[29] Laon's story, which begins at the end of Canto I and continues except for Cythna's interruption until the end (the poet himself never resumes his own narrative, another link between Shelley and Laon), concentrates on the approximate present, since it gives a veiled version of the French Revolution. Both of these revelatory scenes owe something to the epic vision of futurity, but the convention is most clearly used in the scene where Cythna rhapsodically prophesies the "broad sunrise" of the future which is to succeed the present "Winter of the world": "one comes behind, / Who aye the future to the past will bind" (IX.xxv, xxvii). The action is consequential; the lives of Laon and Cythna will be justified by the future triumph they helped prepare:

> "Our many thoughts and deeds, our life and love,
> Our happiness, and all that we have been,
> Immortally must live, and burn, and move,
> When we shall be no more;—the world has seen
> A type of peace." (IX.xxx)

As the future will remember their contribution to ultimate victory, so Shelley makes the two heroic lovers pay homage to the challenging lessons of the past, thus repeating and particularizing the more symbolic version of this point in the first canto. The youthful Laon grows up under tyranny, but is inspired by the memorials of ancient Greece; their message to him is the recurrent epic refrain, that the lessons of the past help us to equal and go beyond it:

> Such man has been, and such may yet become!
> Aye, wiser, greater, gentler, even than they
> Who on the fragments of yon shattered dome
> Have stamped the sign of power. (II.xii)

In the same spirit the Preface to the poem pays homage to the enduring community of poets; the reader is to "be incited to those inquiries which have led to my moral and political creed, and that of some of the sublimest intellects in the world."

As I have mentioned, Shelley recognized the requirement of epic objectivity and promised to observe it in *The Revolt*. Yet, obviously, the poem is as tendentious as it could possibly be. The paradox is not uncommon in the literary epic, which tends to take toward its subject the attitude of a scribe humbly, objectively, even unconsciously recording awesome truth, and toward its audience the superior attitude of the preacher. The prophet serves God but leads his people; the epic poet leads his people while humbly serving the truth. And indeed "truth" is a word that Shelley liked to connect with epic: the phrase "epic truth" occurs twice in *A Defence of Poetry;* Byron was not to compose an epic until he had seen the "truth of things"; in the Dedication of *The Revolt of Islam* the poet exclaims, "Truth's deathless voice pauses among mankind!" (Ded., xiv).

But how much does Shelley really respect the truth? And what justification is there for his implied claims that in this highly propagandistic poem he is being objective? (The second sentence of the Preface calls it an "experiment.") Readers may well wonder, for *The Revolt* seems in many ways utterly alien to what we know about the world and human behavior. Consider, for example, the effects of the speech Laon makes before the Islamic senate in Canto XI. These leaders and the whole population as well are lusting for Laon's destruction, having convinced themselves that only through his death and Cythna's will God remit the plague and other afflictions. But after hearing Laon's speech a large number of the younger men leap up to defend him; they are then, every one, cut down—treacherously, on the spot, without planning —by their reactionary elders (XI.xix–xx). This incredible incident is typical of many others throughout the poem—and I am leaving aside both the allegorical framework and the technically "fabulous" events connected with Cythna's submarine imprisonment.

The skepticism all this occasions can best be met, I believe, by re-examining Shelley's insistent claim that the action of the poem is human rather than supernatural, which claim would also seem to be vitiated, in spirit if not technically, by the unheard-of events in the poem. But we must remember that Shelley is writing an epic, not a novel; his claim to have written a plain human story is not to be read as a guarantee that in the poem things will happen as they usually do. Rather, the poem tries to delineate through external action what Shelley considers the perennial truth of the hu-

man heart. Despite his later statement that the *Faerie Queene* cannot be called a true epic, Shelley's method has something in common with the epic method of Spenser, whose ghost haunts the entire poem and who likewise teaches through far-fetched incidents
a practical program for human perfection. By the standards of
realism, Laon's seemingly miraculous conversions are no harder
to accept than the utter powerlessness of the otherwise resource-
ful Duessa when she is in the presence of Una. I grant the obvious, that Spenser is making a point allegorically, whereas it is not
clear that Shelley is being allegorical (in fact, I believe, *The Revolt* is that only incidentally). But the *Faerie Queene* is not simply allegory, nor does it simply rely on romance's prerogative to
dispense with the laws of reality. Spenser's poem has an epic level
as well, one of somewhat idealized but human action, and on this
level it must observe psychological as well as spiritual truth. On
this more human level, I feel convinced, most readers simply accept Una's uncanny power over Duessa as the kind of dominance
that the truly good person exerts over one whose wholeness is im-
paired by the mutually conflicting stresses of falsehood. In other
words, we accept Una's miraculous supremacy as in some real way
true to what human beings are, though we might also admit that,
statistically, evil persons prevail at least as often as not. At any
rate, the inference does not result simply from allegorical translation.

On the other hand, our suspension of disbelief in the case of
Una's power over Duessa—and I am still considering Una as
portrait rather than abstraction—is intimately related to our whole
awareness of Spenser's religious and Platonic values, whether or
not we believe in God or Platonism. For to the modern reader at
least there is something literally extraordinary about Una's goodness; it is something we are tempted to think of as "heroic" in
the sense which implies that her behavior should not be expected
of *us*. This meaning parallels the commonplace meaning of the
word "saint," which implies exactly the same thing. (That Spenser himself and his contemporary readers saw an immediate per-

sonal and political challenge in the poem I would not deny.) For even that part of Una which does not allegorize divinely granted Truth, that is, the part of her that is idealized natural woman, is distinctly a product of Grace, which is again a motivating force from outside our world. Thus, the example of Una presents to the believer only the challenge of making himself ready to receive Grace when it unpredictably comes; to the nonbeliever, who does not believe in Grace, the counsel of perfection implied in Una's existence makes no sharp or immediate challenge at all, and therefore he is willing to endorse what she stands for in the same piously automatic and impersonal way in which he approves of "saints" while resting secure that they have nothing to do with him.

I am not saying that we should read *The Revolt of Islam* as allegory. The poem is that in certain respects, but these are of secondary importance. The very unlikely benevolence shown toward the Sultan by his oppressed subjects, who dethrone him pityingly after his troops desert, is surely part of Shelley's attempt to represent the French Revolution—the Sultan's bloodless deposition and subsequent treacherous appeal to foreign armies representing the initial leniency toward Louis XVI and the reactionary invasion of France on his behalf. Laon's slaughter of three of Cythna's abductors (III.vi–x) represents the reflex excesses which Shelley says in the Preface must be looked for when a people has been brutalized as the French were under the Old Regime. Such passages can no more be understood apart from their political references than can certain passages in the *Faerie Queene* if we do not advert to Bloody Mary and Philip II. And doubtless both the *Faerie Queene* and *The Revolt of Islam* are somewhat limited in their claims to epic status by the occasionally conflicting demands of allegory.

Yet the incidents which reflect Shelley's more important message about human nature are not really allegorical, just as Spenser's story is not only that. The crucial events in *The Revolt* do not require ideological translation, any more than the equally improbable actions and sufferings of Chaucer's Grisilde. Grisilde is not Patience; she is patient. One point of her story is that, although no one is likely to be so patient as she, people could be so and should. Similarly, Shelley knows that the world will probably not be converted by the unarmed voice of truth, but he believes that the conversion could happen, and in a way not very different from what the poem describes, if men would open their eyes and see things for what they really are. Shelley is trying to dramatize the difference between absurd, unnecessary degradation which men choose for themselves and a happiness and dignity which they could have almost for the asking. In the last analysis, the verisimilitude which both believers and nonbelievers are likely to concede to Spenser more easily than to Shelley does not reflect the difference between allegory and wish-fulfillment that poses as objectivity. The difference lies in the demands the authors make of us. Spenser, humanist and activist though he is, puts much of the burden of human regeneration outside the arena of human powers, whereas Shelley puts it entirely on our shoulders, as a race and as individuals, and then, as it were, insults us by insisting that the weight ought not to seem heavy.

Like so much of Romantic poetry, and like many epics in their own ages, that is, before they are inducted into the formal pantheon, *The Revolt of Islam* cannot be judged apart from its message. If Shelley's view is wrong, the poem lacks verisimilitude in the only important way Shelley wanted the poem to have it and is for that the less worthy of being read. The Shelley who in the Preface sneers at systems "related to mere words" and later in the Preface traces both critics and perverters of minds to the same source among the sophists of ancient Rome, would certainly have accepted those terms. He believes so strongly that he is right, that he is portraying truly the human nature which underlies the crust of custom, that he makes undeflectable demands on the reader's sympathy, demands that are either met or flung back in irritation

at the author. This is the way of the prophets, and such unqualified response is often, in their own day, the response the epic poets
ask for.

Mary Shelley's note to *The Revolt of Islam* states one interesting half-truth about the poem. She suggests in essence that it is
an expression of wishful thinking: Shelley had suffered anguish
in the period just before he wrote the poem and his concomitant
sense of injury led him to embody his feelings "in forms defe-
cated of all the weakness and evil which cling to real life" (*Works,*
I, 409). This sounds convincing, but I suspect it is unfair to Shelley. The occasional shrillness of the poem and (as it may seem to
some readers) Shelley's highhanded way with the facts of experience are not, I believe, the result of immature fantasy-mongering.
But they do, as Mary suggests, spring from a kind of frustration.
It is the kind experienced by a person who has seen something
with his own eyes and whose report of it no one will believe. It
is, perhaps, this most desperate and frustrating of feelings that
prompts the following statement in the Preface:

And if the lofty passions with which it has been my scope to distinguish this story, shall not excite in the reader a generous impulse, an
ardent thirst for excellence, an interest profound and strong, such as
belongs to no meaner desires—let not the failure be imputed to a
natural unfitness for human sympathy in these sublime and animating
themes. It is the business of the Poet to communicate to others the
pleasure and the enthusiasm arising out of those images and feelings, in
the vivid presence of which within his own mind, consists at once his
inspiration and his reward.   (*Works,* I, 240)

The second sentence can be read as aesthetic theory, but I doubt
that it is primarily that. In connection with the foregoing sentence,
it more probably is a request, made in the bland tone of a parent
addressing a self-destructively wayward child, that the reader lis-
ten with a tolerant ear and an open mind to what is likely to make
him happy. For in the poem Shelley tries to show that what for
most men is almost lunatic idealism and optimism is not only
grounded in the facts of human nature, but is quite simply the

commonsense way to happiness. Hence his belief that the poem is human, truthful, objective; he is trying to dramatize his conviction that man's salvation lies well within his ordinary powers.

The traditional epic furnished Shelley with many precedents for preaching, but he goes beyond his models in that his epic not only preaches but is *about* preaching. And the fact that moral persuasion is not only the goal of the poem but also an important subject affects the basic conception of heroism which Shelley embodies in his protagonists. In accordance with his long-cherished views about war, Shelley rejects the martial element in heroism, though he adapts the military metaphor, usually with chivalric overtones, to his new and more spiritual ideal ("linked armour for my soul," "Evil and good, in woven passions mailed"—Ded., v; V.ii). As a substitute Shelley introduces the idea of persuasive eloquence, as Southey had introduced the somewhat similar idea of an all-sufficient personal faith and Wordsworth that of poetic Imagination. Shelley's idea was not a new one for him. In *An Address, to the Irish People* he had implied that language is an effective alternative to force; after warning the Irish about the consequences for the French of their resort to violence, he exhorts Irishmen to let their courage take the form of frank speech: "Speak boldly and daringly what you think; an Irishman was never accused of cowardice, do not let it be thought possible that he is a coward. . . . Leave lies and secrets to courtiers and lordlings; be open, sincere, and single-hearted" (*Works*, V, 226). The strangeness of this passage lies in its combination of the aggressive, passion-rousing rhetoric of the demagogue (the phrase "courtiers and lordlings," flattery of the audience's self-esteem) with the counsel of serenity. *The Revolt of Islam* expresses the same tension between message and tone; the tension is felt, for example, in Shelley's explosive military images of irenicism. I have mentioned the use of these to express his general ideal of heroism as spiritual; appropriately, many of them are also specifically connected with language. The "deathless minds" who inspired Laon with a sense of his mission provided him with "Words which were weapons;—round my heart there grew / The adamantine armour of their power" (II.xx). Laon's tongue, the Hermit tells him, could be "a lance to quell the mailed crest of wrong" (IV. xvii). Cythna too is so armed; she is veiled "In virtue's adamantine eloquence, / 'Gainst scorn, and death, and pain, thus trebly mailed" (IV.xix).

The importance of eloquence in *The Revolt of Islam* almost certainly indicates the growing conviction on Shelley's part that his own role in bringing about reform is to be that of a poet. Since persuasive eloquence is what Shelley is trying to produce in *The Revolt*, we are probably justified in doing what is often done in too facile a way: identifying Shelley with his hero. (His self-conscious claims to objectivity have compensatory overtones.) But this is not to say that Shelley's heroic ideal is in any simple way a projection of his ego. Even within the story the poem tells, Laon and his soul-mate are not the only persons who successfully turn their eloquence to the purposes of good, and the poem explicitly teaches that the task of renovating the world requires the co-operative effort of human beings in many places and ages. It is more likely that Shelley's portrait of heroism is a picture not of what he considers himself to be but of what he wishes to become and do.

I said earlier in this essay that *The Revolt* represents a turning-post in Shelley's career, but that image will be misleading if it is taken to imply no more than a redirection of external energies. As a biographical document the poem is a fascinating, even frightening picture of the convulsion produced in a man, who in many ways is a born extrovert, by the painful decision to turn his energies inward, to renounce direct political action against institutions for much more frustrating indirect battle in the arena of the mind. Doubtless this turning inward was good for Shelley the man and for his poetry, but the turmoil of pain which must have accompanied this smothering of a certain kind of energy should not be glossed over. Shelley stated that while writing the poem he had felt a sense of the precariousness of his life and that his feelings had been those which prompt "the communications of a dying man."[30] These are strong statements, and it seems justifiable to connect them with the extreme tension I have been attributing to the poem, the conflict in it between the style of the political radical and the role of benignant moral physician, between militancy and, in more than one sense, patience.

Shelley's patience, his desire to acquiesce in time's inherent corrective power and also his belief in the redemptive value of passive suffering, explains his espousal of pacific eloquence as a heroic ideal in *The Revolt;* his militancy explains his vehicle, the setting and metaphor of epic warfare. Thus (to return to Dowden's point) the heroic protagonists win their battles through their mere presence and power of speech.[31] Laon's songs

> Peopled with thoughts the boundless universe,
> A mighty congregation, which were strong
> Where'er they trod the darkness to disperse
> The cloud of that unutterable curse
> Which clings upon mankind:—all things became
> Slaves to my holy and heroic verse.   (II.xxx)

The words "holy and heroic" sum up the dual emphases, the substance and vehicle, of *The Revolt.*

Shelley's version of heroism almost inevitably suggests the Southey whom he had once admired so highly.[32] Southey too portrays a heroic ideal of inner integrity which is capable of vanquishing all mere circumstances. And indeed *The Revolt* uses in certain relatively minor ways the technique of serious mock-epic that we find in *Joan of Arc,* though in the most important respects Shelley's epic affirms the value of the past rather than using it as a whipping-boy, which fact crucially distinguishes *The Revolt* from *Joan.* I have already mentioned some of Shelley's calculated reversals of epic tradition; another has to do with Shelley's view of women as it is illustrated by Cythna's role. Southey uses a woman as hero; Shelley uses a woman as one of his heroes and defiantly proclaims her the equal of her male counterpart. It is true that the two, hero and heroine, have somewhat different functions; they represent, as it were, male and female principles, the man being the visionary and the woman the human voice of his poetic insights. Moreover, Cythna has the special role of proselytizing the women. But as human beings they are equal, and one of the more important minor themes in the poem is the liberation of women from lustful domination by men.

Shelley's Laon is inspired with a sense of mission in the way that epic heroes usually are: through a message *ex machina,* Shelley's machine being the enduring memory of great human beings, the continuum of human history. Like other epic heroes, Laon is tempted to forsake his mission—for example, when he nearly commits suicide during his imprisonment atop a column:

> O Liberty! forgive the base endeavour,
> Forgive me, if, reserved for victory,
> The Champion of thy faith e'er sought to fly.   (III.xix)

Moreover, like so many of his contemporaries, Shelley indirectly evokes the convention of woman as an obstacle to duty and, like Landor, utterly reverses its direction. Cythna is absolutely essential to the accomplishment of Laon's mission. She accepts her high function resolutely:

> "Yes, I will tread Pride's golden palaces,
> Thro' Penury's roofless huts and squalid cells
> Will I descend, where'er in abjectness
> Woman with some vile slave her tyrant dwells,
> There with the music of thine own sweet spells
> Will disenchant the captives, and will pour
> For the despairing, from the crystal wells
> Of thy deep spirit, reason's mighty lore,
> And power shall then abound, and hope arise once more."
>
> (II.xlii)

Laon's love for Cythna is as sensual as love could be for any Dido or Armida, but in *The Revolt* as in *Gebir* sexual love is sweet and honest avarice, in no way a dereliction of duty. For Shelley such love is also a symbol, both of the bond of love which should unite all human beings and of the continual regeneration of heroism in history. After a stanza which graphically describes sexual intercourse and the darkness of orgasm, Shelley declares that the sexual act partakes of "the shadow which doth float unseen, / But not unfelt, o'er blind mortality" (VI.xxxvi–xxxvii). Here the darkness is primarily literal description and should not, I think, be too easily identified with the "shadow" in the "Hymn to Intellectual Beauty"; to the extent that the shadow in *The Revolt* is symbolic it represents the general rhythm of history more than a timeless ideal, as the tenor of Cythna's speech in Canto IX shows. In any case, the poem shows woman not as a destructive temptress, but as a free helpmeet, and so far from exerting evil influence over men, she is most often the slave of a tyrannical and lustful husband.[33]

V

Like his contemporaries in their attempts at epic, Shelley both accepts the tradition of epic and in part transforms it. Judged by certain uncomplicated standards of heroism, *The Revolt of Islam* is antiheroic; at any rate, Shelley's definition of heroism emphasizes traits which are exclusively intellectual and spiritual. He is like Southey and Wordsworth in championing values which are opposed to the martial ideal. But, like Wordsworth, Shelley is much closer to being a convincing epic poet than Southey is. For Southey the epic purpose existed independent of subject matter; he was always on the lookout for material which he could work up, without having Wordsworth's and Shelley's sense that they must find definitive themes. For Shelley, despite his occasional excursions into serious mock-epic, which are perhaps conditioned by the rule-mindedness he sometimes reveals, the use of the epic vehicle was not a tour de force. On the contrary, Shelley never in any blatant way invited comparison between his works and those in the orthodox epic canon, though he often did so indirectly. His attempt to be free from rules in general is basic to his literary theory, despite his belief in the continuity of literature. But, in fact, it is this very belief that resolves the paradox; Shelley saw a pattern in literary history paralleling the advancement of the world, and therefore the question of imitation versus originality is unreal as far as his actual practice as a poet is concerned. He both believed and, more important, felt practically that the poet is affected by forces which he cannot escape; he cannot successfully make imitation the basis of his poetry, as Shelley claims Horace, Catullus, and Ovid tried to do, but neither is he a completely free agent, for he is inescapably caught up in the literary current of his age and also in those mysterious forces of cultural progress which span and unify all ages. And thus Shelley, in *The Revolt of Islam,* is neither a dogmatic traditionalist nor a self-conscious rebel. In his epic poem the traditional epic devices are seldom avoided, seldom scrupulously followed; neither resisted nor obviously sought. Shelley seems to have saturated his imagination in the epics of the past and then, without trying laboriously to reproduce details, allowed his own poetic instincts to follow their natural bent.

Five: KEATS AND THE MORTAL TASTE

K EATS'S *Hyperion* is the only English Romantic poem that has always been considered an epic. I believe that it is one, yet I cannot help wondering why the fact is never challenged. That Keats was trying to write an epic can be demonstrated from oblique comments in his letters, but I doubt that even Keatsians are relying mainly on such indirect evidence. Nor have I ever seen a generic definition of epic, however arrived at, that is really applicable to *Hyperion*. (Except where I state otherwise, I reserve this title for the first version.) Its subject is classical, its theme sublime, its style sonorously Miltonic, yet theorists are not likely to accept these qualities consciously as sufficient proof that a work is epic. Part of the answer, doubtless, is that *Hyperion* represents a climax of personally heroic effort by Keats, effort that he could not carry through—a result that conveniently reinforces the belief that the Romantics could not in the nature of things write epics. Some critics, in fact, have come very close to saying that if Keats had finished the poem it would not have been an epic, that it would have had to become something else. But whatever the reason for the secure place of *Hyperion* in the epic gallery, the fact that it is there helps prove the importance of *de facto* rather than *de jure* credentials.

If we look to Keats for even the outlines of a formal epic theory we shall be disappointed. But the general associations he made with epic are fairly clear. In Keats's semi-explicit thought —and he is never really explicit on the subject—the epic meant very nearly what it does for those critics who call *Hyperion* an epic simply because of its elevation and remote grandeur of tone. It meant a little more, though. For Keats the epic implied sternness—of matter as well as approach and viewpoint—sternness in the sense of the word that is opposed to self-indulgence. It meant something ascetic: if not the denial of the senses, at least the rigorous discipline of them. It was a symbol for the magisterial qualities rather than those that were locally, personally intense, and was thus a mode of *general* statement, of what Keats calls "abstraction."[1] It was also a symbol, and not merely a vehicle, for definitive literary greatness and for the fame to which Keats sometimes subordinated literature as means to end.

In his "Epistle to Charles Cowden Clarke" Keats calls epic the "king" of literary modes, a word whose implicit connotations, supremacy and amplitude, are spelled out in the succeeding phrase: "Round, vast, and spanning all like Saturn's ring" (ll. 66–67).[2] In his journal-letter of October, 1818, written just after he had embarked on *Hyperion,* he states in his own characteristic idiom the familiar epic contrast between indulgence and asceticism, between Amaryllis and the Muse.* He tells George and Georgiana Keats that he hopes never to marry, since beautiful creatures, silken carpets, upholstery of cygnet's down, luxurious food (emblems here for both sexual indulgence and a limited, exclusively personal fulfillment) are less attractive to him than "sublime" solitude, where the wind is his wife and the stars are his children; this solitary world can become, he says, a thousand worlds. Then comes the characteristic association with epic, "No sooner am I alone than shapes of epic greatness are stationed around me," and the contrast of such grandeur with "the more divided and minute domestic happiness."[3] We note that this vaguely implied definition of epic has scarcely anything to do with formal aesthetics and that, although the shapes of epic greatness represent a kind of happiness, it is a kind not founded on personal encounter. The view is essentially a religious one; it substitutes for what E. M. Forster is to sum up in the phrase "personal relations" a loftier, more generalized, less individual

---

* In quoting the letters I slightly normalize Keats's carefree spelling, punctuation, and capitalization, but only when I feel sure there is no danger of altering Keats's meaning even slightly.

ideal which is nevertheless self-fulfillment in a high sense. Elsewhere Keats speculates on whether Wordsworth or Milton, the egoist or the poet of suprapersonal vision, has the truer understanding of the human heart, and whether Wordsworth "has in truth epic passion, and martyrs himself to the human heart, the main region of his song."[4] We note again the religious metaphor so typical of Keats's understanding of the epic viewpoint. This viewpoint is not detached in the sense of being insensitive; quite the opposite, since "passion" is essential to epic. Keats implies rather that the epic view is the altruistic, morally heroic one of the martyr, the religious attitude that loves man intensely, individual men deeply but with a detachment that comes from seeing their place in a larger framework. (One wonders how subtly Keats felt the etymological roots of the phrase "epic passion.") *Hyperion* is on one level—not the most important one—a poem about Beauty, but that theme is treated in the poem as a general moral issue rather than, primarily, an aesthetic one. That it treats a moral issue on the level of high generality is one important reason why Keats thought of the poem as an epic.

It is illuminating to compare the attitudes of Keats and Shelley toward epic. Although both *Hyperion* and *The Revolt of Islam* imply a contrast between two levels, one proximate and the other remote, the poets tried to emphasize on the level of narrative action two opposite extremes from among the many complex polarities of epic. Each felt the epic to make demands on him that were opposed to what came naturally. Shelley, who characteristically thought in abstractions, was a moral generalizer, and both acted on and preached categorical imperatives, felt strain in giving his epic matter local habitation relevant to the individual, the age, and the immediate situation; hence his self-conscious insistence that he is writing a human story without systematic argumentation. Keats, whose instincts were to respond personally and with sensuous particularity, and who found most congenial the negative capability which resists dogmatic generalization, had to force himself toward the other epic pole, that of general comment on man's lot; hence he excluded literally human figures from his epic. For both poets, epic was an attempt (salutary, no doubt) to become what they were not, and for Keats this meant moving like many standard epic poets from romance to sterner and more morally general matter. It must be emphasized, though, that both poets were concerned in their epics with deeply human questions which are at the same time universal; they simply approached from different sides the task of combining both emphases.

Keats did not think of epic simply as a tone; he was also vividly aware of epic as a lineage. In the earlier (1815) of the two odes to Apollo he lists the "Bards, that erst sublimely told / Heroic deeds, and sang of fate." The list is almost exactly the orthodox epic canon: Homer, with his "trumpets" and "twanging harp of war," Virgil telling in "sweet majestic tone" of "grief around a funeral pyre," Milton with his "tuneful thunders," Shakespeare the master of the Passions (an anomaly among epic poets, though as a poet of suffering man he figures in the epic tradition as Keats saw it), Spenser with his "martial notes" and hymn to "spotless Chastity," Tasso ardently rousing youth from "idle slumbers" and "Pleasure's lair." Significantly, Keats's synopsis of epic history oscillates between emphases on stern valor and on tenderness or seductiveness, sometimes specifically contrasting the two motifs within the work of a single author. Like many of the Romantics and like most of the standard epic poets, he implies some kind of tension in the heroic tradition between love and war. And it is noteworthy that all the poets in the list, along with his relatively late love Dante, figured significantly in Keats's development: he had translated the entire *Aeneid* during his adolescence; two sonnets testify to the impact of Homer on his imagination; Fairfax's translation of Tasso he knew so well that its rhythms became an integral part of his own style, notably in *Isabella*. That he loved Spenser goes without saying. I will add that Mickle's translation of the *Lusiad* was one of the books in Keats's small private library.[5]

It is partly Keats's sense of epic continuity that leads him to use certain of the traditional imitative devices of epic—for example, the council and the *medias res* opening. As in the other Romantic poets I have discussed, some of these devices serve Keats's theme while others do so marginally or not at all. Most of the narrowly imitative detail comes not from the epic tradition as a whole, but directly and exclusively from Milton. In its larger epic strategies, *Hyperion* draws somewhat more eclectically on the tradition, though even in this area Keats's ear is tuned to only two or three epic voices. Milton, the semi-epic Dante, and Shakespeare are the prime movers of the poem, especially in that most crucial of epic concerns, the message itself.

II

Although one can hardly avoid using Keats's letters to help interpret his poetry, they are admittedly a risky guide. The opalescent mind they reveal was capable of glancing at a dozen deeply felt, often conflicting ideas in a single fairly short letter, and it is easy to exaggerate the importance of any one of them. The danger is compounded because the brevity of Keats's life invites us to divide into fallaciously distinct periods what might well have been considered a single period had he lived another forty years. We cannot afford to forget that Keats's life was pre-eminently normal, that is, true to the norm of human development. That he understood the issues and processes in his own growth more imaginatively and accurately than almost anyone else has done at any age should not obscure the fact that when he died at twenty-five he had had only those insights and experiences available to a young man. Or perhaps it would be more exact to say that the universal human questions took for him the forms they normally take for a young man.

Almost all readers of Keats's letters would agree, however, that in 1818 and 1819 or during some part of that period his

often volatile mind was the arena of especially sharp conflict on
an obsessively recurrent question. Keatsians have given various
names to the conflicting ideas, and I do not wish to suggest that
the differences in nomenclature are unimportant. There can be
little question, though, that in one form or another Keats's conflict was between attitudes of tension and relaxation. I believe
that in his own unique way he was experiencing the inevitable
young man's quandary: "What is my true vocation? Which of
my capacities shall I, through work, objectify as my definitive
self?" Keats's overwhelming desire was to be a poet, but he knew
he could be a number of other things, and he was growing sus-
picious of poetry; part of him, in fact, despised it, though he
sometimes believed it was the summit of human achievement
and the highest road to fame, a goal which in certain moods he
could place above any means to it, including poetry. But the crux
of the matter was his uncertainty of poetry's value. Some kind of
doubt would seem to have been inevitable for anyone whose
background, like Keats's, had been intellectually unself-conscious
and in a sense healthily lowbrow. But this reason is trivial, and
in any case debatable, compared with the more fundamental problem Keats had come to feel: there seemed to be something im-
moral about art, for it turns what is alive into something dead
and static, it disturbs the equilibrium of nature and of definitive
human experience, it *uses* people and their human values and
therefore hampers immediate, normal responses. Furthermore, it
impedes our knowledge of truth, since to see the world in terms
of its potential as art is to falsify it in the very act of perceiving
and experiencing it. The threat art-consciousness poses to true
understanding is both moral and aesthetic, moral because plain
truth is obviously a moral norm, and aesthetic because at its best
art itself originates in an accurate, unmediated response to what
truly is. Keats did not always feel such doubts, of course; he
often thought of poetry as a thoroughly humane activity, perhaps
the most highly so, and at still other times he acknowledged that
poetry is trivial but surrendered himself to it in a spirit of defiance—defiance, that is, of his nagging conscience.

I have been stating Keats's problem both too narrowly and too broadly. Keats's concern with the value of poetry had become part of his more general concern, both emotionally and intellectually, with the enigma of physical evil, or suffering; his letters reveal him as almost nightmarishly vexed by that perennial riddle. Against the cosmic background of pain, art appeared to be a frivolous giggle. On the other hand, if one somehow accepted art as not contemptible, he was again faced with the problem of pain, this time within the limits of art itself. True, the whole problem of poetry versus life could be skirted if poets declined to compete with life on the level of high seriousness; they could then write narcotic, sensuously pretty poetry, which Keats had come to associate with romance, and leave alone the "deep eternal theme" of human tragedy. But this Keats was unwilling to do. In both versions of *Hyperion* the general human theme of heroic suffering is to the theme of escapism as, on a more restricted and autobiographical level, serious poetry is to frivolous poetry. Since for Keats as for Wordsworth the problem of how to live one's life was only partly separable from the desire to be a poet, Keats fused in *Hyperion* the themes of suffering and of tragic art, but he wished, I believe, to emphasize more strongly the universal human theme. To see *Hyperion*—either version—as a poem about poetry is to mistake a variant of the theme for the theme itself.

One can trace forms of these ideas and problems far back in Keats's life, but they began to appear unmistakably in 1818. In January he told Haydon that *Hyperion* would have less of the "deep and sentimental cast" of *Endymion* and more of the "naked and grecian" manner; Apollo, the new hero, would as a foreseeing god be superior to circumstance. The new poem would portray an undeviating "march of passion and endeavour,"[6] and one thinks of Keats's identification, four months later, of passion with martyrdom to the human heart. Admittedly, the tone of these statements in January is optimistic, even a little brash, but that the theme of suffering had struck Keats deeply is shown by the exactly contemporary sonnet on *King Lear*, wherein

Keats turns from the "golden tongued" siren of romance and embraces Shakespeare's "bitter sweet" theme, "the fierce dispute, / Betwixt Hell torment & impassioned Clay," asking to be saved from "barren dream."[7]

During his walking-tour the following summer, Keats wondered why the mountains of the Isle of Annan did not "beckon Burns to some grand attempt at Epic";[8] once more we find Keats identifying epic with magnitude and remoteness. But the ordeal proper began in September, when Keats went to nurse his brother Tom, who was to die three months later. It was also in September that Keats began to write *Hyperion,* which he twice described as an escape from the agonizing sight of his brother's suffering. "I am obliged to write, and plunge into abstract images to ease myself of his countenance his voice and feebleness. . . . Imagine 'the hateful siege of contraries'—if I think of fame of poetry it seems a crime to me, and yet I must do so or suffer."[9] The same conflict between ease and pain and the same guilty feeling about the "crime" of poetry appear in his letter to the recently married Reynolds: "Gorge the honey of life. I pity you as much that it cannot last for ever, as I do myself now drinking bitters.—Give yourself up to it—you cannot help it—and I have a Consolation in thinking so—I never was in love—Yet the voice and the shape of a woman has haunted me these two days—at such a time when the relief, the feverous relief of Poetry seems a much less crime —This morning Poetry has conquered—I have relapsed into those abstractions which are my only life—I feel escaped from a new strange and threatening sorrow.—And I am thankful for it."[10] Keats's statements that he had plunged into "abstractions" or "abstract images" as a relief from suffering can easily be misread; the statements were almost surely not meant to imply that *Hyperion* is an escapist or easily optimistic poem. "Abstractions" was probably for Keats as for Shelley[11] a near-synonym for "poetry," of which any kind would seem abstract by comparison with an actual scene of mortal suffering, but especially the kind of generalized statement of human suffering, represented in divine actors, that *Hyperion* is. Keats's statements are not to be read as implying that the *subject* of his poem is an escape from suffering. There are many things one might do in order to divert one's thoughts from the subject of pain, but one can hardly take up an epic theme out of such a motive. And if *Hyperion* is what it is sometimes called, a paean to beauty and progressive optimism, would its poet while writing it have referred twice to poetry and once to love as a crime? It seems much more reasonable to assume that the presence of unrelenting suffering in Keats's daily life found its way into his epic. Fortunately, we do not have to assume this, for there is good evidence in the poem, as I shall presently try to demonstrate.

Tom died on December 1, and thereafter Keats seems to have worked more sporadically on the poem.[12] In February he wrote that he had done no recent work on *Hyperion;* he had not been "in great cue for writing lately" and must wait for the spring to rouse him.[13] In March he was still listless, in a "qui [cui] bono temper, not exactly on the road to an epic poem."[14] The Latin phrase was not being used casually, for it asks exactly the question that Keats had been asking himself about suffering and about poetry. In April he sent the manuscript, two books and part of a third, to Woodhouse, declaring according to the latter that he would work on it no more.[15] And from February to May Keats was writing his great journal-letter which contains his description of the world as a "vale of Soul-making," his closest approach to a solution of the problem of physical evil.[16] This letter expresses a number of ideas which had been and were to be crucial themes in *Hyperion* and its revised version. I shall mention these ideas later.

The conflict between artistic concerns and an awareness of the suffering world continued in an even more intense way during the following months. In June Keats considered renouncing poetry for a medical position at sea; his training had been medical and he needed money, but in addition one suspects the notion of having a symbolic content, since the problem of suffering, vividly felt, typically prompts either desperate escapism or a determination to take heroically direct action—as a doctor or missionary, for example. In the same letter Keats broods over the disappointments suffered by the English poets: Boiardo "had a Castle in the Apennine. He was a noble Poet of Romance; not a miserable and mighty Poet of the human Heart." But besides leading him to mourn the martyrdom of serious poets, his gloom glances at the value of poetry itself: "I have been very idle lately, very averse to writing; both from the overpowering idea of our dead poets and from abatement of my love of fame. I hope I am a little more of a Philosopher than I was, consequently a little less of a versifying Pet-lamb."[17] The term "philosopher" was, of course, one that Keats often used as an antonym for the self-indulgent dreamer; in the spring he had expressed a preference for philosophy over poetry because philosophy strives for truth while poetry may be "fine" but "erroneous."[18] A letter to Fanny Brawne in late July reveals that he had been working on "a very abstract Poem," certainly one of the two versions of the Hyperion poem, almost certainly, in view of the September letter to Woodhouse, *The Fall.*[19]

The emotional tension was building up to a number of explosive statements by Keats. On August 23 he was truculently and self-consciously asserting what he himself called "pride and egotism"; he had decided to sacrifice humanitarian concerns to poetry: "Pride and egotism will enable me to write finer things than anything else could—so I will indulge it." He referred sneeringly to the "commonplace crowd of the little-famous," a "myriad aristocracy in Letters."[20] The passage has Keats's invariable honesty, but there is also something shrill, almost desperate about it. The climax came with his declaration in September that he had abandoned the poem, presumably the second version. There were too many Miltonic inversions in it; Miltonic verse could only be written "in an artful or rather artist's humour" (Keats's self-correction is helpful); he drew a contrast between the "false beauty proceeding from art" and "the true voice of feeling."[21] "The Paradise Lost though so fine in itself is a corruption of our Language—it should be kept as it is unique—a curiosity. . . . I have but lately stood on my guard against Milton. Life to him would be death to me."[22] The artist's humour, something antithetical to honest, vital experience, had been rejected, but Keats had solved nothing, either philosophically or emotionally.

According to Charles Brown, Keats did not entirely give up the poem in September.[23] This is understandable, since both versions of *Hyperion* had been in effect one large arena wherein he had tried to work out his deepest problems ever since the preceding September, and he had not yet worked them out. But his efforts at further composition were apparently half-hearted, and we hear no more from Keats about work on the poem. The serene mood of "To Autumn" had been no more than a brief respite, and in November Keats wrote a letter that both confesses and illustrates his continuing confusion. The letter both denies and asserts the author's poetic ambitiousness. Keats had decided to revert to romance, the fanciful, the "marvellous." On the other hand, he confessed: "I and myself cannot agree about this at all. Wonders are no wonders to me. I am more at home amongst Men and women. I would rather read Chaucer than Ariosto." He had retreated, it seems, from the high eminence of Moneta's shrine and of epic endeavor, defeated not by a literary form but by the insoluble enigma of pain. Now he was once more at the bottom of the stairs, uncertain whether to quit the temple entirely by going back to romantic themes or to begin the weary climb toward greatness all over again. Certain of the poems he was contemplating would, by combining the coloring of romance with human drama, be a "famous gradus ad Parnassum altissimum," and the metaphor, in connection with Moneta's stairs, has a muted ring of despair that mixes uneasily with the poet's determined tone. His plan, in any case, appealed to him only when he felt ambitious; "I am sorry to say that is very seldom."[24]

III

Readings of *Hyperion* have generally taken one or more of three approaches. The oldest view, which still survives though in relatively sophisticated forms, is that *Hyperion* is a poem about historical progress, either in politics or in general culture. Most of these theories lean heavily on the speeches of Oceanus and Clymene in the council of fallen Titans.[25] Apart from the fact that such optimism is belied by Keats's general mood during most of 1818 and 1819, the trouble with these theories is that they ascribe to Keats an interest in public affairs and a powerful belief in the value of culture for which there is very little evidence in his letters.[26] Keats was interested in such matters, but no more than in a score of others, and certainly not enough to write an epic poem about them. Furthermore, as critics have often observed, the Titans are not described as oppressors, but rather in the most sympathetic of terms; conversely, the Olympians are in certain ways unattractive. The difficulty might seem to be resolved by assuming that Keats is using an *a fortiori* argument: if the old order was beautiful, how much more so the new one, now first in might as in beauty? The answer to this defense is that Keats would hardly have overshot his mark so far; there is too much emphasis on the Titans' beauty for even an *a fortiori* demonstration. Furthermore, the emphasis on the Titans' prelapsarian glory and beauty is Keats's contribution; the mythographers he drew on generally depict the deposition of the Titans by the newer gods as a triumph of sweetness and light over barbarity.[27]

More helpful are the interpretations which identify Titans and Olympians with different sets of values or with conflicting tendencies in Keats; Miltonism versus Shakespeareanism, humanism versus humanitarianism, passion versus humanitarianism.[28] My own reading has much in common with these views. I have only one objection to most of them: they imply that the conflict between Titans and Olympians reflects insights and concerns too exclusively Keats's own; such interpretations tend to solemnize as definitive, technical labels the literary shorthand of Keats's utterances. Keats's ideas are less idiosyncratic than his half-private symbolism of names and terms might suggest.

A third view, which sometimes blends with forms of the second, is one that is becoming more widespread but has not been developed in detail. This third view, which I share, sees *Hyperion* as dramatizing the difference between innocence and experience, between the idyll of childhood and the knowledge and pain that come with maturity.[29] All too often, however, critics have found this tragic depth in *The Fall of Hyperion* but not in *Hyperion* itself.[30]

How well can this theme be assimilated to epic? That is one of Keats's big questions and one we must try to answer as well. In fact the theme has definite epic possibilities. I have mentioned that the epic tradition includes a number of polarities. There is, for one, the antagonism, in authors and in their heroes, between what comes easily and what high duty exacts. Wordsworth had adapted this ordeal pattern, Shelley had merely hinted at it (Laon has only the rudiments of an internal struggle); it is distinctly present in *Hyperion,* where Keats implies that human beings can choose, as poets can in their own special sphere, whether they shall be perennial children or grow to responsible awareness of reality. Another form of epic polarity, one illustrated in Wordsworth and Shelley both, is the contrast between human and more remote levels; for Keats this becomes a two-way metaphor by which both the loss and acquisition of deity are in different ways initiations into humanity. The contrast between near and far also dictates the inverted allegory, often implied in the diction of the poem, by which Keats represents what is most vitally human as almost indescribably remote. This is the Miltonic "accommodation" in reverse. The poet tells us that Thea's words are "in our feeble tongue . . . how frail / To that large utterance of the early Gods!" (I.49–51) and that Hyperion enters his palace with a "roar, as if of earthly fire" (I.215). The rhetorical and psychological technique is Raphael's, except that ultimately the truth Keats wants to express is human truth; his story is an "accommodation" of earthly insight to the narrative level of the supernatural.

But the most important way in which Keats's theme in *Hype-*

rion aligns itself with the epic tradition is less schematically theoretical: Keats is re-evoking for his own purposes the themes of
several particular poets, especially Milton and Dante. Despite a
few relatively brief suggestions by recent critics that in *Hyperion*
Keats is thematically in Milton's debt,[31] readers tend to find in
the poem only textural imitations of Milton's style and structure
—which are indeed pervasive, as De Selincourt and Bate have
definitively shown.[32] Symptomatic of this oversight is the claim,
often made even by admirers of *Hyperion,* that the poem's subject is unfit for epic or for Keats's message.[33] The style is often
regarded as the poem's greatest and most epic achievement. Actually *Hyperion* is in the epic line mainly because like other epics it
places its message in competition with those of earlier works, the
most important of which is the definitive English epic, *Paradise
Lost.*

Milton's epic describes in Christian terms the fall from innocence and joy; the definitive pagan expression of the same theme
is the myth of the golden age, the decline of the world after the
reign of Saturn. Keats imaginatively blends the two accounts,
along with important overtones from Shakespeare and Dante.
This kind of imaginative fusion is the kind of synthesizing tour
de force that Keats was master of; it is illustrated again and
again, in both casual and central matters, in his letters. To this
imaginative power Keats, perhaps paradoxically, joined the analy-
tic detachment of the modern comparative mythologist, as his
"Soul-making" letter shows. There he suggests that a world of
pain is necessary in order for men to acquire individual identi-
ties, and that his theory may have been the archetype after which
several religious popularizations were fashioned: "It is pretty
generally suspected that the Christian scheme has been copied
from the ancient Persian and Greek Philosophers. Why may they
not have made this simple thing even more simple for common
apprehension by introducing Mediators and Personages in the
same manner as in the heathen mythology abstractions are personified." He adduces illustrations from Zoroastrian, Christian,

Hindu, and Greek religion. "For as one part of the human species must have their carved Jupiter; so another part must have the palpable and named Mediator and saviour, their Christ their Oromanes and their Vishnu."[34] Whatever the merit of Keats's idea, the man who arrived at it was capable of far-ranging thematic counterpoint.

One preliminary example, examined in detail, will show Keats's dependence on the *matter* of his models. I choose a passage which is thematically important but not especially obtrusive. In Book I Hyperion, the only Titan not yet deposed, is described as sensing, even in his "palace bright," the impending change:

> Also, when he would taste the spicy wreaths
> Of incense, breath'd aloft from sacred hills,
> Instead of sweets, his ample palate took
> Savour of poisonous brass and metal sick.   (I.186–89)

Undoubtedly the bold locution "Savour of poisonous brass and metal sick" refers elliptically to the classical metaphor describing the decay of the world in terms of the four symbolic metals: gold, silver, brass, and iron. The words *gold* and *silver,* as we shall see, are often used in *Hyperion* to characterize the Titans and their prelapsarian life. Thus gold and silver are probably considered as together representing the first, most happy state of man; the odor of brass, then, would appropriately suggest the first decline from the state of pristine joy. In *The Fall of Hyperion* Keats is to make the "golden age" theme more explicit by having the poetic suppliant conjure Moneta "By all the gloom hung round thy fallen house, / By this last temple, by the golden age," by Apollo, and by herself, "The pale Omega of a withered race" (I.284–88). In *Hyperion* Keats's reference to "brass and metal sick" gives his version of the Titans' fall the overtones of immemorial mythic insight. The standard expression of this insight in classical literature is, of course, Ovid's *Metamorphoses,* Sandys's translation of which Finney cites as one of the sources Keats used for *Hyperion.*[35]

But the classical myth is only one thread in Keats's fabric. The

word "snuff'd" which occurs a few lines before the passage
quoted has been linked with the incident in *Paradise Lost* where
Death "snuffd the smell / Of mortal change on Earth" (X.272–
73).[36] (Milton's lines are part of a thematic inversion of his
own; before the fall the still-innocent living creatures "send up
silent praise / To the Creator, and his Nostrils fill / With grate-
ful Smell"—IX.195–97.) Keats's echo, however, is more than
a casual attempt at Miltonic overtones; the analogy between Hyperion's action and Death's is thematically and dramatically very
close. Both figures "snuff" from unimaginably remote places the
odor of mortality that so dearly concerns them. In both poems an
old way of life, one of joy and wholesomeness, is dying and being replaced by a world of suffering. It is true that in the long run
of his poem Keats will interpret this change as salutary, as Milton does too in his way, but at these two particular moments both
poets are describing the change pessimistically.

Thus Keats tactfully and without ostentation assimilates the
classical and Christian associations. But the counterpoint is to include still another Christian voice. In the summer of 1818, just
before writing *Hyperion*, Keats had read intensively Cary's
Dante, which was the only book he took with him during his
walking tour,[37] and he heavily marked Cantos IX to XV of the
Inferno, cantos which as Gittings shows are especially suggestive
of the vale of the fallen Titans in *Hyperion*. Keats marked especially heavily Dante's description (in Canto XIV) of the statue
of the Old Man of Crete, which follows by only a few lines a
reference by Dante to efforts by Rhea, the spouse of Saturn, to
conceal the birth of her son Jupiter. Gittings points out the parallel with Keats's characters and finds a reminiscence of the Old
Man of Crete in part of Keats's description of the dejected Saturn (I.20–24).[38] But once again we find the echo to be more
than textural. For Dante's Old Man is the most direct symbol in
the *Inferno* for the lapsed and suffering world; the statue represents with its split body the theologians' "wound of nature" after
the fall.[39] "In midst of ocean," says Virgil in the Cary version,

"A desolate country lies, which Crete is nam'd,
Under whose monarch in old times the world
Liv'd pure and chaste. A mountain rises there,
Call'd Ida, joyous once with leaves and streams,
Deserted now like a forbidden thing.
It was the spot which Rhea, Saturn's spouse,
Chose for the secret cradle of her sons; . . .
                              Of finest gold
[The statue's] head is shap'd, pure silver are the breast
And arms; thence to the middle is of brass,
And downward all beneath well-temper'd steel,
Save the right foot of potter's clay, on which
Than on the other more erect he stands.
Each part, except the gold, is rent throughout;
And from the fissure tears distil."[40]

Keats draws heavily on details in Cantos XIV and XV, and there can be little doubt that Dante's Old Man, which in the *Divine Comedy* itself explicitly assimilates the classical myth of Saturn and the symbolic metals to the poem's Christian theme, is relevant to Keats's own version of the Fall and more specifically to the "poisonous brass" and "metal sick" snuffed by Hyperion. It deserves to be noticed that Keats's allusions to both Milton and Dante are to passages which even in the sources had drawn thematically on other passages or works. This essentially epic technique, the mutation on a mutation, is almost exactly the same that we observed earlier in Wordsworth's evocation of Miltonic and pre-Miltonic gardens.

That in *Hyperion* Keats drew thematically on Milton is understandable in view of Keats's associations with him. As we know, Keats came to make some kind of identification between Milton and an "artful or rather artist's humour" (a phrase I shall try my hand at explaining later) which he contrasted with "the true voice of feeling." He also associated Milton with the devoted statesman and great poet as opposed to the venal public figures and trivial poetasters of his own day, "all Bucks Authors of Hengist and Castlereaghs." Leaving aside the problematical reference to the artist's humour, we can infer that for Keats Milton was both a

literary and extraliterary symbol; he was a hero because he could
put aside literature for worldly action and because, within literature, he represented lofty moral concerns as opposed to ease.
These two sides are summarized in Keats's description of him as
"an active friend to Man all his Life and . . . since his death."[41]

Perhaps the most interesting of all his comments on Milton is
one that Keats wrote in his copy of *Paradise Lost*. Here he doubtless draws on Milton's own statements associating great poetry
with asceticism, but Keats's exaggerated version of Milton's
moral struggle between luxury and duty is clearly a projection of
his own conflicts:

> The Genius of Milton . . . calculated him, by a sort of birthright, for
> such an 'argument' as the Paradise Lost: he had an exquisite passion
> for what is properly, in the sense of ease and pleasure, poetical Luxury;
> and with that it appears to me he would fain have been content, if he
> could, so doing, have preserved his self-respect and feel of duty per-
> formed; but there was working in him as it were that same sort of
> thing as operates in the great world to the end of a Prophecy's being
> accomplish'd: therefore he devoted himself rather to the ardours than
> the pleasures of Song, solacing himself at intervals with cups of old
> wine; and those are with some exceptions the finest parts of the poem.[42]

The view of Milton as having abandoned his birthright, poetical
luxury, and devoted himself "rather to the ardours than the
pleasures of Song" is a very accurate description of Keats's self-
imposed task in writing *Hyperion* and, within the poem, of
Apollo's agonizing metamorphosis in Book III to tragically heroic
poet. We can also say literally of Apollo what Keats said of Milton, that "there was working in him as it were that same sort of
thing as operates in the great world to the end of a Prophecy's
being accomplish'd," for Apollo is the fulfillment of Mnemosyne's prophetic visions. During Apollo's anguish "Mnemosyne
upheld / Her arms as one who prophesied.—At length / Apollo
shriek'd;—and lo!" (III.133-35).

Having given and analyzed my preliminary example, I turn
now to a more systematic examination of *Hyperion*. Let me ex-

plain what the system is, however. As the example was partly intended to show, Keats's method is contrapuntal and allusive; in this respect *Hyperion* closely resembles *The Waste Land*. Therefore, one cannot easily discuss any one passage in isolation, any more than in Eliot's poem, since many passages reflect several of the themes and several other passages. My method will be somewhat analogous to the meteorologist's when he draws a weather-map: I shall look closely at the beginning of the poem and examine the way in which the major themes are introduced, then draw isobars, as it were, to the other parts of the poem where the same theme is repeated or developed.

As many critics have observed, *Hyperion* begins like the traditional epic, in the middle of things. (There is no other trace of the epic "opening formula"—invocation, statement of theme, rhetorical question, and so forth.) But there is no need to associate this technique with the general epic tradition, for the whole initial scene is a close imitation of *Paradise Lost,* though the tense quietude of the mood is distinctively Keats's own. The numbed desolation in which we discover Saturn recalls the nine days during which Satan and the fallen angels lay confounded on the lake of fire (*PL,* I.50–52). It is true that Saturn has been separated from the other gods, but when we meet these others in Book II we find them in the same state of immobile helplessness as the angels and Saturn. And there are many other detailed echoes of Milton's phrasing and descriptive strategy, echoes that must have been deliberate. Milton had himself prepared the way for Keats by comparing Satan's enormous, prone figure to beings

> whom the Fables name of monstrous size,
> *Titanian,* or *Earth-born,* that warrd on *Jove,*
> *Briareos* or *Typhon,* whom the Den
> By ancient *Tarsus* held. (*PL,* I.197–200)

This brief catalogue of Titans and the mention of a "Den" that holds them (Milton again applies the word to Hell in his second Book—"dark opprobrious Den of shame"—II.58) awake sympathetic diction in Keats's first description of the assembled fallen Titans,

> Coeus, and Gyges, and Briareüs,
> Typhon, and Dolor, and Porphyrion,   (II.19–20)

in their "den where no insulting light / Could glimmer on their tears" (II.5–6).

But in themselves parallels like these help to prove only what scholars have long been aware of, the stylistic and structural debt which *Hyperion* owes to Milton's epic. They do not throw much light on the meaning of *Hyperion*. In fact Keats is drawing on the Miltonic *theme,* the theme of lost innocence; Saturn and the other Titans have lost something analogous to what Satan and the fallen angels lost. The thematic parallel is subtly emphasized in another echo of *Paradise Lost* early in *Hyperion.* Milton's Satan and the devils are

> As farr remov'd from God and light of Heav'n
> As from the Center thrice to th' utmost Pole.   (*PL,* I.73–74)

Keats likewise describes Saturn's horrifying loss of the old world in terms of light and the heavenly bodies which administer it:

> Far sunken from the healthy breath of morn,
> Far from the fiery noon, and eve's one star, . . .
> Forest on forest hung about his head
> Like cloud on cloud.   (I.2–7)

This passage is also a good illustration of Keats's repeated attempts to direct our attention back to his ultimately human theme from the supernatural beings who enact it, for at the same time that the passage echoes the fallen angels' alienation from light it also echoes Milton's own doubling of his image when later in *Paradise Lost* Adam asks the forests to hide him from the accusing presence of heavenly light:

> those heav'nly shapes
> Will dazle now this earthly, with thir blaze
> Insufferably bright. O might I here
> In solitude live savage, in some glade

Obscur'd, where highest Woods impenetrable
To Starr or Sun-light, spread thir umbrage broad,
And brown as Eevning: Cover me ye Pines,
Ye Cedars, with innumerable boughs
Hide me, where I may never see them more.

(*PL*, IX.1082–90)

Keats once remarked, in connection with *Paradise Lost* and the *Inferno*, that the opening of great poems had "great charm . . . , more particularly where the action begins."[43] This statement emboldens me to suggest that the word "vale" in the first line of *Hyperion* shares some of the overtones it has elsewhere for Keats. In the same copy of *Paradise Lost* in which he inscribed the note I have just quoted, he praises the sound of "vale" and Milton's choice of it to describe his Heaven and Hell. (The passage Keats is annotating concerns the banishment of the fallen angels from "the vales of Heaven.") "The English word"—as distinguished from Latin, one presumes—"is of the happiest chance. Milton has put vales in heaven and hell with the very utter affection and yearning of a great Poet. It is a sort of Delphic Abstraction—a beautiful thing made more beautiful by being reflected and put in a Mist."[44] Thus "vale" has Miltonic associations. But in the "Soul-making" letter "vale" is linked also to Keats's justification of heroic suffering. And the letter does what *Hyperion* itself does with the Miltonic theme of a fallen world, that is, converts a Christian commonplace into Keats's own version of it: "The common cognomen of this world among the misguided and superstitious is 'a vale of tears' from which we are to be redeemed by a certain arbitary [sic] interposition of God and taken to Heaven—What a little circumscribed straightened [sic] notion! Call the world if you please 'The vale of Soul-making.' "[45] It seems to me revealing that the contexts of all three of these references to "vale" express the same theme: the transition from a world of innocence or joy or both to a world of tragic suffering.

There are a number of other Miltonic echoes in the early lines of *Hyperion*. Most of them are casual, but occasionally there are more thematically relevant touches. The term "margin-sand"

(l. 15), another that Gittings traces to Canto XIV of Cary's *Inferno,* evokes Dante's Campaneus, who according to Gittings bears a general pictorial similarity to Keats's Saturn.[46] Campaneus's defiance of God resembles both Satan's defiance of Him and the defiance of Jupiter by Keats's Enceladus. In a passage which again illustrates Dante's own assimilation of pagan and Christian worlds, Campaneus boasts:

> "If Jove
> Weary his workman out, from whom in ire
> He snatch'd the lightnings, that at my last day
> Transfix'd me, if the rest he weary out
> At their black smithy labouring by turns
> In Mongibello, while he cries aloud;
> 'Help, help, good Mulciber!' as erst he cried
> In the Phlegraean warfare, and the bolts
> Launch he full aim'd at me with all his might,
> He never should enjoy a sweet revenge."
>   (Cary's *Inf.,* XIV.48–57)

Enceladus uses much the same imagery:

> 'Not thunderbolt on thunderbolt, till all
> That rebel Jove's whole armoury were spent,
> Not world on world upon these shoulders piled,
> Could agonize me more than baby words
> In midst of this dethronement horrible.'   (II.311–15)

Like Satan and like Keats's Titans, Campaneus has been struck down by divine power, and like Milton's fallen angels he is supine on a fiery bed. All three poets are describing defiant alienation from an older, happier existence. But the thematic point of all this for Keats becomes clearer if we recall Virgil's subsequent statement to Campaneus that his histrionics represent a failure to understand the real nature of the situation, and that his punishment is the greater for his refusal to acknowledge reality (*Inf.,* XIV.63–72; Cary, XIV.59 ff.). In just the same way Milton originally portrays Satan as a heroic figure but finally reveals him as stupidly recalcitrant to reality, a hero who, unlike the redeemable Adam, is a slave to his past. These emphases are centrally relevant to Keats's own epic, for the main difference between Titans, including Enceladus, and Olympians is in their power to grow, to acknowledge the new painful facts of life.

In lines 20–21 Keats underlines Saturn's inability to accept the new world, his exclusive concern with the past, in the words "his bow'd head seem'd list'ning to the Earth, / His ancient mother, for some comfort yet." The latent image of childhood, which is soon to suggest childishness as well, anticipates the explicit introduction of the infancy image in line 26, where Thea is called "a Goddess of the infant world." In the poem such imagery is two-edged, for it suggests both innocent happiness and the childish ignorance which must in time be put away if one is to become a mature person. The child imagery always refers to the old order, either the Titans' lost world or the Apollo who has not yet been deified by suffering. In calling for the return of the old life, Saturn daydreams of "Beautiful things made new, for the surprise / Of the sky-children" (I.132–33). Hyperion, anticipating his downfall, asks, "Am I to leave this haven of my rest, / This cradle of my glory?" (I.235–36). Oceanus utters tones which "his first-endeavouring tongue" had "Caught infant-like from the far-foamed sands" (II.171–72). Enceladus scoffs at Clymene's "baby-words" (II.314). Apollo's capacity for growth, on the other hand, is symbolized in Mnemosyne's contrast between his "infant hand" and his power to bend the heroic bow. She has watched over him

> 'From the young day when first thy infant hand
> Pluck'd witless the weak flowers, till thine arm
> Could bend that bow heroic to all times.' (III.73–75)

"Witless" is also a key word, since Apollo is deified by "knowledge enormous" of suffering.[47] In the background of the passage are the naïve Telemachus and the wise, experienced, bow-bending Odysseus. And the whole image and theme of infancy are an elaboration of Keats's "chambers" analogy, in which he describes the growing man as moving from the "infant or thoughtless

Chamber" of life to the initially exhilarating Chamber of Maiden-
Thought, which then darkens through man's consciousness of
"Misery and Heartbreak, Pain, Sickness, and oppression."⁴⁸

Keats's description of Thea includes his most obvious adaptation of the "Miltonic turn":

> But oh! how unlike marble was that face:
> How beautiful, if sorrow had not made
> Sorrow more beautiful than Beauty's self.   (I.34–36)

The stylistic virtuosity should not, however, distract us from the
meaning of the lines, which summarize the central idea of *Hyperion*. They narrowly skirt euphuistic nonsense, but if we recognize the complex ambiguities in the terms they are meaningful
and thematically powerful. Sorrow is more beautiful than Beauty's
self because through sorrow men in general are given the oppor-
tunity for soul-making and the poet learns to hear the "deep, au-
tumnal tone" that characterizes supreme poetry. These new possibilities, on both levels, are superior to the simple and obvious
beauty which is based on naïveté and ignorance.

Keats's insistence that despite her statuesque appearance Thea's
face is unlike marble is the first explicit mention in the poem of
the new and ungodlike suffering which the Titans must now endure, the first sign of "mortal change." A few lines later Keats
plays on the same theme, again using the technique of reverse accommodation to emphasize the human relevance of the poem:

> One hand she press'd upon that aching spot
> Where beats the human heart, as if just there,
> Though an immortal, she felt cruel pain.   (I.42–44)

A variant of the same humanizing emphasis then follows, in the
words "poor old King" which Thea addresses to Saturn—an
echo of *King Lear*.⁴⁹ Again Keats is using literary allusion to en-
rich his theme. Both Saturn and Lear are old, deposed kings, and
there is a scenic parallel between Thea and Cordelia as comfort-
ers. But a more important parallel is the similarity (up to a
point) in spiritual experience. Both monarchs, Saturn and Lear,

react with at least initial childish bravado to their humanizing, their exposure to the common lot of man. Both stories tell of revolt against its elders by a generation which is both wiser and tougher than they. Keats is turning from romance, which in the *"King Lear"* sonnet he had called "golden tongued," "Queen of far-away," to the "bitter sweet" Shakespearean fruit, the powerful beauty that comes from a tragic embracing of suffering. He is also *describing* such a turn in his poem. The tragic spirit, and the epic note which Keats identifies with martyred asceticism and tragedy, is not only grander but more truly beautiful than romantic escapism.[50] This is a deepened form of the view Keats had once expressed in a letter to his brothers in which he claims that intensity, "the excellence of every Art," can make "all disagreeables evaporate, from their being in close relationship with Beauty & Truth—Examine King Lear & you will find this exemplified throughout."[51] The more general, human aspect of Keats's turning from romance is reflected in another statement he once made: that it was not "skyey Knight errantry" that could heal the "bruised fairness" of suffering women.[52]

Thea's address to the still unawakened Saturn describes in some detail the new signs of disorder in nature since the Olympians' accession. For in the early parts of the poem, and in the Titans as distinguished from the Olympians, the emphasis is on loss seen in retrospect, not on soul-making or the tragic poetry which can reconcile creatures to their loss. Thea's words are an echo of the two Miltonic passages which show nature as sighing and weeping in response to human sins. Thea says:

> 'For heaven is parted from thee, and the earth
> Knows thee not, thus afflicted, for a God;
> And ocean too, with all its solemn noise,
> Has from thy sceptre pass'd; and all the air
> Is emptied of thine hoary majesty.
> Thy thunder, conscious of the new command,
> Rumbles reluctant o'er our fallen house;
> And thy sharp lightning in unpractis'd hands
> Scorches and burns our once serene domain.'   (I.55–63)

The words "Our once serene domain" are typical of the consistent emphasis on the tranquillity and innocent thoughtlessness
which had characterized the Titans' prelapsarian life, which values suggest in their turn the "innocent" world men know before
they grow into suffering and heroic acceptance of it. The "reluctant" thunder (Keats marked the word admiringly in his *Paradise Lost*[53]) is another thematic glance at Milton, who heralds
with "reluctant flames" (VI.58) the visitation of divine wrath
on the angels who are to be cast out of Heaven.

   Like Milton, Keats stresses that one important result of the
fall from innocent glory is new domination by unruly passion;
Finney has mentioned the resemblance between Satan's disordered
passion in his Mount Niphates soliloquy, where his borrowed
visage is marred by the passions of ire, envy, and despair, "dis-
tempers foule" from which heavenly minds are clear (*PL*, IV.
114–19), and the "frailty" of grief, rage, fear, anxiety, revenge,
remorse, spleen, hope, "but most of all despair" which Saturn
now feels for the first time. A "mortal oil," a "disanointing
poison" has been poured on his head.[54] (One thinks too of the
identical imagery in Shakespeare's *Richard II*, another work with
a prominent "fall" theme.) Similarly, Clymene's words later in
the poem, "all my knowledge is that joy is gone, / And this thing
woe crept in among our hearts" (II.253–54), express the baffled
wonder of the Titans over their new painful condition and have
the cadence of several phrases in *Paradise Lost*, including Satan's
mock-innocent "whatever thing Death be" (IX.695), Adam's
appalled reference after the fall to "this new commer, Shame"
(IX.1097), and, obviously, the reference to the tree whose mortal taste brought Death and "all our woe" (I.3).

   The awakening in the Titans of novel, ungodlike passions is,
as Caldwell has shown, one of Keats's most insistent points in
Hyperion.[55] Coelus states it definitively in his speech to the
doomed sun-god:

> 'For I have seen my sons most unlike Gods.
> Divine ye were created, and divine

In sad demeanour, solemn, undisturb'd,
Unruffled, like high Gods, ye liv'd and ruled:
Now I behold in you fear, hope, and wrath;
Actions of rage and passion; even as
I see them, on the mortal world beneath,
In men who die—This is the grief, O Son!
Sad sign of ruin, sudden dismay, and fall!' (I.328–36)

When the Titans are first introduced in Book II, they are pictured in Dantesque, twisted attitudes which, as often in the *Inferno*, illustrate heroic vindictiveness combined with a suggestion of absurd ineffectuality. Creüs in his rage has shattered a rib of rock, Iäpetus has strangled a serpent because it "could not spit / Its poison in the eyes of conquering Jove," Cottus is grinding his skull on the flint (II.41–51). The change from the old calm demeanor is most evident in Enceladus:

once tame and mild
As grazing ox unworried in the meads;
Now tiger-passion'd, lion-thoughted, wroth,
He meditated, plotted, and even now
Was hurling mountains in that second war . . . (II.66–70)

All these signs of emotional upheaval represent, as in Milton, the difference between the innocent and fallen worlds.[56]

Thea's speech fails to awaken Saturn, and the mourning figures retain their motionless *pietà* attitudes for a whole lunar cycle. When Saturn finally awakes and speaks he introduces a number of new variations on Keats's theme. One is the benignity and beauty of the gods in their old dispensation; heretofore their former serenity has been more strongly emphasized. Saturn now mourns his lost "influence benign on planets pale,"

'peaceful sway above man's harvesting,
And all those acts which Deity supreme
Doth ease its heart of love in.' (I.108–12)

Soon he envisions a new victory, with trumpets of triumph, festival hymns, soft voices, the stir of stringed instruments, in short "Beautiful things made new" (I.126–32). The same atmosphere

of luxuriant beauty pervades Hyperion's former way of life and
his palace, with its "bowers of fragrant and enwreathed light"
(I.176–220). The speech in which he bids farewell to "this soft
clime, / This calm luxuriance of blissful light," to "splendour"
and "symmetry," and sees in their stead "death and darkness" is
Keats's reworking of Satan's speech bidding farewell to the happy
fields of Heaven and acknowledging the exchange of "this mourn-
ful gloom / For that celestial light" (*PL*, I.244-45). Later Enceladus is to bemoan not so much the loss of his old realm as that

> 'The days of peace and slumberous calm are fled;
> Those days, all innocent of scathing war,
> When all the fair Existences of heaven
> Came open-eyed to guess what we would speak.' (II.335–38)

Such passages as these make it impossible to interpret *Hyperion*
as a simple statement of progress. There is a kind of progress—
not secular or cosmic—in the coming of the new gods, but their
coming destroys a wondrously attractive thing, the state of innocence itself.

A second motif introduced by Saturn in his opening speech is
a metaphorical expression, through the imagery of gold and silver, of the Titans' former beauty and goodness. As I have already
suggested, the precious metals are identified with the old uncom-
plicated world that has been lost, so that Hyperion "snuffs" the
change to "brass and metal sick." (Incidentally, it is typical of
Keats and indicative of his vision of innocence that he should
describe a moral insight through an olfactory image.) Saturn introduces the gold-silver image by calling Thea "tender spouse of
gold Hyperion" (I.95); the restoration he envisions is to be a
"golden victory," with

> 'hymns of festival
> Upon the gold clouds metropolitan,
> Voices of soft proclaim, and silver stir
> Of strings in hollow shells.'   (I.126–31)

Hyperion's luxurious palace is "his own golden region" (I.224).
It is important, however, that in the course of the poem these

precious metals change their symbolic direction. The change begins, approximately, when Oceanus makes his reconciliatory speech. Before that, gold and silver have connoted retrospective nostalgia for the Titans' vanished ease; now they begin to be applied to the Olympians instead. The new gods are "not pale solitary doves, / But eagles golden-feather'd" (II.225–26). Clymene describes Apollo's music, which she has overheard, as "that new blissful golden melody" (II.280). In Book III the image occurs with insistent frequency. A form of the self-conscious epic invocation which Keats had avoided in Book I occurs at the beginning of Book III: "Apollo is once more the golden theme!" (III.28). (The precedent for Keats's autobiographical references in this passage is Milton's reference to himself in the course of his hymn to light at the beginning of his own third Book; if one sees in Keats's relatively personal tone a sign that he is wearying of his epic vehicle, one must in logic say the same of Milton.) Apollo's tears go "trickling down the golden bow he held" (III. 43); Mnemosyne tells him that after dreaming of her (we are possibly meant to compare Adam's prophetic dream in *PL*, VIII. 292–311) he awoke and found "a lyre all golden" by his side (III. 63); Apollo yearns to inhabit a star and "make its silvery splendour pant with bliss" (III.102); during his agonized metamorphosis his "golden tresses famed / Kept undulation round his eager neck" (III.131–32).

But this shift in imagery is not inconsistency; it mirrors a deliberate change of direction in Keats's theme. Before Oceanus's speech in which he urges his fellows to accept their new state, Keats has asked us to share the Titans' grief over their loss. It is truly a sad thing, he seems to be saying, that men cannot remain forever in the infant and thoughtless chamber. But, like Wordsworth's "Immortality" Ode, *Hyperion* goes on to stress that the pain of loss is only half of the full truth, the less important half. Keats, like Wordsworth, modulates to an optimism which does not contradict the earlier expression of pain but rather sees it in a new light. Hence the imagery of gold and silver remains, its new overtones assuring us that the world of pain has possibilities for greatness and true humanity, for soul-making and heroic poetry, which were not available in the thoughtless world of immaturity.

Apollo becomes a god in Book III, a change that balances Keats's emphasis on the Titans' fall to a more human status. We first meet the hero-to-be wandering in uncertainty and confusion, full of vague aspirations and half-insights, questioning his role in life. His deification requires a critical agony, which he undergoes in the last lines of the fragmentary poem, agony accompanied by the acquisition of the new power that is knowledge; hence he reverses the two most distinctive traits of the Titans' old world, ignorance of real life and placid immunity to pain. We remember that Keats had promised Haydon early in 1818 that the hero of his new poem would not be led by circumstance, but, "being a fore-seeing God will shape his actions like one."[57] Keats's prognostication is fulfilled in the metamorphosis wherein Apollo gains the heroic and painful knowledge he wants and needs:

> 'Knowledge enormous makes a God of me.
> Names, deeds, grey legends, dire events, rebellions,
> Majesties, sovran voices, agonies,
> Creations and destroyings, all at once,
> Pour into the wide hollows of my brain,
> And deify me . . .' (III.113–18)

The metaphor of deification is intimately associated with the Keatsian doctrine of identity. Saturn has also introduced that motif in his opening speech; like King Lear he appeals to external authority in order to find out who this "naked" person, he himself, is (his brow is "Naked and bare of its great diadem"— I.101); he confesses that he has left "My strong identity, my real self" (I.114). But, paradoxically, "identity" implies for Keats not only deity but also, as his "Soul-making" letter makes clear, high individual humanity: "How then are these sparks [i.e., human intelligences] which are God to have identity given them—so as ever to possess a bliss peculiar to each one's individual existence? How, but by the medium of a world [of suffering] like this?"[58] That Keats should use in *Hyperion* a metaphor of deification to express the attainment of essential humanity is only superficially a paradox, though it is a rich one. It is, for one thing, part of his general epic strategy, the strategy by which he consistently expands, distances, and generalizes his basically human concerns in *Hyperion*. And, more specifically, he is drawing on Milton's similarly rich Christian paradoxes. Adam and Eve try to be "divine" in a sense that denies the truth of their nature and consequently reduce themselves, like the Titans, to a state that is "human" in that it is disordered and pain-ridden. But there is a different sense in which their fall does earn them a share in divinity, through the Incarnation which is to link man and God more profoundly. It is significant that the passage I have just quoted from the "Soul-making" letter comes after a reference to *King Lear* and another to Eve's leaving Paradise. Keats's theme is not Christian; it is even anti-Christian in important ways. But the way of the epic poet is to imitate or evoke earlier epic themes with the aim of going beyond them.

Apollo illustrates also the special implications of soul-making for the poet. Saturn's response to his fall is not simply frustrated indignation; he contemplates creativity as a solution:

> 'But cannot I create?
> Cannot I form? Cannot I fashion forth
> Another world, another universe,
> To overbear and crumble this to naught?
> Where is another chaos? Where?' (I.141–45)

Again to the accompaniment of Miltonic overtones, this time relatively casual ones, Keats is attacking escapist art, which in the context is part of Saturn's incapacity for growth through suffering. When Apollo appears he is described as "the Father of all verse" (III.13) and as a musician who is transformed by knowledge and suffering into a heroic and tragic poet, in effect into a "miserable and mighty Poet of the human Heart."

The increased depth and scope, the *true* beauty, attainable in the poetry of a fallen world are symbolically expressed by Oceanus in his speech in Book II, where he interprets to the Titans the meaning of the new gods' accession. I think it is somewhat risky to base interpretations of the whole poem on this episode, since Keats is still copying Milton pretty faithfully, and his echoes are not invariably thematic. Oceanus's advice, in its quietism and apparent reasonableness, is almost certainly based on Belial's speech in the Miltonic council, just as Enceladus's inchoate wrath and his emphasis on the sensuous aspects of the old life are Keats's evocation of Moloch and Mammon. Keats may well have intended this scene to be, like Milton's, objectively dramatic; hence we cannot simply identify the speakers' ideas with Keats's own. The lines that immediately follow Oceanus's speech tend somewhat to distance the Titan's sentiments, to objectify them as his own:

> Whether through poz'd conviction, or disdain,
> They guarded silence, when Oceanus
> Left murmuring, what deepest thought can tell? (II.244–46)

But let us assume (as I in fact believe is true) that Oceanus's speech is thematically important. The crucial lines are these:

> 'We are such forest-trees, and our fair boughs
> Have bred forth, not pale solitary doves,
> But eagles golden-feather'd, who do tower
> Above us in their beauty, and must reign
> In right thereof; for 'tis the eternal law
> That first in beauty should be first in might.' (II.224–29)

The last line, when used to document interpretations of the poem as a manifesto of cosmic or political progress, is almost always cited without consideration of its whole context and of the specific image it caps. The contrast between pale solitary doves and golden-feathered eagles cannot possibly express the difference between rude barbarism and culture or between tyranny and political progressivism. The image of the two birds expresses rather a contrast between prettiness and grandeur, between an innocent view of the world and the somber insight of a mature man. And, in poetic terms, the contrast is between merely romantic prettiness and tragic profundity.[59] It is important that the eagle, prior to the painful events which have followed the new gods' accession, had been "Unseen before by Gods or wondering men" (I.183) and that in the *"King Lear"* sonnet the contrast between a forest and soaring wings occurs as part of a contrast between romance and tragic poetry. Both for men in general and for the poet, sorrow is to make Sorrow more beautiful than Beauty's self.

But what of Clymene's speech? The Apollonian music she overhears, which awakens despair in her and tells her that the Titans must yield to new beauty, is not sternly tragic, but soft and sensuous, "full of joy and soft delicious warmth." Apollo's song is a "blissful golden melody"; its notes are "rapturous," like strung pearls; each note is "like a dove leaving its olive perch"; the "morning-bright Apollo" is proclaimed by a voice "sweeter, sweeter than all tune" (II.266–94). Such diction does not suggest the poetry of pain or the stern courage that accepts a world of woe; it seems to describe exactly the kind of etherealized sensuousness which Keats is condemning along with "romance" in general. But we must bear in mind—it is crucial, I believe, to an understanding of *Hyperion*—that the contrast between Titans and Olympians and between Hyperion (or Saturn or Clymene) and Apollo does not always symbolize the difference between two ways of life; more often the contrast reflects two different *responses* to the challenge of growth and pain. When we first hear of Apollo from Clymene he is experiencing the same kind of innocent beauty that the Titans had enjoyed before their fall. At the beginning of Book III we find him still young, innocent, ignorant—except that, unlike the Titans, he is filled with the desire for knowledge of life and new experience, which comes to him a little later in his agonizing transformation. He has responded positively to exactly the same challenge that the Titans refuse. It is partly for this reason, though also because at times gold does represent the higher beauty of tragedy and suffering, that Keats can describe Apollo in the same gold-and-silver imagery he has earlier applied to the Titans' prelapsarian state and to lost innocence. Keats's structural plan is again thematically relevant to *Paradise Lost,* for the positive response to their fallen state ultimately made by Adam and Eve takes meaning in that poem from the failure of Satan and the devils to acquiesce in the truth of things. The structural contrast between Olympians and Titans has a similar function.[60]

IV

For a number of reasons, I am less concerned with *The Fall of Hyperion* than with Keats's first version of the myth. For one thing, a good many of my comments on *Hyperion* are easily transferable to *The Fall,* where Keats is dealing with the same themes and using much of his former material. In addition, the recent article by Stuart Sperry interprets *The Fall* almost exactly as I have interpreted *Hyperion,*[61] a fact that makes elaborate analysis unnecessary here. But obviously *The Fall* throws light of some kind on the earlier version, and therefore the revision deserves at least brief consideration here.

That on one level of *Hyperion* Keats is trying to say something about poetry and its function is made even more certain by the explicit discussion of this problem in the revised version. Similarly, the solution outlined in *Hyperion*—the idea that poetry not only can find a place in a world dominated by suffering but can even help to justify suffering by the celebration of it in heroic or tragic poetry—is made clear by contrast with Keats's ideas in the revision. In *The Fall* Keats is much less confident about the poet's role; he does not say quite consistently that poetry is intolerable in a world scarred by suffering, but he must strain not to say that, since he no longer trusts his original *felix culpa* solution of the problem. The poet's ordeal at the shrine of Moneta involves him in a problem essentially identical with that explored in *Hyperion,* the relative value of those who "feel the giant agony of the world" and "Labour for mortal good" and those "who find a haven in the world, / Where they may thoughtless sleep away their days" (*Fall,* I.150–59). As a poet, Keats falls into a contemptible intermediate group; he is superior to the "thoughtless" men in that he has felt the miseries of the world, and therefore, after entering the temple (which I take to represent artistic or mental achievement in general and the Fame that can spring from it), he is allowed to approach the shrine (which I believe is symbolic of specifically poetic achievement), but he is less worthy than those true humanitarians who do good for the world and therefore forsake fame, being content to remain outside the temple along with common, ungifted, healthy men for whom artistic or imaginative fame was never a possibility. Those outside the temple seek no wonders but "the human face" and no music "but a happy-noted voice"; Keats is like all thinkers and creators in that he "venoms all his days," neither acting for the benefit of humanity nor being able to experience joy and sorrow separately as every healthy man does, whether he be a humanitarian hero or just an ordinary man—"Whether his labours be sublime or low." (I.162–76). But among those who enter the shrine are both poets and fanatics (I.17), that is, true and false poets, true and false visionaries. Keats's ability to climb the steps to the shrine, which proves that he is capable of poetic achievement in the tragic or painful vein, distinguishes him from the false poets as in *Hyperion* Apollo had been distinguished from the poet of pretty sensuousness. But even to succeed in this climb—that is, to be a true poet, a true visionary—does not make the artist equal in value to the nondreamers outside the temple, whatever advantage he may have over other men in the narrow area of imaginative achievement. Artists are admitted into the temple only as a kind of recompense for their paltry exchange of life for visions:

> 'Therefore, that happiness be somewhat shar'd,
> Such things as thou art are admitted oft

Into like gardens thou didst pass erewhile,
And suffer'd in these temples.'   (I.177–80)

In short, Keats has virtually abandoned his attempt to justify the
ways of poetry to himself and to men; at this level of his theme
he is now fighting to show merely that the poetry of pain is greater
than the poetry of prettiness.

Admittedly, *The Fall* can more easily be interpreted this way
if we omit the disputed lines (I.187–210) in which Keats contradicts everything else he has said in the poem and makes the
poet a sage, a humanist, a physician, the "sheer opposite" of the
dreamer. It seems to me that the combination of external evidence and internal, logical evidence for omitting the lines ought
to be conclusive.[62] The fact that Keats wrote the lines in the
poet's defense shows, however, that Keats as a man could not entirely accept the despairing and contemptuous attitude toward
poetry which the rest of the poem implies.

Keats has narrowed his emphasis somewhat, and he now responds less hopefully to the questions about poetry and suffering
which he had raised in *Hyperion*, where, after a struggle, he had
adopted a reconciling attitude toward pain, though he had not
falsified the magnitude of the problem. In the early version the
advent of pain into a person's world is taken so seriously that
Keats calls on definitive treatments of the theme in earlier literature, especially Milton, in order to underline his message. The
reasons Keats gave for abandoning the poem in September, 1819,
are intimately connected with the Miltonic effect of what he had
already written. Furthermore, his statements that he has abandoned *Hyperion* refer, almost certainly, to the whole project and
not, as most authorities believed before the recovery of the "lost"
letter to Woodhouse, to the first version only.[63] But it is also generally agreed that the second version represents a systematic attempt to remove the specifically Miltonic flavor of the earlier
poem. Why, then, should Keats have abandoned the *second* attempt as too Miltonic? And, since Milton was thematically so
useful to Keats's exploration of the transition from bliss to suffer-

ing, why should Keats have thrown away in the second version one of his most powerful poetic strategies, the evocation of *Paradise Lost?*

The answer to the first question is, I believe, fairly clear. In recasting the poem Keats tried to remove the Miltonic style of the first version, but he found that the task was too great for him. In other words, he was not, in September, 1819, suddenly rejecting Miltonic style which he had earlier tried to achieve or tolerated in the second version, but simply conceding that the Miltonic qualities he was trying to remove were too deep-rooted. Most of his criticisms of Milton—in fact, virtually every one—in the letters of September 21, 1819,[64] are very specifically concerned with style and language in a narrow sense. His confession to Reynolds that he could not "make the distinction" between the false beauty of art and the true voice of feeling suggests that he was having a problem in critical discrimination, not a problem in composition. He was saying to Reynolds, in effect, "*You* try to root out the artificial-sounding lines in my first version, which I have been revising; *I* have not been able to decide what to change and what to retain."

As for the second question, I do not believe that Keats ever rejected thematic Miltonism as a strategy in the Hyperion poems, though he rejected the Miltonic style in the second.[65] The rejection of Miltonism *in general* would have been synonymous with giving up all attempts to finish *Hyperion* or its sequel, which is what Keats temporarily decided to do in September; Milton was too deeply involved with the issues he was discussing for Keats to abandon the Miltonic themes as such and still go on with either version. In *manner The Fall* is more Dantesque than *Hyperion,* but Dante had been in the first version all along and Milton remains in the second. There is, of course, a change in their weights, but this change ought not to be exaggerated. Let me summarize what I believe happened in 1819.

In April, 1819, Keats gave up *Hyperion* and at some time in the next few months began *The Fall,* in which he felt free to use his own stylistic idiom rather than Milton's. In addition, he had grown even more skeptical than before about the value of poetry, and in *The Fall* he wanted to express a new solution in which he exalted the value of poetic sternness of matter over sensuousness but only after conceding that all poetry, even the best, is a dreaming thing, a fever of itself. In other words, he had rejected the Miltonic *felix culpa* solution *as it applies to the poet*, though he could not always accept his new judgment any more than he could any other. But it does not make much sense to write a serious poem about the frivolousness of art, and Keats was to recognize the paradox more clearly as the year went by.

During the spring and summer he seems generally to have regarded life as far better than art, though in the late summer he began to reassert the value of poetic egoism of some kind. These views may seem mutually contradictory, but they are not necessarily so; the only really illogical thing is to try to write a high-serious poem to express such views. Keats was moving toward his decision to abandon the whole impossible attempt to solve the greatest philosophical problem in the world and his own most urgent personal problem at the same time. By September this decision had crystallized, and Keats at that time decided to pursue the career of poetry on a less ambitious, more easy-going level which abandoned statement and solution and did not attempt to justify poetry's role in the world. *Paradise Lost*, he wrote to George and Georgiana, "though so fine in itself is a corruption of our Language . . . I have but lately stood on my guard against Milton. Life to him would be death to me. Miltonic verse cannot be written but in the vein of art—I wish to devote myself to another sensation." The last clause is the crucial one, I believe; apart from the question of Miltonic style, which for technical reasons Keats believed to be a corruption of English, he was not condemning Milton or what he stood for; he was simply declaring his own incompatibility with Milton at the moment. He now preferred to relax for a while and to give up large projects— perhaps in favor of melodious, completely nonintellectual lyrics like "To Autumn." But his statements are not a philosophical anathema hurled against Milton. *Paradise Lost* is "fine in itself," and what would be death to Keats is, after all, "life" to Milton. Poetic art could not, Keats now felt, be justified with relation to life, nor could he himself sustain the "artist's humour"—the dedication to the ardours of song which attempts at the same time to be philosophy—after so many exhausting months. But none of this establishes a clear-cut difference between the *subjects* of *Hyperion* and *The Fall of Hyperion,* both of which are included in what Keats thought he was abandoning, half defiantly and half in despair. He had simply been defeated—not by epic but by the problem of evil and by his honest contempt for poetry which attempts to justify its dignity in rivalry with life. Now he could turn eagerly to poetry (or so he thought—he went back to the chronic problem and the chronic poem later in the autumn) because he was no longer trying to convince himself that poetic art had great value or nobility. He was attempting to leave Moneta's temple, the hall of visionaries, and by way of cultivating the honest, unpretentious *craft* of poetry, to join those happy and useful men who find their pleasure in the immediacy of experience. Two months later he was again glancing self-consciously at Parnassus, but in September Keats felt he had made his decision.

Thus to the Keats of September, 1819, the "vein of art," the "artist's humour," was not quite a synonym for aestheticism, but rather for that kind of aestheticism which takes itself too seriously, specious profundity as distinguished from unpretentious, honest craftsmanship. It is interesting to compare his letter to Shelley of August, 1820, which does not necessarily criticize Shelley for social-consciousness, as it might seem to do, but does criticize him for confusing the roles of poet and humanitarian: "There is only one part of it [*The Cenci*] I am judge of; the Poetry, and dramatic effect, which by many spirits nowadays is considered the mammon. A modern work it is said must have a purpose, which may be the God—*an artist* must serve Mammon—he must have 'self concentration' selfishness perhaps. You I am sure will forgive me for sincerely remarking that you might curb your magnanimity and be more of an artist, and 'load every rift' of your subject with ore."[66] The passage is full of ironies, intentional and (one suspects) unintentional. The "Mammon" is the New Testament's, but I suspect it is Milton's and Spenser's as well; the allusion to "rifts" of subterranean gold suggests so, especially when one remembers the "vein" of art Keats had mentioned eleven months earlier. "Spirits" and "magnanimity" are sarcasm, but also, perhaps, sardonic irony at Keats's own expense, for largeness of soul is what Keats, in certain of his fluctuating moods, had come to associate with the "artist's humour," with poetry that claims more for poetry than it is capable of. "Magnanimity" is exactly what Keats had half-guiltily renounced when he abandoned the Hyperion poems. And, although "artist" would seem to have changed its meaning significantly since the preceding September and to suggest in 1820 the kind of poetic craftsmanship with which Keats had contrasted it earlier, this inference is not to be counted on, for in the phrase *"an artist* must serve Mammon" the italics give "artist" an aggressive, tauntingly ironic tone that the word had not had in the letters of September, 1819. It is as if Keats were throwing the word at Shelley in quotation marks and asking him how he had convinced himself that art is consistent with high, ameliorative didacticism—all this, of course, under the cloak of elaborate civility. The prescription need not mean that Keats was committing himself wholeheartedly to "Mammon"; he was saying that Shelley could not serve two masters, humanitarian social-mindedness and the demands of the poet's relatively lowly craft; one must either enter the temple or stay outside. During most of 1819 Keats had been readier, even in his poetry, to serve "God," that is, profundity. In any case, one of the most interesting ironies in the letter to Shelley is that there we see Keats doing what he had done in the "Soul-making" letter and the Hyperion poems: adapting a traditional Christian formula to his own purposes.

V

The Fall of Hyperion makes an impression different from that of *Hyperion,* but it is easy to exaggerate the dissimilarity of the two poems. Their tones, styles (in a narrow sense), and atmospheres differ, not because in *The Fall* Keats was embarking on a new subject but because he was giving a different answer to his earlier question about poetry and because he was exploring the question from a different narrative viewpoint. It is a mistake, for example, to think of *Hyperion* as a poem about cosmic beauty or progress and *The Fall* as a poem about evil and suffering. The first *Hyperion* is as deeply concerned with suffering as is the revision, and although it attempts to "solve" the problem (the solution is experiential, existential, rather than rational) it does not underrate or understate that problem, either in the form it takes for all men or in the form it takes for the artist. If *Hyperion* seems to be more detached, to take a colder view of actual human suffering, that is not because the poem is escapist praise of idealized beauty or general progress; indeed, *Hyperion* is one of the most somber poems in our language. The real reason lies in Keats's too exclusive identification of the epic with such qualities as remoteness, elevation, and—in tone and scene and character—superhumanity, which are only half of the epic picture. Like Shelley's *Revolt of Islam, Hyperion* plays proximate and remote levels of action against each other, but the human level is present in *Hyperion* only by implication and indirection, even though Keats's hints make it perfectly clear that the poem is not really about gods or abstractions. *Hyperion* addresses itself to the most human of subjects, but Keats felt he must go the long way around and treat the human in terms of the divine, which is different from showing what is in some sense a real interaction between man and superior forces. In his self-consciousness about epic, Keats tried to avoid vivid, obvious human appeal on the level of action.

Such an approach was artificial, and it produced a great but unnecessarily artificial poem—artificial, I emphasize, not in its theme and ideals, but in its form, its texture, and its tone. I do not believe that Keats in deciding to write a second version of *Hyperion* was giving up epic; he was rather taking the more permissive, flexible, *human* view which is the one actually sanctioned by those most pragmatic of visionaries, the great epic poets. In *The Fall* Keats sacrificed the relatively superficial "epic" elements such as the Miltonic magniloquence and grandeur of character for a more eclectic inspiration that, as we have seen, had been at work in *Hyperion* as powerfully as in the second version, but less freely and less obviously. And in the second version he took another step toward less self-conscious and truer epic by allowing himself the prerogative which, Aristotle notwithstanding, epic poets have generally allowed themselves: he put himself in the poem. In this way he gave *The Fall* a tone of personal urgency that is entirely typical of epic poets after Homer.

The most serious liberty Keats took with the epic tradition was to divorce it from the theme of temporal continuity in history. I think it is quite possible that the lines in *Hyperion* which have caused some critics to misread it as a poem about cosmic progress spring from Keats's sense that, although the poem is not about history, at least the *metaphor* of historical progress is called for in an epic. His real theme is another kind of progress, the progress in individual development which every man experiences if he survives the ordeal of growth in the world. Wordsworth too had made this subject heroic argument, but he had combined with his concern for what is changeless in man a sense of historical urgency in preaching the doctrine of changelessness to a generation that had forgotten it and had therefore lost hope and nerve. But neither version of *Hyperion* contains such a sense of historical charisma; the two poems are doctrinal to man but not to an age or nation. Dante and Spenser took the epic a long way toward the form which today we call myth, but at the same time they tried to relate their messages to a distinctive need of a certain historical time. Milton himself wrote with a sense that his message was especially relevant to the "evil days" on which he and England had fallen. Whether Keats's total and unprecedented unconcern with history and his moment in it is compatible with the development of epic remains to be seen, and although debate will help to influence the final verdict, the decisive grounds are more likely to be the *de facto* judgments of later poets and readers. In the meantime, until this issue and some of the others we have been concerned with are faced, the name of epic will doubtless be reserved for the first version of *Hyperion* alone and will be conceded to it entirely on the vague grounds of consciously noble sonority.

Six: BYRON AND THE EPIC OF NEGATION

O F the major English Romantic poems none reminds us of
its debt to epic tradition so often or insistently as Byron's *Don
Juan*. At the same time the poem is obviously unheroic, though
not simply mock-epic. This is only one of the countless puzzles
and contradictions which criticism of the poem must deal with.
If criticism's task is to elucidate the central meaning of a work
and the principles of order that give it coherence, then surely
Don Juan is one of the most recalcitrant of subjects for the critic.
Almost any interpretation of its "meaning" must ignore a good
deal of conflicting or anomalous evidence. It is sometimes said
that *Don Juan*, while lacking formal unity, has a thematic unity
which arises from Byron's repeated harping on the same strings:
the baseness and hypocrisy of marriage, the meanness of despo-
tism, and so forth.[1] This critical point is useful, but even on
many of his pet themes Byron is far from consistent. His attack
on marriage hardly wavers at all, but his commitment to, say,
popular rule is not nearly so firm; he surmises, for example, that
if monarchs were in fact overthrown he would probably become
an ultra-Royalist (XV.23).[2] Nothing is so easy as to catch Byron
in the act of contradicting himself—except that "catch" is the
wrong word, since Byron admits his inconsistency and even makes
a virtue of it.

> Also observe, that like the great Lord Coke,
>   (See Littleton) whene'er I have expressed
> Opinions two, which at first sight may look
>   Twin opposites, the second is the best.
> Perhaps I have a third too in a nook,
>   Or none at all—which seems a sorry jest;
> But if a writer should be quite consistent,
> How could he possibly show things existent?   (XV.87)

Don Juan is sometimes treated as a great poem *manqué*, a brilliant achievement which might have been far better if Byron had devoted himself to it with more serious single-mindedness, if he had labored more zealously to order his heterogeneous material in the way that great poems do. But such regrets ignore what Byron insistently implies or states, both in *Don Juan* itself and in his comments on it, namely that the poem is calculatedly formless, aesthetically and in its ideas. It is one of the very few poems which truly assert and exemplify philosophic nihilism. Although statements of skeptical relativism come thickest in the later parts of the poem, they appear in the early cantos too, and such philosophizing comprises much of what is sometimes called the digressive material of the poem. Deliberate, considered statements denying the possibility of knowledge or certainty are so frequent that illustration seems unnecessary. One needs to be aware, however, that the motif of skepticism is constantly recurring in the kind of casual detail which in some ways is even more revealing than overt and lengthy discussion. What will happen to Juan and Johnson in the battle of Ismail is "According to the artillery's hits or misses, / What Sages call Chance, Providence, or Fate" (VII.76); that the Irish language is descended from Punic is "rational / As any other notion" (VIII.23); Don Juan is "real or ideal,— / For both are much the same" (X.20); Woman is "thou nondescript" (IX.55); the great end of travel is not arriving but the act of driving itself (X.72); to prove any point is "A thing with poetry in general hard" (XII.13); the statue of the Virgin at Norman Abbey makes the earth below seem holy, for "even the faintest relics of a shrine / Of any worship, wake some thoughts divine" (XIII.61); whether Juan and the Duchess of Fitz-Fulke behaved virtuously is left "a problem, like all things" (XVII.13). And, lest any statement or episode be taken as expressing a leading truth, Byron repeatedly throws the reader off balance by his notorious habits of digression and of incongruous tone-shifting.[3]

The corelessness of *Don Juan*[4] is actually reinforced by Byron's

rollicking good humor in many passages and by his occasional
irony at the expense of his own Pyrrhonism. For example, after
citing and endorsing the skepticism of Montaigne, he concludes:
"So little do we know what we're about in / This world, I doubt
if doubt itself be doubting" (IX.17).[5] The same reflexive irony
emerges from another passage, in which Byron comically portrays
himself as totally confused, juggles skillfully the implications of
relativism, and extricates himself through an epigram that would
seem to describe fairly his actual attitude:

> If people contradict themselves, can I
> Help contradicting them, and every body,
> Even my veracious self?—But that's a lie;
> I never did so, never will—how should I?
> He who doubts all things, nothing can deny.   (XV.88)

Without such undercutting of skepticism itself, Byron's attitude
would emerge as a kind of consistent position after all, dark and
self-consciously tragic. And this vein is only one of a dozen Byron wants to exploit in the poem, since it is only one of many
mutually incongruous elements in life. Byron wants to write so
comprehensive a poem ("De rebus cunctis et quibûsdam aliis"—
XVI.3) that it will have no message except to assert a radical disorder.

Byron was capable of caviling over the details of *Don Juan;*
printers' errors enraged him, for example, and versification (form
in its moment-to-moment aspects) was a subject he was avidly
interested in. But he was scarcely concerned with larger structure
except to the extent that he took pains to avoid it.[6] Analogously,
he seems to have cared about the particular points he made in
particular stanzas; if we allow for his irony, we need not doubt
that at any one moment Byron believed what he was saying, however contradictory his ideas may seem when we take a bird's-eye
view of them. But the effect of the whole poem, or rather of the
sixteen cantos that Byron finished, is entirely independent of any
particular stanza or episode. *Paradise Lost,* like most great poems,
creates, partly through the accumulation of details, a vision which

subsumes those details; it is greater in statement and pattern than the sum of its parts. *Don Juan* is in this sense less than the sum of its parts, and Byron intended it to be so. His intention was to state an endless series of particular truths which did not add up to any Truth. Consequently, the poem is not a promising one for the critic. To the extent that one finds meaning and significance in it, one finds either what Byron tried deliberately to neutralize or the kind of order that the statistician induces from random behavior. And in fact the explication of *Don Juan* almost inevitably commits the critic to using the technique of classification, at least much of the time.

Byron's statements about the poem were often made in jest or partly so, and this is especially obvious in his discussions of possible "plans." What seems to be his most serious statement on the subject is one he made late in 1822, when he declared that *Don Juan* would eventually be seen for what it was, "a *Satire* on *abuses* of the present states of Society, and not an eulogy of vice."[7] I wish to return later to the subject of the poem's satire, but we can note immediately that the quotation describes an intention rather than an organizing idea. Furthermore, the context here is one of Byron's defenses of the poem's morality, a fact that limits the statement's applicability to the poem as a whole. More often Byron's statements imply that the poem was to be comprehensively aimless, a point he sometimes suggested through rather ironically elaborate outlines of an actual and coherent plan. During its early stages he described the poem as meant to be "a little quietly facetious upon every thing."[8] Here Byron's confession of aimlessness has a casual ring, but his more aggressive jesting later continued to make the same point. He wrote to Murray, "You ask me for the plan of Donny Johnny: I *have* no plan—I *had* no plan; but I had or have materials . . ." (The distinction between plan and materials is accurate and revealing.) "Why, Man, the Soul of such writing is its licence . . ."[9] Later he declared, again to Murray, that the plan was to have Juan tour Europe and finish his career in the French Revolution, the poem in the meantime exposing the ridiculous aspects of the various European countries. Juan's last state was to be Hell or an unhappy marriage, which Byron suggested are equivalents.[10] There is a good deal of mock-solemn joking late in the poem about the earlier parts having been a mere introduction and the real plan being a closely guarded secret (XII.54, 55, 87, 89). And several times, in the poem and in comments on it, Byron defiantly promised to make it endless or nearly so.

As usual with Byron, it is impossible to distinguish clearly between earnest and jest. But, jest or no jest, it would have been easy for Byron to hit on an effective organizing plan, either the satiric tour of Europe or the restatement of the traditional legend or some other scheme. But Byron was not aiming at a well-made poem, and he therefore avoided narrative continuity as well as other patterns. (*Don Juan* as we have it reflects to some extent all the patterns Byron mentioned, but none is more than desultory.) As for the ending, it could hardly have been important for Byron at all, since he promised to delay it until after a hundred or so cantos. But, to repeat what I have said, the absence of pattern was itself deliberate.

Byron's often-repeated jest or promise that *Don Juan* would run to inordinate length is symptomatic of his general tendency to discuss and evaluate the poem in quantitative terms which again imply aesthetic as well as ideological formlessness. At the end of Canto III he humorously tells the reader that he is cutting the third canto into two parts, simply because it is too long; critics, Byron remarks, will find a way to rationalize the division as a virtue. This passage would almost surely be taken as facetiousness if we did not know from Byron's correspondence that his account is exactly accurate.[11] In reply to Murray's judgment that only half of *Don Juan* was good, Byron argued, "if *one half* of the two new Cantos be good in your opinion, what the devil would you have more? No—no: no poetry is *generally* good— only by fits and starts—and you are lucky to get a sparkle here and there. You might as well want a Midnight *all stars* as rhyme all perfect."[12] This is very much like his cynical comment on Canto III: "The *third* canto of *Don Juan is dull*, but you must really put up with it: if the two first and the two following are tolerable, what do you expect? particularly as I neither dispute with you on it as a matter of criticism, or a matter of business."[13] Such statements are of a piece with the flippancy Byron often showed toward *Don Juan* and the career of poet, but more specifically they were meant to have a slight and half-humorous shock effect because of their audacious disregard of form and essential content as criteria of literary quality.

II

If *Don Juan* was to be a pointless poem, why should its author have written and published it? Why should any author do so? Byron gives one answer himself:

> But "Why then publish?"—There are no rewards
> Of fame or profit, when the world grows weary.
> I ask in turn,—why do you play at cards?
> Why drink? Why read?—to make some hour less dreary.
>
> (XIV.11)

There is no reason why we should regard this answer as sheer irony; it accords very well with the other evidence that Byron's aim was aimlessness and his message relativistic skepticism. But, although Byron thought of his poem as empty of essential message, its very aimlessness and formlessness were not to be seen as mere irrelevancy, except perhaps at the very beginning of the poem, where his aim was to "giggle and make giggle."[14] The poem in general is written in a polemical spirit, the enemy being sham, which for Byron includes almost everything, every institution and systematic code of manners or belief.

> I think that were I *certain* of success,
> I hardly could compose another line:
> So long I've battled either more or less,
> That no defeat can drive me from the Nine.

This feeling, 'tis not easy to express,
And yet 'tis not affected, I opine.
In play, there are two pleasures for your choosing—
The one is winning, and the other losing.   (XIV.12)

Byron's point that life is aimless and the world a chaos is not a
point he is making in a vacuum; he is trying to evaluate, in relation to the myriad ideas and persons he opposes, the true nature
of man and the true place of Byron's own age in the continuum
of human life. It is for this reason that *Don Juan* evokes the epic
tradition so often, epic being a definitive vehicle for charismatic
utterance concerning man's place in the cosmos and the relationship between present and past. One of the many good reasons for
admiring *Don Juan* as a tour de force is that in it Byron pits man
against the cosmos (or, alternatively, Providence) and the present against the past with the result that laurels are bestowed nowhere.

As I have mentioned, Shelley tried strongly to persuade Byron
to write an epic. Several other people made the same suggestion,
a fact that, incidentally, contradicts the notion that epic had lost
its appeal and prestige by the time of the Romantics. Byron's response was usually indignant refusal. To Murray he wrote an-
grily, "So you and Mr. Foscolo, etc., want me to undertake what
you call a 'great work?' an Epic poem, I suppose, or some such
pyramid. I'll try no such thing; I hate tasks. . . . You have so
many '*divine*' poems, is it nothing to have written a *Human* one?
without any of your worn-out machinery."[15] The "Human"
poem was, of course, *Don Juan*. Medwin records a conversation
in which Byron responded in a similar way, except that this time
he suggested defiantly that *Don Juan* actually was an epic:

People are always advising me to write an epic. You tell me that I shall
leave no great poem behind me;—that is, I suppose you mean by great,
a heavy poem, or a weighty poem. . . . As to epics,—have you not got
enough of Southey's? There's 'Joan of Arc,' 'The Curse of Kehama,'
and God knows how many more curses, down to 'The Last of the
Goths.' If you must have an epic, there's 'Don Juan' for you. I call

that an epic: it is an epic as much in the spirit of our day as the Iliad was in Homer's. Love, religion, and politics form the argument, and are as much the cause of quarrels now as they were then.

Byron added that the poem should have twenty-four books, "the legitimate number; and my spirits, good or bad, must serve for the machinery. If that be not an epic, if it be not strictly according to Aristotle, I don't know what an epic poem means."[16] On still another occasion he is reported to have said in response to the usual question about an epic by him that "he would never attempt any thing which approached it nearer than Don Juan"; all the great subjects were exhausted and the most celebrated epics were no longer read.[17] Another account, apparently based on the same authority, shows him as having made essentially the same answer and then adding, "I shall adapt my own poesy, please God! to the fashion of the time, and, in as far as I possess the power, to the taste of my readers of the present generation; if it survives me, *tanto meglio,* if not, I shall have ceased to care about it."[18] Perhaps in jest, Byron seems to have thought of *Don Juan* in the light of the epic tradition, by regarding it either as a modern epic or as the most viable alternative to epic in his day. Even if he was jesting, however, a jest must have a point, and this one has none if it does not at least partially reflect Byron's actual attitude. Moreover, the same "jest" recurs over and over again in the poem itself.

Serious students of Byron do not need to be reminded of the remarkable frequency of epic echoes in *Don Juan,*[19] but more casual readers, I believe, tend to think almost entirely of the exuberant clowning about the epic which occurs near the beginning of the poem—the burlesque of the *medias res* convention (I.6–7), of the unity of time (I.120), and of epic clichés in general:

> My poem's epic, and is meant to be
> Divided in twelve books; each book containing,
> With love, and war, a heavy gale at sea,
> A list of ships, and captains, and kings reigning,
> New characters; the episodes are three:

> A panorama view of hell's in training,
> After the style of Virgil and of Homer,
> So that my name of Epic's no misnomer.   (I.200)

Actually the epic echoes continue throughout the poem and, though less obvious than the early ones and often less funny, they take on an even richer meaning and relevance to their contexts. They become more truly witty. The passage just quoted is followed by a succinct parody of the technique by which the epic poet, while paying to earlier epics and earlier ages the tribute of evocative imitation, claims to have gone beyond the limited horizons of the past:

> There's only one slight difference between
>   Me and my epic brethren gone before,
> And here the advantage is my own, I ween; . . .
>   They so embellish, that 'tis quite a bore
> Their labyrinth of fables to thread through,
>   Whereas this story's actually true.   (I.202)

This is funny, but the joke is not a rich one; it consists entirely in the anomaly of such irreverence toward the poet's august ancestry and in Byron's audaciously false claim to be telling a true story. (Whether or not it is based on actual events, the reader is supposed to assume that it is fiction.) As yet little in the poem has labeled it an epic or mock-epic, apart from a few casual remarks like those about the indecent "Aeneids, Iliads, and Odysseys" and Julia's Armidan charms (I.41, 71) and the more serious opening stanzas explaining the choice of Juan as hero. There are a few other clever adaptations of epic material in Canto I, and I shall mention them briefly later, but their epic pointedness depends on their sharing a pattern which asserts itself clearly only after one has read further. Byron's claim to true heroic argument is at this early point a tall tale and little more. But compare with this passage the following one, from the end of Canto VIII; here Byron makes a very similar statement, but its humor and weight are entirely different because we now know the poem retrospectively:

Reader! I have kept my word,—at least so far
    As the first Canto promised. You have now
Had sketches of love, tempest, travel, war—
    All very accurate, you must allow,
And *Epic*, if plain truth should prove no bar;
    For I have drawn much less with a long bow
Than my forerunners. Carelessly I sing,
But Phoebus lends me now and then a string, . . .
But now I choose to break off in the middle,
    Worn out with battering Ismail's stubborn wall.

                                                    (VIII.138–39)

Again we hear an appeal to epic tradition coupled with a boast to
have transcended it—with the added fillip of plunging *out* of the
middle of things. But the tone is no longer farcical; it is dry—
even grim, in the light of the Ismail cantos we have just read,
where frequent comparisons of the modern action to Homeric
epic have raised fundamental questions about heroism in both
modern and ancient worlds. Although Byron is capable throughout the poem of resuming his earlier, more broadly humorous
tone, the contrast between the two passages typifies the general
shift in epic technique as the poem progresses.

Don Juan has often been called a mock-epic, and it is one. But
it is not only that, and except now and then, mainly in the first
canto, even the mock-epic approach is complex or ambiguous.
Few questions are so problematical as that of Byron's seriousness;
one must in the first place decide whether he is concerned with
Byron the man or Byron the poet, and indeed whether the usual
distinction between biography and art should be observed in his
case; one must then define *seriousness*, an ambiguous word in almost any context. Since the refinements of Byron's seriousness
are so varied, I shall give myself a good deal of latitude by defining very broadly the word as I use it here: as the opposite of
giggling and making giggle. And whatever may be its value in
general, the distinction between author and persona seems to me
artificial when applied to *Don Juan;* I shall assume that there is

no important distinction between the narrator of *Don Juan* and Byron himself. The distinction seldom applies to epic; in *Paradise Lost* it is not primarily a persona who says he has fallen on evil days and evil tongues.[20]

The epic elements in *Don Juan* manifest themselves with bewildering variety. But common to nearly all Byron's epic allusions, especially the more serious ones, is the assumption that traditional epic makes uncompromising statement and urges on its own age an inspiriting and inspired program. Byron himself never does any such thing, and the ironies that emerge from this failure to fulfill the epic poet's prophetic role are sometimes mildly teasing, sometimes darker. Byron's general technique in the poem is to hit and run, to evoke in himself and his audience "genuine," apparently unironic responses which are never allowed to stand unqualified. The idyll with Haidée is deflated (though not completely, of course) by the reminder that Juan has been unfaithful to Julia (II.208); the savage attack on war in Cantos VII and VIII ends with Byron's arbitrary statement that he has wearied of "battering Ismail's stubborn walls." In the same way the reader's associations with epic are played against one another. In *Don Juan* Byron uses almost every possible variation of epic tone, from the frivolous to the almost entirely serious. I should like to mention four different attitudes which Byron takes toward epic in the poem. But I must emphasize that these attitudes often blend, overlap, or conflict with one another; there are certain passages in *Don Juan* which would fit any or all of the four categories I mention. I make this reservation partly in self-defense; if the reservation is not understood the reader is certain to be convinced that I have at the very least an imperfect ear for irony.

Beginning with Byron's least serious use of epic, we have first of all his fairly straightforward use of comic mock-epic. Here the joke is almost entirely a literary one, its target being the epic as an august literary mode, its method the incongruous association of epic with innocuous trivia. When he is using this technique

Byron relies heavily on the clichés of epic theory and on those details of actual epic practice which have been most rigidly schematized by critical dogma. As it must, this technique over-simplifies and caricatures epic tradition.

As I have already mentioned, most of this relatively uncom-plicated mock-epic clowning comes near the beginning of the poem, and although it is funny it has little bite.

> Most epic poets plunge in "medias res,"
>   (Horace makes this the heroic turnpike road)
> And then your hero tells, whene'er you please,
>   What went before—by way of episode,
> While seated after dinner at his ease,
>   Beside his mistress in some soft abode,
> Palace, or garden, paradise, or cavern,
> Which serves the happy couple for a tavern.

But his own way, says Byron, is to begin at the beginning and to avoid "wandering." (1.6–7.) The narrative leap from June to November in the first canto occasions an apology to "Aristotle and the Rules" for the breach of unity (I.120–21). The list of epic devices which I have already quoted (I.200) is likewise followed by a promise that they will be used in accord with Aris-totle's rules and by a reference to the great neoclassic debate (which takes off from Milton's strictures on rhyme) about verse form:

> Prose poets like blank-verse, I'm fond of rhyme,
>   Good workmen never quarrel with their tools.

The third canto begins, "Hail, Muse! *et cetera.*—We left Juan sleeping," and ends with an offer to justify the arbitrary division of the canto into two parts on the basis of Aristotle's *Poetics, passim.* The end of the second published installment (Cantos III, IV, V) implies jestingly that epic principles of composition are taking precedence over matter:

> Thus far our chronicle; and now we pause,
>   Though not for want of matter; but 'tis time,

According to the ancient epic laws,
    To slacken sail, and anchor with our rhyme.
Let this fifth canto meet with due applause,
    The sixth shall have a touch of the sublime;
Meanwhile, as Homer sometimes sleeps, perhaps
    You'll pardon to my muse a few short naps.

A second general way in which Byron draws on the epic tradition is by using older heroism as a yardstick against which to
measure the decadence and pettiness of his own age. This is a
standard satiric technique, of course; it also resembles in certain
of its strategies the technique of ordinary comic mock-epic. Like
the latter, it depends for its effectiveness on an oversimplified
view of the heroic tradition. The difference is that this second
technique is not concerned with *belles lettres* thought of as such,
but rather with values, with heroic performance itself. The de-
sired response is laughter, but in this case contemptuous laughter
directed at ridiculous degeneracy rather than amusement occasioned by the lighthearted twitting of an overconventionalized
literary mode. Poetry may be included in the catalogue of modern degeneracy, but the emphasis is on poetry as socially relevant
statement rather than on poetry as art. Since this type of ridicule,
especially when it is most serious, is not directed against the epic
as a genre, Byron tends with infrequent exceptions to avoid references to the theory of epic or of literature in general, though he
often cites older authors and poets as precedents and standards.
On the other hand, the technique I am describing is like comic
mock-epic in being a distinct reversal of the epic practice by
which earlier values and heroes are evoked in order that the poet's
own matter may be vaunted as truer and loftier heroic argument.

This second, satiric technique usually appeals to earlier epic in
a loose and general way, by merging it with older heroism in
general. An unusually specific echo of the epic tradition is the
opening section, added by Byron to the original draft, in which
the choice of Juan as the hero is placed in the tradition of the
search for a theme.[21] With an implicit and ironic glance at Mil-

ton's list of rejected subjects, Byron mentions a multitude of contemporary celebrities who have distinguished themselves only to be soon forgotten. Their recent great popularity and the oblivion into which they have since fallen support two of Byron's main points, for through his list of failed heroes he indicts both the mediocrity of their achievement and the contemptible fickleness of an age which is extravagant in bestowing laurels and as quick in withdrawing them. Some of these heroes, Byron suggests, are unworthy of praise and therefore illustrate the degradation of heroism in an age which no longer knows what real greatness is. Others, Nelson for example, deserve lasting fame but have been forgotten. A similar point—that modern heroism is degraded or sham—emerges though in widely varying tones from the discussions of modern heroism as exemplified in Lambro (III.53–55), the Duke of Wellington (IX.1–13), and Tom the highwayman (XI.19–20), and from the reflection that revolutionary patriots need to secure the financial backing of Rothschild and Baring (XII.5).

Byron's many attacks on what he considered the wretched poetry of his age ought to be seen as part of his larger, epic-conditioned attack on the falseness of the age in general. When he is reviling bad poetry simply as bad poetry he is likely to present Pope and Dryden as his standards:

> "Pedlars," and "boats" and "waggons"! Oh! ye shades
> Of Pope and Dryden, are we come to this? . . .
> The "little boatman" and his "Peter Bell"
> Can sneer at him who drew "Achitophel"! (III.100)

Evocations of the epic poets or those of romance-epic are likely to have a broader human and social context, like the lament of the poet-trimmer in Canto III:

> The heroic lay is tuneless now—
> The heroic bosom beats no more!
> And must thy lyre, so long divine,
> Degenerate into hands like mine?
> ("The Isles of Greece," stanza 5)

or the following:

> To the kind reader of our sober clime
>   This way of writing will appear exotic;
> Pulci was sire of the half-serious rhyme,
>   Who sang when chivalry was more Quixotic,
> And revell'd in the fancies of the time,
>   True knights, chaste dames, huge giants, kings despotic;
> But all these, save the last, being obsolete,
> I choose a modern subject as more meet.   (IV.6)

The most savage attacks in the poem are, of course, directed at Southey, the "Epic Renegade," who for Byron represented not simply bad poetry, but the diseased condition of the age.[22] Not only is Southey the official spokesman of modern English values by virtue of his post as Laureate; he is also a man who, since his specialty is epic poetry, implies that his values are the definitive, "epic" ones for which he and his age will be immortalized by posterity. Hence Byron's ridicule of Southey's belief that time will vindicate him.[23] In fact, by giving him the epic place of honor in the Dedicatory Stanzas, Byron is acknowledging Southey's spiritual "leadership" of his age, much as in *The Prelude* Wordsworth does to Coleridge in a spirit of sincere admiration. I do not think it is entirely fanciful to regard Southey as Byron's equivalent of the epic patron-addressee. Southey, "that incarnate lie," typifies changeability, persons who "veer round with every breath" (X.13); what better emblem than he for the kind of shifting, protean poem which Byron (though in a spirit of truthfulness and candor) is trying to write? That Byron thought in terms of such symbolic dedications is borne out by his decision to make a special dedication of the war cantos to Wellington:

> As these new Cantos touch on warlike feats,
>   To *you* the unflattering Muse deigns to inscribe
> Truths that you will not read in the Gazettes.   (IX.10)

A third way in which Byron approaches epic contradicts the second flatly. This third way consists in treating modern life as something truly adventurous, sometimes almost noble. *Almost* that; Byron never entirely commits himself, even temporarily, to so positive a view, and even if he did the effect of such high seriousness would be neutralized by his other, more jeering references to epic and to modern heroism. But, though we must make qualifications like these, it remains true that certain passages or sections of *Don Juan* show modern life and actions as far from trivial. What is more, the samples of modern heroism are often justified in precisely the way which epic has made familiar: through asserting their superiority or at least equality to epic heroism in the past. It is probably no accident that in *Don Juan* and in his epistolary references to it Byron is constantly quoting and citing precedents; his technique is simply one more, thinly disguised variation on the technique of epic imitation. And in no area does he use the technique more sustainedly than in his assertion of the quality of high adventurousness in modern life.

Byron's stanzas attacking Wellington (IX.1–13) are a damning indictment of the age, and the personal portrait, though less simply contemptuous than the character of Southey in the Dedication, is as powerfully mordant as anything in the poem. Yet in this very passage Byron asserts the possibility of heroism in the modern world, just as he does elsewhere in discussing George Washington (VIII.5; IX.8) and Daniel Boone (VIII.61–67). To Wellington Byron writes:

> Never had mortal Man such opportunity,
>   Except Napoleon, or abused it more:
> You might have freed fall'n Europe from the Unity
>   Of Tyrants, and been blest from shore to shore.   (IX.9)

The same earnest note usually characterizes Byron's statements in *Don Juan* championing war waged in the cause of liberty.

Byron's relatively serious treatment of modern heroism is mainly concentrated in two extended passages, of which one is the shipwreck passage in Canto II. Readers have tended to find only sensationalism and grim clowning in the episode and to overlook Byron's engrossment in the action as a very serious and awesome thing. The general similarity between the episode and various shipwreck scenes in epic literature has been recognized (Haidée, for example, being a re-creation of Nausicaa), but too often readers have assumed that the shipwreck is simply one more detail in Byron's mock-epic strategy, a whimsical fulfillment of his promise in Canto I to explore each of the standard epic situations. But Byron actually treats the incident with almost unparalleled seriousness. The disabled ship presents

> a scene men do not soon forget;
> For they remember battles, fires, and wrecks,
> Or any other thing that brings regret,
> Or breaks their hopes, or hearts, or heads, or necks.   (II.31)

The flippant note in the last line recurs many times in Canto II, but it is far from neutralizing Byron's general seriousness of tone. The grim plight of the survivors in the lifeboat evokes ancient parallels, the point of which seems to be that modern fact is at least as impressive as ancient fable:

> 'Tis thus with people in an open boat,
>   They live upon the love of life, and bear
> More than can be believed, or even thought,
>   And stand like rocks the tempest's wear and tear;
> And hardship still has been the sailor's lot,
>   Since Noah's ark went cruising here and there;
> She had a curious crew as well as cargo,
> Like the first old Greek privateer, the Argo.   (II.66)

The shipwreck episode is especially full of allusions to Dante. Juan's heroic speech to the sailors who raid the liquor in the hope of dying drunk, "No! / 'Tis true that death awaits both you and me, / But let us die like men, not sink below / Like brutes" (II. 36), was inspired partly by one of the sea narratives which Byron used as sources,[24] but the addition of the word "brutes" indicates that Byron was probably thinking of Ulysses' noble speech to his own sailors ("Consider your origin; you were not made to live like brutes, but to follow virtue and knowledge"—*Inf.*, XXVI. 118–20). The scene on the sinking ship is described in a fairly close paraphrase of Dante's description of despairing souls whom Charon is to ferry across the Acheron.[25]

> Some cursed the day on which they saw the sun,
>   And gnash'd their teeth, and, howling, tore their hair. (II.45)

The parallel is strengthened by a later passage which compares the four last survivors in the boat to "Charon's bark of spectres, dull and pale" (II.101). Byron reminds those readers who find Pedrillo's fate too horrible that "Ugolino condescends / To eat the head of his arch-enemy" after he "politely ends" his narrative, so that the scene in the lifeboat is not "much more horrible than Dante" (II.83). The sons who die before their fathers' eyes (II.87–90) also recall the Ugolino incident. The stanza in which Byron explains that Catholics who died in the wreck have to wait several weeks before "a mass / Takes off one peck of purgatorial coals" (II.55), which has been criticized as in indecorous bad taste,[26] is probably part of this web of Dantean associations. Later we are told that Juan and Haidée, because of their love, "Had run the risk of being damn'd for ever," though Haidée (as well as the definitely Christian Juan, it is implied) "Had, doubtless, heard about the Stygian river, / And hell and purgatory" (II.192–93). The exhausted people in the boat are cheered by the apparition of a rainbow and a bird, which seem good omens ("an old custom of the Greek and Roman . . . of great advantage when / Folks are discouraged"—II.93), but their joy is misleading and all of them except Juan perish; we think of the false hope which cheers Ulysses' men just before their final shipwreck.[27] The whole episode implies, especially through its allusions to past literature and its sardonic indictment of the Christian Providence, that great suffering commands respect and can occasion extraordinary heroism at the same time that it occasions such base but predictably natural acts as cannibalism.

The other principal episode in which Bryon treats modern heroism with a fair measure of high seriousness is the siege of Ismail in Cantos VII and VIII. In one sense the seriousness of this section is unmistakable; in its savage sarcasm about the brutality and

wastefulness of war it maintains a relatively consistent tone for a
longer time than any other part of *Don Juan*. But with his diatribe
against war Byron mixes a certain amount of genuine admiration
for the individual combatants whose fate it is to have their iden-
tities lost in the vastness and gruesome impersonality of the battle.
Byron treats the warriors with a mixture of pity, loathing, and awe,
and, while he refuses to praise what they are doing and insists that
the "glory" they supposedly earn is a nine-days wonder at best, he
finds something truly impressive in their conduct.

   The older traditions of heroism are repeatedly invoked. While
there is something absurd in the Russians' unpronounceable names,
which Byron tries to weave into an epic "catalogue" beginning
with an ironically traditional invocation ("But oh, ye Goddesses
of war and glory!"), he insists that "Achilles' self was not more
grim and gory / Than thousands of this new and polished nation"
(VII.14–17). The catalogue continues with the soldiers from
allied nations, including a number of Englishmen, "Sixteen called
Thomson, and nineteen named Smith," and continues the serious
parody of epic by providing the traditional glances at individual
biographies—"Jack Smith / Was born in Cumberland among the
hills, . . . his father was an honest blacksmith." (VII.18–20). This
is not true mock-epic, for we are not being asked to find a simple
incongruity between these modern soldiers and Homer's warriors.
A little later Byron cites a historian's opinion that the Prince of
Ligne, Langeron, and Damas are "Names great as any that the roll
of Fame has," and although Byron then uses this extravagant claim
made about men who have already become obscure for ironic
comment on the longevity of fame, his ultimate judgment of them
is genuinely admiring:

> But here are men who fought in gallant actions
>   As gallantly as ever heroes fought,
> But buried in the heap of such transactions
>   Their names are rarely found, nor often sought.
>
> (VII.32–34)

Potemkin's message ordering imperiously that Ismail be taken, had
it been issued in support of a better cause, would have been

"worthy of a Spartan" (VII.40). The dominance in war of strong minds over the multitude is illustrated by a conscious series of similes which include the familiar epic bull and sheep images (VII.48). The cannonade is "As terrible as that of Ilion, / If Homer had found mortars ready made";

> Oh, thou eternal Homer! I have now
>   To paint a siege, wherein more men were slain,
> With deadlier engines and a speedier blow,
>   Than in thy Greek gazette of that campaign;
> And yet, like all men else, I must allow,
>   To vie with thee would be about as vain
> As for a brook to cope with Ocean's flood;
> But still we Moderns equal you in blood;
>
> If not in poetry, at least in fact,
>   And fact is truth, the grand desideratum!   (VII.78–81)

Johnson is "a noble fellow," whose likeness will not soon be seen, though "his name, than Ajax or Achilles / Sounds less harmonious" (VIII.39). The defense put up by the Sultan and his five sons is clearly modeled on epic precedent, especially Book II of the *Aeneid;*[28] Byron is not describing "Priam's, Peleus', or Jove's son," but "a good, plain, old, temperate man, / Who fought with his five children in the van" (VIII.105). The Pasha sits calmly smoking his pipe while "Troy / Saw nothing like the scene around" (VIII.121); the friends of the orphan Leila, "like the sad family of Hector, / Had perished in the field or by the wall" (VIII.141). All this is a long way from the usual tone of the standard epics, but the Ismail cantos are no mock-epic belittlement of modern triviality. Byron is awed by the sheer scope of the action he is describing, and also by certain rare examples of true magnanimity which somehow, incongruously, emerge from the chaos of war.

The fourth of Byron's main epic strategies is directed against the tradition of epic heroism itself. When he is writing in this vein Byron suggests that heroism has never been more than a sham and glory never more than a mockery even in the past. This attitude might well impress itself on the reader as the net effect of Byron's three other views—irreverence toward the epic as a supposedly sacrosanct literary form, the belief that heroism is no longer what

it used to be, and the contrary belief that, after all, modern times
have witnessed some impressive actions. But the frequency with
which Byron expresses this fourth view explicitly or nearly so marks
it as his most characteristic one; like the mixture of tones and the
mutually contradictory statements in the poem as a whole, this
fourth epic strategy generalizes into an attack on the nobility and
meaningfulness of all human life, anywhere and in any age. Since
the essence of this fourth strategy is to evoke the epic tradition in
order to show scorn for its false values (not, as in standard epic,
superiority to good but now superseded values), one is strongly reminded of the serious mock-epic as used by Southey and Landor.
And indeed there is a strong similarity. The difference is that,
while Southey and Landor champion antiheroic values with at least
some positive content, Byron champions nothing at all of general
significance.

When we read that "Troy owes to Homer what whist owes to
Hoyle" (III.90), the poet's facetiousness may suggest that the quip
is part of the relatively simple irreverence toward epic that he shows
so often in the early parts of *Don Juan*. But the next stanza, which
discusses the deflation of Milton's heroic image by certain shabby
facts related in Johnson's biography, makes us take the point about
Troy a little more seriously; we now see it as part of a general
comment on epic and greatness, especially since Byron goes on to
cite similarly deflating facts about Shakespeare, Bacon, Caesar,
Burns, Titus, and Cromwell. (Milton and Dante have been singled
out earlier for commiseration about hapless nuptials—III.10–11.)
Juan's voyage past the site of ancient Troy reinforces the point
about Homer. On this "vast, untill'd, and mountain-skirted plain"
is entombed Achilles, "the bravest of the brave" (though "Bryant
says the contrary");

> The situation seems still form'd for fame—
> A hundred thousand men might fight again
> With ease; but where I sought for Ilion's walls,
> The quiet sheep feeds, and the tortoise crawls.
>
> (IV.76–77)

The same idea is elaborated near the end of the canto (IV.100–4).

In general, the belief that heroic achievement wins glory is one that Byron repeatedly denies; Time always makes a jest of glory, the future is simply a question mark. Even early in the poem this is Byron's view; in the following passage, for example, he evokes the tradition of purposeful heroic progress through an ordeal only to imply that no real goal is ever reached:

> Few mortals know what end they would be at,
> But whether glory, power, or love, or treasure,
> The path is through perplexing ways, and when
> The goal is gain'd, we die, you know—and then—

"I do not know, no more do you," Byron concludes (I.133–34).

I have already remarked that in the Ismail cantos Byron often insists that modern warriors are really made of the same stuff as were Achilles and Hector. But this statement is often intended to be a compromising admission rather than a boast, and for that reason the equating of modern and ancient heroism in the war episode preserves Byron's antiwar message reasonably intact. For in the Ismail cantos some of Byron's most acid sarcasm is reserved for the whole tradition of heroic warfare, including epic warfare. He introduces the episode with a clever twisting of Spenser's declaration that war and love are to "moralize" his song:

> "Fierce loves and faithless wars"—I am not sure
> If this be the right reading—'tis no matter;
> The fact's about the same, I am secure;
> I sing them both.   (VII.8)

Here, as Ridenour has mentioned, Byron's target is not simply modern war, but the basic belief that prowess in war is heroic argument.[29] Suwarrow's drilling, we read, makes "each high, heroic bosom" burn "For cash and conquest," but then Byron diversifies his attack with a sudden shaft of sarcasm directed at the Crusades:

> as if from a cushion
> A preacher had held forth (who nobly spurned
> All earthly goods save tithes) and bade them push on
> To slay the Pagans . . .   (VII.64)

No lines in the entire poem are so devastatingly ironic as the invocation of the "bulletins of Bonaparte," along with the "less

grand long lists of killed and wounded," the shade of Leonidas,
and Caesar's Commentaries that they may lend to Byron's Muse "A
portion of your fading twilight hues, / So beautiful, so fleeting"
(VII.82), and his admission that in the war cantos his rhymes are
a little "scorched" with

> the blaze
> Of conquest and its consequences, which
> Make Epic poesy so rare and rich.   (VIII.90)

One of Byron's most frequent insinuations is that poetry, especially great epic poetry, serves the interests of falsehood by
glossing over the realities of war. Before his rather lengthy apos-
trophe to Homer Byron apologizes for the cacaphonous vocabulary
of modern military tactics: "Bombs, drums, guns, bastions, batteries,
bayonets, bullets; / Hard words, which stick in the soft Muses'
gullets"; this is the kind of language modern poets must use rather
than write of "slaying Priam's son" (VII.78). In the context
("But still we Moderns equal you in blood"), such statements are
surely as much an indictment of Homeric warfare as of the ignoble
jargon of modern military tactics. "Souls of immortal generals!"
Byron continues, "Phoebus watches / To colour up his rays from
your despatches" (VII.81). At the beginning of Canto VIII Byron
transforms the invocatory prayer sanctioned by epic into a curse:[30]
"Oh blood and thunder! and oh blood and wounds"; then, after
apologizing to the reader for these "vulgar oaths," he shrugs:
"Call them Mars, / Bellona, what you will—they mean but wars."
A similar conviction inspires the poet's outrage at Wordsworth's
having called Carnage "God's daughter," a blasphemy to which
Byron replies in kind by remarking that in that case she must be
Christ's sister (VIII.9). The two climactic statements of Byron's
position include one piece of angry sarcasm and one emotionally
straightforward attack on poetry's role in the glorification of
murder:

> Yet I love Glory;—glory's a great thing;—
> Think what it is to be in your old age
> Maintained at the expense of your good king:

> A moderate pension shakes full many a sage,
> And heroes are but made for bards to sing,
>   Which is still better; thus in verse to wage
> Your wars eternally, besides enjoying
> Half-pay for life, make mankind worth destroying.
>
>   (VIII.14)

> . . . *one* life saved, especially if young
> Or pretty, is a thing to recollect
>   Far sweeter than the greenest laurels sprung
> From the manure of human clay, though decked
>   With all the praises ever said or sung.   (IX.34)

III

I have been trying to show that in *Don Juan* Byron wanted to create a poem that was deliberately and in every sense inconclusive, since he wanted to show life itself as ultimately without meaning, despite its enthralling variety and the high flavor its particular episodes could have. For the last two or three hundred years this view of life has been common among thinking men, and for such men in our own day it is probably the most common of all. But one does not usually write a long narrative poem to assert such a philosophy. Byron did so because, it would seem, he felt the pressure of what he considered specious orthodoxies and systems all around him—some of them old, many of them new. Therefore the fact of life's insignificance was something that urgently needed to be asserted in his day. Byron's comments on *Don Juan* stress again and again its relevance to the age; in his own way Byron was trying to be doctrinal to a nation. But his doctrine was to be the denial of particular doctrines and of the very notion of doctrine, even that last infirmity of the noble skeptic, defiant fist-shaking curses at the gods who are not there. (There is plenty of this in Byron's other late poems, of course, a fact that renders even more significant the generally tolerant skepticism of *Don Juan;* the rule dramatizes the exception.) And what more striking vehicle could Byron have used to assert the emptiness of man's enterprise than

the epic, a form in which the statement that after all there is no
final Truth, or that if there is one we have no way of knowing it,
has the kind of jarring effect it would have if one heard the statement from a pulpit?

I have also been arguing that one of Byron's basic strategies for
emptying *Don Juan* of meaning is to play against one another
different attitudes toward epic. Just as important, though, are his
ironic adaptations of more specific traditional epic devices. Most
of these are directed against epic values themselves, and not simply
against Byron's own age, though of course at times and for particular satiric effects Byron does choose to compare modern life unfavorably with the past in the way I have outlined earlier. But
although he sometimes feels the satirist's impulse to correct contemporary abuses, that purpose is, I beleive, subordinate to the
basic philosophic message of the poem.

For the most part, Byron's twisting of epic conventions involves
the hero and his function. The central fact about Don Juan is that
he has no mission. Except in Canto I, where Byron wants to show
him as a green adolescent, the Don is not an absurd figure at all;
he shows himself capable of noble and generous-minded behavior,
as in his exhortation to the sailors to die like men rather than like
brutes, his defiance of Gulbeyaz, and his rescue of Leila. Nor, if
we except his amours, is he usually passive in any ordinary sense;
he responds with instant action to the holdup by Tom and is in-
strumental in turning the tide of battle at Ismail. His passivity,
so-called, strikes us only when we think of him as an epic protagonist, and even then not because he is not active enough but
because his actions do not form a meaningful sequence leading
him toward definitive achievement. The disjointedness of his
"progress" is nowhere better illustrated than in Byron's mystifying
and cavalier silence about how the harem episode turns out—this
after he has created more narrative suspense than in any other part
of the poem. As a man of action, an adventurer, Don Juan is not
so totally unlike Byron's swashbuckling protagonists as he has been
said to be; as an epic protagonist, however, his aimlessness is dearly
felt.

Nor, on the whole, is the Don's lack of a mission a satiric comment on the impossibility of modern heroism, as is the portrait of Lambro (III.53–55) or (more facetiously or indirectly) those of Tom the highwayman and Lord Henry Amundeville (XI.10, 19–20; XIV.70–72). Don Juan's most impressive derring-do is evident in the siege of Ismail, where more than anywhere else in the poem Byron draws a serious equation between modern and ancient heroism. Moreover, one of the most striking facts about Juan is his ability to live in the world while somehow remaining unaffected by it. Byron shows him as having been a little spoiled and over-sophisticated by his tenure as Catherine's favorite, but not very significantly (XII.49). Nowhere, in fact, are Juan's polite distance from the group and superiority to the fiats of modern convention and fashion more strongly emphasized than in the English cantos, where for satiric purposes he might most easily have been shown as corrupted or limited by the triviality of the world he is part of. Juan's failure to have a mission is, rather, part of Byron's attempt to depict realistically the actual conditions of all heroism, the fact that although a hero may be admirable and do some impressive things, his deeds cannot lead to any meaningful result. And this, of course, is just the opposite of what epic usually tries to demonstrate.

"You have so many *'divine'* poems," Byron wrote to Murray, "is it nothing to have written a *Human* one? without any of your worn-out machinery." And part of his aggressive jesting about his epic plan for *Don Juan* was the statement that "my spirits, good or bad, must serve for the machinery." That there is a pun here on *spirits* is borne out by the poem itself, where Byron sometimes claims to be writing while half-drunk or suffering from a hangover (perhaps we are meant to compare the nocturnal visitations of Milton's Muse) and also plays at introducing ghosts as machinery:

> And now, that we may furnish with some matter all
> Tastes, we are going to try the supernatural.   (XV.93)

But—to mention the most obvious meaning last—by "spirits" Byron also means his whim and disposition. He would seem to have introduced "machinery" into his epic in the only form he could accept—random, calculatedly digressive speculations, notably on metaphysical and religious subjects. For it is precisely through "machinery" that the epic poets have most imaginatively stressed the meaningful, destined role that their heroes play. Byron's hero is under tutelage to no fore-seeing gods; his progress—or lack of progress—is determined by the merest whim of his creator, Byron himself, who repeatedly appears *ex machina* to explain the cosmic meaning—that is, lack of meaning—of his poem and of his hero's actions. If we regard the author's almost never-failing comments on his own digressiveness and tendency to metaphysical speculation as in themselves a joke, we must admit that it becomes frayed by the time Byron has repeated it five or six times. The joke is richer, I believe, if we see his digressiveness and highhanded manipulation of his action as analogous to the oscillation of epic narrative between the hero and his guiding destiny, between earth and heaven. This idea might also explain Byron's occasional references to his poem as "fiction,"[31] which seem to contradict flagrantly his more typical insistence that he is being factual or truthful. But it is important to Byron that he have it both ways, for he is trying to say, in effect, that if we are honest, if we respect truth and fact, we must see epic heroism as a poet's pipe-dream; truth is fact, and that heroism is a fiction is *a* fact. Was Aeneas guided by supernature toward awesome achievement? Was Milton, as he claimed to be, a taker of divine dictation? "Very pretty poems, Messrs. Milton and Virgil, but you must not call them truth."

For choosing a legendary epic hero Byron had good precedents in epic and its theory. Don Juan is, specifically, a legendary lover, and this fact too is intended to have epic reverberations. When Juan and Johnson are parting from the women before plunging into gruesome, nightmarish battle, Byron observes that Juan never left women "Unless compelled by fate, or wave, or wind, / Or near relations" (VIII.53–54). In the background, I believe, is the memory of Aeneas's abandonment of Dido so that he may fight and found an empire and perhaps of Hector's farewell to Andromache. In the context, which is Byron's savage attack on war and the ideal of martial glory through explicit parallels with epic tradition, the further implication is obvious: Byron is endorsing love as the alternative to war and thus reversing the antifeminism which is implied in one form or another by almost every traditional epic. Ridenour has accurately observed that many of the heroines in *Don Juan* are queenly figures;[32] the fact is significant, for Juan's relationship to them is in a general way a mocking reversal of such foolhardy "heroism" as Aeneas shows when he renounces his regal mistress and her love, which are existent facts, for that wispiest of fools' fires, the glory of empire. The point is suggested as early as the scene involving Julia's letter, which shows its author as having, womanlike, given all for love while Juan is free to achieve "Pride, fame, ambition" through "Sword, gown, gain, glory" (I.194). It is interesting that most of what remains of Canto I is devoted to elaborate mock-epic clowning and a discussion of the hollowness of fame and glory, and that Canto II shows Juan setting forth into the Mediterranean of epic memory under the handicap of unheroic queasiness. The humor and irony of the scene are deepened if we compare him with Aeneas leaving Carthage.

Byron continues throughout the poem to suggest the same point —that love is a higher calling than war and other types of conventional prowess—and to evoke ironically the cliché of woman as an obstacle to heroism. Haidée is doubtless a Nausicaa, but she is also a Dido, giving herself unreservedly to her shipwrecked lover and dying for it. The "nuptials" stanzas (II.188–90, 204), the mention of the Stygian river (II.193), the fatalistic tone ("deeds eternity can not annul" II.192)—all these make the parallel fairly convincing. An ironic reflection on conventional heroism follows once again, however; almost immediately after the consummation of the "nuptials" Byron writes a stanza celebrating "worthies Time will never see again," including Caesar, Pompey, and Belisarius, all of whom were "heroes, conquerors, and cuckolds" (II.206). Sex, in short, is a reality, a fact, which Juan and Haidée have confronted in their private, human way; the same force, in a degraded

form, returns upon conventional heroes to remind them—and
Byron's readers—of facts of life which are ignored at one's peril.
To cap the irony (though the effect is also to alter and embitter
the irony, to direct it at life rather than at heroism), Fate inter-
venes—not to set the hero back on the high path of heroism but
to despatch him over the heroic Mediterranean waves to a slave
market. That Byron thought out the parallel as schematically as I
have described it is admittedly doubtful, but that he wrote in this
spirit seems fairly certain.

Gulbeyaz, Lady Adeline, and Catherine are Didos too in their
own ways. The scorned Gulbeyaz is terrible in her frustrated passion, like "A tigress robbed of young, a lioness, / Or any interesting beast of prey" (V.132). But Juan's defiance of her (he "heroically stood resigned, / Rather than sin—except to his own wish")
melts when she weeps and proves herself a woman (V.141); again
his conduct reverses the Dido-and-Aeneas pattern. Adeline is "the
fair most fatal Juan ever met . . . ; Destiny and Passion spread the
net" (XIII.12). We never learn why she is fatal; the reversal of
epic pattern in Catherine is clear, though. She is literally a queen;
she is (what Dante stresses about Dido) unfaithful to "her lord, /
Who was gone to his place" (IX.54). Unlike Aeneas, Juan is
docile to her whims; his later success in London he owes to his
youth, his valor, his dress, his beauty, "but most / He owed to an
old woman and his post" (X.29). The departure from Catherine
is again ironic and unheroic, the cause being "a feverish disposition" which with a naughty *double entendre* Byron suggests is due
to "the fatigue of last campaign" (X.39–40). And, unlike Dido,
Catherine is consolable; "Time, the comforter" relieves her distress
after "four-and-twenty hours" (X.48). Byron's simplest statement
of this whole ironic attitude is his claim that woman, far from
being the " 'teterrima Causa' of all 'belli,' " is the *best* cause
(IX.55–56). He pleads with Death,

> Suppress then some slight feminine diseases,
> And take as many heroes as Heaven pleases.   (XV.9)

IV

Byron's contemporaries often accused him of degrading human nature:

> They accuse me—*Me*—the present writer of
> The present poem—of—I know not what,—
> A tendency to under-rate and scoff
> At human power and virtue, and all that;
> And this they say in language rather rough.　　　(VII.3)

In the lines following these Byron defends himself by citing the examples of Dante, Solomon, Cervantes, Swift, and a number of other writers of the past, but (here, at least) he does not deny the charge. The current trend in criticism is to regard these contemporary objections, with which Keats, for one, agreed,[33] as short-sightedness which mistook satire for scurrility. But Byron's critics were not so blind as we sometimes assume they were. It is true that Shelley, whom one would expect to be sensitive on such a point, defended Canto V as containing nothing which "the most rigid asserter of the dignity of human nature could desire to be cancelled," but that he should make this defense at all is significant, and, besides, Canto V would have appealed to Shelley because of its idealistic speeches about love and its defiant attitude toward tyranny.[34] But in many crucial ways *Don Juan* does subvert the idea that man is noble, especially through attacks on heroism's clay feet, both today and in the past.

What his contemporaries really did fail to appreciate was Byron's reluctance to destroy such illusions. His defense against the public outcry was that truth must be served first. His Muse, he maintains,

> mostly sings of human things and acts
> And that's one cause she meets with contradiction;
> For too much truth, at first sight, ne'er attracts;
> And were her object only what's call'd glory,
> With more ease too she'd tell a different story.
> 　　　(XIV.13)

These last lines were no empty boast, as Byron's early exotic tales could testify. Byron believed that the heroic ideal had never been more than a dream. But, although the dream was based on false values, it nevertheless could be bracing and invigorating. He could not or would not abandon any of these conflicting views, and he states his dilemma poignantly in the "Aurora Borealis" stanzas. Man's highest ideals are love and glory, which "fly / Around us ever, rarely to alight."

> Chill, and chained to cold earth, we lift on high
>   Our eyes in search of either lovely light;
> A thousand and a thousand colours they
> Assume, then leave us on our freezing way.

Such, too, is his own "non-descript and ever varying rhyme . . . Which flashes o'er a waste and icy clime."

> When we know what all are, we must bewail us,
>   But, ne'er the less, I hope it is no crime
> To laugh at *all* things—for I wish to know
> *What* after *all*, are *all* things—but a *Show?*   (VII.1–2)

Byron's italics, which he always uses skillfully and accurately, are often important to his mood and meaning; here the italicizing in *"all* things" suggests that Byron intends the phrase to mean, not the total of discrete things and experiences, but rather the "allness" of things, the sum of things considered as having or not having coherent meaning. So defined, *"all* things" are simply appearance, a show, a spectacle, like the Aurora Borealis. True love and glory, which if they existed might give meaning to life, are so foreign to its actual conditions as to be pure illusion. The overtones of Byron's statement are, in different ways, Dante's pity, when he first leaves Hell, for the "northern widowed clime" which does not know the stars he now can see, and Milton's gloomy apprehension that his epic enterprise may be defeated by cold climate and an age too late.[35]

But for Byron the "cold and icy clime" is not so much his own age as the human lot in general, earthbound but prone to find beauty in its illusory visions. Byron too finds these illusions beautiful, even beneficent. And therefore he sometimes feels that his campaign for honesty is misguided; though glory and high ideals be will-o'-the-wisps, to expose them as sham is to destroy the illusions without which nations and individuals cannot flourish. *Don Quixote* is the saddest of all tales; its "hero's right, / And still pursues the right,"[36] but

> Cervantes smiled Spain's Chivalry away;
>   A single laugh demolished the right arm
> Of his own country;—seldom since that day
>   Has Spain had heroes. (XIII.9, 11)

This reluctance by Byron to smash even false idols helps account for certain especially insistent paradoxes in the poem.

The English cantos, for example, have often irritated, bored, or puzzled critics. The treatment of England seems anticlimactic. Byron has skillfully whetted our appetites for this section; throughout the first ten cantos England is often the subject even when she does not furnish the setting or the actors. The sharpness of Byron's frequently interpolated attacks on England makes us expect savage satire in the English cantos themselves, but on the whole this is not what we get. We get delicate social satire at most, and often not even that; Byron sometimes seems to have turned into a novelist, with the novelist's minute and relatively neutral interest in the workings of a social group.[37]

Much of this is true, but it is important to recognize that Byron is still writing an epic. *Don Juan*, despite its inclusive European setting, is very much a national epic poem; that is, it comes close to being one in the negative sense applicable to *Joan of Arc*— through its vilification of the poet's own country. Hence (ironically in more than one way) Byron's dedication of the poem to the official spokesman for English values, the epic renegade Southey, and hence his bitterness toward the other false poetic prophets of his country, his obsession with the dirt of English politics, his rhetorical celebration of England as a nation which has traded its sometime greatness for universal abhorrence and the status of "first of slaves" (X.66–68)—all of which is an inversion of the usual epic rhetoric. But Byron cannot use an inverted epic tradition in the service of a positive cause; he does not have one. Since by Canto X he has thoroughly deflated ancient as well as modern heroism, the false values of men in general as well as English illusions, he cannot consistently adopt the attitude of moral superiority he has implicitly promised to assume and which the satirist and the Southey of *Joan* do assume. He cannot compare the English unfavorably with an idealized alternative group.

But neither does Byron simply become a novelist; at the same time that he is probing the minutest details of English life, often tolerantly or with bemused fascination, he never allows society to become the unquestioned framework of his action; he maintains his epic vista by keeping us aware of the totality of time and of the place of Englishmen in their heroic tradition, such as it is. He conjures up the Black Prince, Thomas à Becket, Cressy, and the Druids; he reminds us of British achievements in the cause of liberty; he traces the history of Norman Abbey and of its personages.[38] References to epic tradition are very many: the bluestockings ask Juan if he saw Ilion, matchmaking ladies are implicitly compared to the Virgilian gods (" 'Tantaene!' Such the virtues of high station"), there are the Cervantes stanzas calling *Don Quixote* a "real Epic," there is a subtle comparison of the Menelaus-Paris-Helen triangle to Lord Henry-Adeline-Juan, a parallel is drawn between the feast at Norman Abbey and the battles and feasts in Homer.[39]

The result of all this is an ambivalent treatment of the English. To the extent that he has undermined the whole notion of heroism Byron can be tolerant toward the English; to the extent that they make pretensions to the loftiest heroism or significance and to the extent that Byron himself feels the need to believe in a heroic ideal, he shows the English to be seriously inadequate. But neither of these judgments is that of the vitriolic satirist; even Byron's criticisms of the English in the later cantos are sad rather than angry or stridently contemptuous in tone. Byron is no Swift, even when he is criticizing; while he denounces he often seems to be asking, candidly and without rhetorical self-righteousness, how anything can really be expected of so frail a being as man.

Byron's criticism of the English returns again and again to the same point: that they lack individuality. Society is "smooth'd" so that "manners hardly differ more than dress" (XIII.94). Society has "a sameness in its gems and ermine, / A dull and family likeness through all ages," "A kind of common-place, even in their crimes," "a smooth monotony / Of character" (XIV.15–16). There is "little to describe"; Byron says he could more easily "sketch a harem, / A battle, wreck, or history of the heart" (XIV. 20–21). High life is "a dreary void" (XIV.79). Formerly "Men made the manners; manners now make men— / Pinned like a flock, and fleeced too in their fold" (XV.26);[40] Lord Henry lacks the indefinable qualities of Paris (and presumably Juan) that were capable of starting an epic war (XIV.72). One thinks of Byron's loathing of Suwarrow because he tends to think of men and of things "in the gross, / Being much too gross to see them in detail" (VII.77) and the leveling of the same charge at History:

> History can only take things in the gross; . . .
> The drying up a single tear has more
> Of honest fame, than shedding seas of gore.   (VIII.3)

The reason, Byron explains, is that such an act of individual kindness "brings self-approbation," and by contrast we think of the oblivion which, he is constantly telling us, awaits the hero who looks for that generalized, immortal good will called Glory.

This concern with the individual as superior to and more real than the mass is only one aspect of Byron's championing of "fact" as opposed to wider, more generalized vision and doctrine, which he associates not only with philosophy but also with poetry. "But still we Moderns equal you in blood," he apostrophizes Homer,

> If not in poetry, at least in fact,
> And fact is truth, the grand desideratum!
> Of which, howe'er the Muse describes each act,
> There should be ne'ertheless a slight substratum.
>   (VII.80–81)

Elsewhere he declares:

> But then the fact's a fact—and 'tis the part
> Of a true poet to escape from fiction
> Whene'er he can; for there is little art
> In leaving verse more free from the restriction
> Of truth than prose . . .   (VIII.86)

His own Muse "gathers a repertory of facts" (XIV.13).

Byron uses the word *fact* in a curiously ambivalent way. It sometimes means "truth" as distinguished from lies or fiction or sham. To use the word so is to use it in the satirist's, or corrective, sense. But it can also have a more philosophical sense; here *fact* refers to the isolated, unrationalized phenomenon, frequently in opposition to the "ideal." When Byron writes, "fact is truth, the grand desideratum," he is not so much stating that the two words are semantically equivalent as hazarding a definition of the nature of things, which are what they are without reason or connection with one another, without a unifying "Idea." This is where the emotional conflict in Byron becomes apparent. In *Don Juan* Byron repeatedly sneers at philosophical idealism, especially in its Platonic form, though also in others—Berkeley's, for example (XI.1–3). Yet almost as often Byron states or implies that the world is a tawdry place compared with what one can imagine its being. His view, of course, is that such imagining is simply dreaming; there is virtually no serious attempt to say that what exists as thought must have an analogue outside the individual mind or that whatever is thought is *ipso facto* real.[41] But Byron cannot help feeling a deep sense of loss because reality is so much less than dream. From the satirist's viewpoint *fact* is a word to be used with angry gusto; from the viewpoint of the epic poet-prophet *fact* suggests the dreariness of the human lot. Yet, Byron seems to be saying, fact is all we have and we must live with it.

It is this stubborn insistence that in spite of the temptation to dream we are dupes if we go beyond isolated phenomena to a systematic belief in a "Truth" behind the phenomena that makes *Don Juan* a sad and frightening poem; clearly, fact is all that

Byron will admit, but it is not always enough for him. In this respect he is similar to many twentieth-century existentialists. But he differs from many, perhaps most, of them in that he feels sadness rather than anger at man's lonely meaninglessness and in his avoidance of the position that by egoistic fiat one can create a valid kind of reality. He refuses, that is, to turn his kind of skepticism into what is popularly called a "philosophy." I am still referring to *Don Juan*, be it understood; in other poems Byron is capable of taking both of these existentialist positions.

Perhaps, after all, *Don Juan* does imply a certain kind of heroic ideal. It is not the heroism of the scientist, for whom "fact" is of utterly no consequence except as it contributes to system and generality; the kind of heroism Byron implies is much more consistent with technology, which deals with limited facts and situations and leaves ultimate questions alone. The two passages in praise of Newton (VII.5; X.1–2) emphasize respectively Newton's modest denial of having discovered ultimate truth and his usefulness to progress in mechanics; it is Wordsworth rather than Byron who admires the Newton of "strange seas of thought." On the other hand, we cannot attribute heroism to the mean sensual man whose respect for facts arises from mere unreflectiveness. The heroism implied by *Don Juan* is that of the man who can think and think and think and be a skeptic. It consists in tolerant, unembittered unbelief accepted in spite of a serious need for a sense of meaning and direction in life.

In a way it is surprising that Keats should have denounced Byron so severely, for Byron is very close to preaching—and in *Don Juan* exemplifying—the Negative Capability that Keats had once urged. The Keats who had once endorsed that attitude later became, as we have seen, a diligent seeker for answers. But even if, with his Shakespeare and thrush, he had never fretted after knowledge, his uncertainty would have been different from the uncertainty Byron acknowledges. Keats advocated Negative Capability in a spirit of optimism; he assumed that one could gain positive knowledge by not interposing labels and formulas be-

tween oneself and the object. He also assumed, though, that there
is an order in the world and especially in life which, independent
of the formulas of thought, will make itself apparent to a person
who is patient and alertly perceptive. Byron's negative capability
is more negative and also, in a way, more heroic. Without a flag
to fight under, without goal or obvious reward, it skirmishes end-
lessly against protean falsehood—and without even the adrenal
stimulus of the will to disbelieve.

But although *we* may call this heroism, Byron does not; he
endorses no heroic ideal as such, this one or any other. And this
fact brings me to some final comments pertinent to him and to the
three other major poets discussed in this book.

In my introductory chapter I claimed that when they were working in the tradition of epic the Romantics generally expressed
heroic values that were not relativistic. Byron is obviously an exception; in *Don Juan* we find precisely that typically modern distrust of objective values to whose influence the decline of epic and
epic heroism, along with a host of other vanished certainties, is
so often attributed. It is true that when critics or historians, especially those antipathetic to the Romantics, bring the charge of
relativism against them, the complainants usually have in mind
what they would consider a vague and specious spirituality in the
Romantic creeds and are not adverting to Byron's considered, hard-
nosed Pyrrhonism. Often, indeed, critics make a reservation in
Byron's favor as for a man who appreciated better and cherished
more dearly than his contemporaries the threatened heroic standards of earlier ages. Nevertheless, it must be admitted that Byron
helps corroborate the actual substance of the charge.

Surely there is an irony here. Byron appears, in different poems
and in different parts of *Don Juan,* both as the Romantic poet who
broke most violently with the moral values of the past and as the
last exponent of larger-than-life, "traditional" heroism; the poet
of titanic defiance of God and man is the same poet who created
the most unheroic of epic heroes. Is this irony simply one more to
be added to the long list of unresolved paradoxes concerning By-

ron? Perhaps, but I think there is a plausible solution. It has to do with the paradox of progressivism and conservatism in epic outlined in the first chapter of this book. The fact is that although Byron does not really believe in heroism, past or present, he defines this nonexistent thing to himself in a curiously rigid way. Both when he is denying the possibility of heroism and when he is portraying a titanically powerful figure capable of shaking earth's foundations and the firmament, Byron regards heroism as something alien to the familiar norms of human experience, as something either contemptibly fake or superhuman. Heroism is for him one specific *style* of action rather than the *substance* of a code of values. But in the great literary epics there are different styles of action and, which is more important, such styles are by-products of heroism, not values themselves identifiable with heroism. Both Aeneas and Turnus can defy, boast, fight, and kill, but for Virgil Aeneas is a true hero and Turnus at best a hero *manqué*. Byron, in short, makes in some ways the same erroneous estimate of traditional heroism as do many writers on epic today; he identifies heroism too exclusively with certain of its manifestations in some particular age or ages. (The matter is complicated, of course, by the fact that such misunderstanding is functional to his deliberate, undermining skepticism in *Don Juan*.) It is interesting to notice how consistently Byron associates heroism with such terms as "fame" and "glory," which two values he systematically contrasts with the familiar realities of human experience and with such aspects of individual inner life as "self-approbation" (VIII.4). Where in *Don Juan* Byron comes closest to asserting positive values they do not differ radically from the pacific and spiritual ones preached by other poets we have been considering. The difference between them and Byron is that they did not find such essentially human values at odds with their understanding of heroism, while Byron did. One may say that they understood the heroic tradition more flexibly than he did (or, perhaps, than he *chose* to); I should prefer to say that they understood it better.

Byron, then, exemplifies the paradox of the epic in a negative way. The definitive epic poets and those Romantic poets who tried to place themselves in the tradition believed in the possibilities of their own ages because they also believed that greatness had existed in the past and could therefore provide a foundation on which to build newer and grander structures. One can also state this the other way around: their belief in progress committed them to an appreciation of the values of the past; even Keats, who in *Hyperion* was not much interested in any doctrine of historical continuity, implicitly salutes the past by calling up earlier statements paralleling his own statement of an essentially timeless truth. But Byron plays past and present against each other, denying that there has been greatness in the past, yet also evoking an illusory idea of earlier greatness as a judgment on his own uninspired age. Heroism, according to this view, cannot evolve; neither can the epic; nothing can come of nothing. The traditional view, the one which, despite their frequent and impatient claims to reject the past, is sanctioned by the great poets of literary epic, is to see heroism as a human reality whose development is from good to better.

REFERENCE MATTER

NOTES

Chapter One

1 The most useful summary of neoclassical epic theory in England is H. T. Swedenberg, *The Theory of the Epic in England, 1650–1800,* University of California Publications in English, Vol. XV (Berkeley and Los Angeles, 1944).

2 *The Spectator,* Everyman's Library ed. (New York, 1945), No. 273 (Jan. 12, 1712).

3 *Spectator,* No. 369 (May 3, 1712).

4 *A Defence of Poetry,* Julian ed., VII, 130. (See ch. 4, n. 5.)

5 *Poetics,* trans. Ingram Bywater, 23–24, 1459a–60a.

6 E. M. W. Tillyard, *The English Epic and Its Background* (London, 1954), p. 5.

7 Karl Kroeber, *Romantic Narrative Art* (Madison, 1960), p. 86.

8 Homer's "two poems are each examples of construction, the *Iliad* simple and a story of suffering, the *Odyssey* complex . . . and a story of character." *Poetics,* 24, 1459b.

9 *The English Epic,* pp. 6–7.

10 *Definition* (Oxford, 1950), pp. 113–14. For their advice on the applicability and import of this passage I am indebted to Timothy J. Duggan and Bernard Gert of the Dartmouth College Philosophy Department.

11 Tillyard has stated *(The English Epic,* p. 5) that to be valid the definition of a literary term must be arrived at inductively, that any-one who tries to define a term for himself will discover that he is relying on unconsciously selected samples. He concedes that this kind of induction cannot be rigidly systematic, and that one must go back and forth between the works he definitely wants to include and those that are more doubtful. But the criteria for epic that Tillyard arrives at in this manner seem to me excessively general and (because the exemplars first determined on are arbitrarily chosen) unconvincing. One ought to start with works that the world in general calls epic. On the other hand, to make any really distinctive and specific trait a *universal* requirement for *all* epics is to insure the omission of at least one work which nearly everyone regards as an epic. Unless one is content to define an epic as a long narrative poem

229

(and this is the way some people use the word) or to accept very general criteria like Tillyard's (high quality, expansiveness, disciplined control, the "choric" quality) one cannot draw universal inductive generalizations about the epic at all.

Incidentally, it is interesting that the word *tragedy* is allowed to have many meanings, but this tempting solution is generally rejected where epic is concerned except for the general agreement to distinguish between the folk epic and the art epic. Aristotle and Fielding distinguish different types, but in this they are atypical.

12 *Spectator,* No. 267 (Jan. 5, 1712). Addison actually claims to waive the question whether *Paradise Lost* is an epic, but the tenor of his series of papers and their frequent appeals to principles of epic theory contradict his rather haughty disclaimer. The important point, in any case, is that the *Spectator* papers on Milton did help greatly to establish the poem's canonicity.

13 Cf. Karl Kroeber, *Romantic Narrative Art,* pp. 102–3, and my own doctoral dissertation "The English Romantic Poets and the Epic" (Madison, 1959), pp. 1–3.

14 Cf. Frederick A. Pottle (who cites Alan Clutton-Brock and A. C. Bradley), "The Case of Shelley" (orig. publ. 1952), reprinted in *English Romantic Poets: Modern Essays in Criticism,* ed. M. H. Abrams (New York, 1960), pp. 289–93; and Harold Bloom, *Shelley's Mythmaking* (New Haven, 1959), pp. 65–90.

The blowing of a trumpet is a recurrent image in the Prophets, where as in Shelley's ode it can have both dire and irenic associations, since the trumpet-call announces both military attack and a summons to worship.

15 The texts of Homer and Virgil cited in this book are the following: *The Aeneid,* ed. J. W. Mackail (Oxford, 1930); *The Iliad,* with trans. by A. T. Murray, Loeb Classical Library, 2 vols. (London, 1924); *The Odyssey,* with trans. by A. T. Murray, Loeb Classical Library, 2 vols. (New York, 1919).

16 It is not impossible, however, that Virgil knew the Biblical account of the Exodus, which has many striking parallels with the *Aeneid* and expresses a conception of history as purposeful and divinely ruled which is much like what Virgil expresses in his epic. Many classicists now believe that Virgil was directly influenced in the Fourth Eclogue by the Book of Isaiah.

17 *Os Lusiadas,* ed. J. D. M. Ford, Harvard Studies in Romance Languages, Vol. XXII (Cambridge, Mass., 1946). In references hereafter the abbreviation *Lus.* refers to this edition; capital Roman numbers denote cantos, lower case Roman numbers denote stanzas. I

have used various translations of this and other ancient and Renaissance epics, but citations have been checked against the original texts.

18 *Gerusalemme Liberata*, with notes by Pio Spagnotti and introduction by Michele Scherillo, 5th ed. (Milan, 1918), hereafter abbreviated as *GL*. Capital Roman numbers refer to cantos, lower case Roman numbers to stanzas. I have generally used the Fairfax translation.

19 *Paradise Lost*, IX.13–47 (hereafter abbreviated *PL*). The edition used is *The Poetical Works of John Milton*, ed. Helen Darbishire, 2 vols. (Oxford, 1952, 1955).

20 They are discussed by C. M. Bowra in *Heroic Poetry* (London, 1952), pp. 34–35.

21 See, for example, Addison, *Spectator*, No. 273 (Jan. 12, 1712).

22 The generalization is based mainly on my own experience. Brief discussions of the Romantic epic appear in Kroeber's *Romantic Narrative Art*, pp. 84–88; with reference to *The Prelude*, in Abbie Findlay Potts, *Wordsworth's "Prelude": A Study of Its Literary Form* (Ithaca, 1953), *passim*, and in Herbert Lindenberger, *On Wordsworth's "Prelude"* (Princeton, 1963), pp. 9–15 and *passim;* with reference to *Don Juan*, in George M. Ridenour, *The Style of Don Juan* (New Haven, 1960), *passim*.

23 Robert Langbaum, *The Poetry of Experience: The Dramatic Monologue in Modern Literary Tradition* (London, 1957).

24 My argument here may remind the reader of the argument developed by Langbaum in his first and last chapters. According to Langbaum, the scientific emphasis in the Enlightenment destroyed the solidity of earlier tradition. Early, sentimental Romanticism (eighteenth-century sentimentalism and the early work of many nineteenth-century Romantics) reacted to this by exalting feeling and denying the scientific ideals of intellect and objectivity. The later, more mature Romanticism represented by the great poets of the nineteenth and twentieth centuries responded more positively to the challenge of science by creating new formulations of tradition (as in Eliot) and objectivity (as in Yeats), out of individual, empirical experience rather than sentimentalism. Thus the definitive modern poets are akin to the definitive Romantics; both groups of poets affirm the value of tradition because they are concerned with its loss.

For the most part, I agree with this thesis. But my own point is a different one. The ambiguity toward tradition felt in the epic is different from what Langbaum is describing, and in their attempts at epic the Romantics proclaimed a progressive ideal in much the same way as had the great epic poets in earlier ages. Langbaum stresses the revolutionary break between the Romantics and the past and the consequent kinship between the Romantics and the poets of our century, and although he defends the Romantics he agrees with their critics that the traditional forms really had broken down. My position is that, however revolutionary the Romantics may have been in some of their poetry or in their poetry in general, the progressivism they express in their epics is more conservative and evolutionary.

25 Swedenberg, *The Theory of the Epic in England* (n. 1 of this chapter); Donald M. Foerster, *The Fortunes of Epic Poetry* (Washington, 1962).

26 For a discussion of them, see Raymond Dexter Havens, *The Influence of Milton on English Poetry* (Cambridge, Mass., and London, 1922), pp. 290–313.

27 *Poetics*, 24, 1459b.

28 *Ibid.*, 4, 1449a.

29 *The Reason of Church-Government*, in *The Works of John Milton*, Columbia ed., III, 237.

30 *Faerie Queene*, Introductory Letter to Raleigh.

31 This is the criterion applied by Peter L. Thorslev, who argues that heroism is completely dead in literature today, killed largely by the forces of naturalism and the cult of the common man inherent in Romanticism. *The Byronic Hero* (Minneapolis, 1962), pp. 185–99.

32 The mutually contradictory charges are analogous to that other paradox, remarked by Langbaum (*The Poetry of Experience*, p. 10), by which the Romantics are attacked both for a false sentimentality toward the values of the past and for breaking with the main tradition of European culture.

33 Tillyard, for example, argues cogently that it is not. *The Epic Strain in the English Novel* (Fair Lawn, N.J., 1958), pp. 17–24.

34 Preface to *Joseph Andrews*, Modern Library ed. (New York, 1939), p. xxxi.

35 *Tom Jones*, XII, xii; *Aen.*, I.441–95.

Chapter Two

1 *Southey's Common-Place Book*, ed. John Wood Warter, 2nd ed., 4 vols. (London, 1850), IV, 206—hereafter abbreviated as *C-PB*.

2 *The Life and Correspondence of Robert Southey,* ed. Charles Cuthbert Southey, 6 vols. (London, 1849–50), May 20, 1808—hereafter abbreviated as *L and C.*

3 *L and C,* Aug. 5, 1810, to John May. Southey also believed in a perennial standard of English diction, citing in support of this belief the authority of Wordsworth; see *L and C,* Nov. 22, 1808, to Lieut. Tom Southey.

4 "I am fully convinced that a gradual improvement is going on in the world, has been going on from its commencement, and will continue till the human race shall attain all the perfection of which it is capable in this mortal state." *L and C,* Nov. 30, 1814, to Dr. Gooch.

5 *Don Juan,* III.79.

6 *L and C,* April 21, 1807; *C-PB,* IV, 259.

7 *L and C,* Dec. 22, 1802, to C. W. W. Wynn.

8 See Jack Simmons, *Southey* (New Haven, 1948), p. 75.

9 *C-PB,* IV, 205.

10 *L and C,* Nov. 13, 1793.

11 *L and C,* May 2, 1808.

12 Preface to the *Madoc* volume of the 1837–38 collected edition, quoted in *Poems of Robert Southey,* ed. Maurice H. Fitzgerald, Oxford Edition (London, 1909), p. 10. Except for *Joan of Arc,* of which I have used the original 1796 edition, references to Southey's poems and prefaces are to the Fitzgerald edition except where otherwise stated.

13 See the General Preface to the 1837–38 collected edition and the prefaces to the *Madoc* volume and to *The Curse of Kehama* prepared for the same edition (*Poems,* pp. 1, 10–11, 16). For Byron's criticism see *Don Juan,* Dedication, stanzas 5–9.

14 *L and C,* May 5, 1807, to G. Bedford; Dec. 22, 1802, to Wynn.

15 "Nothing can be more absurd than thinking of comparing any of my poems with the Paradise Lost. With Tasso, with Virgil, with Homer, there may be fair grounds of comparison." *L and C,* Feb. 16, 1815, to Dr. H. H. Southey. In the Preface to *The Curse of Kehama,* Southey acknowledges as his stylistic masters, even in this oriental poem, "our own great masters and the great poets of antiquity." *Poems,* p. 16.

16 See H. T. Swedenberg, *The Theory of the Epic in England, 1650–1800* (above, ch. 1, n. 1.), esp. ch. 11.

17 *Poems,* pp. 15–16.

18 *C-PB,* IV, 10.

19 See William Haller, *The Early Life of Robert Southey* (New York, 1917), p. 99.
20 *C-PB*, IV, 17.
21 *C-PB*, IV, 11.
22 *L and C*, Aug. 11, 1806, to Joseph Cottle.
23 Cf. Swedenberg, *Theory of the Epic, passim,* esp. p. 242; for the Pantisocratic ideas in *Madoc,* see Herbert G. Wright, "Three Aspects of Southey," *RES,* IX (1933), 38–40.
24 For example, Simmons (pp. 210, 212) calls both *Thalaba* and *Kehama* epics.
25 He once described a projected poem on the subject of Robin Hood as a "pastoral epic." *C-PB*, IV, 17–18.
26 For a summary of this critical debate, see Swedenberg, *Theory of the Epic,* esp. ch. 10.
27 *L and C*, Feb. 21, 1801, to Wynn; notes on the romance *Pharamond,* in *C-PB*, IV, 280.
28 Cf. Swedenberg, *Theory of the Epic,* ch. 9.
29 Cf. *ibid.,* esp. pp. 335–36; for a summary of English neoclassic theory on the question of blank verse or rhyme in the epic, see pp. 340–42. Most of the theorists favored blank verse.
30 *Poems,* p. 23 (Preface to first edition of *Thalaba*) ; *C-PB*, IV, 14. In a letter to G. Bedford (*L and C*, June 17, 1806), Southey wrote: "I have been inserting occasional rhymes in Kehama. . . . It gains by rhyme, which is to passages of no inherent merit what rouge and candle-light are to ordinary faces. Merely ornamental parts, also, are aided by it, as foil sets off paste. But where there is either passion or power, the plainer and more straightforward the language can be made the better."
31 *L and C*, Nov. 25, 1809, to Lieut. Tom Southey.
32 "I shall write this romance [*Kehama*] in rhyme, thus to avoid any sameness of style or syntax or expression with my blank verse poems, and to increase my range and power of language." "Blank verse has long appeared to me the noblest measure of which our language is capable, but it would not suit Kehama. There must be quicker, wilder movements; there must be a gorgeousness of ornament also,—eastern gem-work, and sometimes rhyme must be rattled upon rhyme, till the reader is half dizzy with the thundering echo." *C-PB*, IV, 14; *L and C*, May 20, 1808, to Landor.
33 In referring to his romances Southey sometimes showed indifference which borders on cynicism, an attitude which contrasts strikingly with the solemnity of his pronouncements about his epics. He ex-

pressed hope that the "anti-Jacobin criticasters" might spare *Thalaba* because it was "so utterly innocent of all good drift" (*L and C,* Feb. 21, 1801, to Wynn) and boasted to Coleridge of the ease with which the poem had been written and of the money it had made (*L and C,* July 11, 1801). Once he called *Kehama* "a sort of episode to my main employments" (*L and C,* March 20, 1810, to Sharon Turner). For similar statements about *Kehama* see *L and C,* June 12, 1803, and June 17, 1806, to G. Bedford; May 2, 1808, to Landor.

34 See, among other references to this plan, *L and C,* Nov. 4, 1812, to J. M. Longmire.

35 *C-PB,* IV, 182; *L and C,* Nov. 4, 1812, to Longmire.

36 Southey once implied that one of the distinctions between his romances and epics was at least partly an accident. "My aim has been to diffuse through my poems a sense of the beautiful and good . . . rather than to aim at the exemplification of any particular moral precept. It has, however, so happened that both in Thalaba and Kehama, the nature of the story led me to represent examples of faith." *L and C,* Nov. 4, 1812, to Longmire. But in the romances the "examples" of faith are fabulous rather than natural.

37 *C-PB,* IV, 258. See also his comments on the romance *Gyron le Courtoys* in *C-PB,* IV, 281.

38 *C-PB,* IV, 182.

39 *Thalaba* has twelve books, *Kehama* twenty-four. Both poems have episodes in the underworld, and in *Kehama* the incident is filled with literary echoes, especially of Virgil and Dante. Also, *Thalaba* was at one time meant to contain a vision of the future; see *C-PB,* IV, 185.

40 1805 Preface to *Thalaba,* in *Poems,* p. 460.

41 See the account and discussion by Raymond Dexter Havens in *The Influence of Milton on English Poetry* (Cambridge, Mass., and London, 1922), pp. 284–87, 278*n.*

42 *L and C,* Nov. 13, 1793, to H. W. Bedford; Havens, *The Influence of Milton,* p. 280.

43 *L and C,* II, 121–22, Oct., 1800, to John Rickman.

44 *L and C,* May 9, 1799. Coleridge's plan for an epic is mentioned by R. C. Bald, "Coleridge and *The Ancient Mariner,*" *Nineteenth Century Studies,* ed. Herbert Davis and others (Ithaca, 1940), pp. 15 ff.

45 *L and C,* Sept. 22, 1799, to Joseph Cottle.

46 *L and C,* April 1, 1800, to Coleridge.

47 L and C, April 26, 1808, to G. Bedford.
48 1831 Preface to "Gebir," "Count Julian," and Other Poems, quoted
in The Complete Works of Walter Savage Landor, ed. T. E. Welby
and Stephen Wheeler, 16 vols. (London, 1927–36), XIII, 344. The
poems (ed. Wheeler) comprise Vols. XIII–XVI.
49 Joan of Arc, an Epic Poem (Bristol, 1796), p. vii. Unless otherwise noted, all references to Joan and its Preface are based on this
edition.
50 Works, XIII, 344. References to Gebir are to the 1803 edition as
reproduced in Wheeler. There are many variations between this and
the 1798 edition, but none of them affects significantly what I am
saying about the poem, and line references to the 1798 edition
would be meaningless in terms of the definitive edition. The 1803
text differs from that of 1798 mainly in elucidating obscure passages in it and in making more emphatic the original liberal principles of the poem. Landor, furthermore, had not seen the first edition adequately through the press; see Addenda to the canceled
1800 Post-Script to Gebir, in Works, XIII, 365. Where Landor's
Preface, Notes, or other comments on Gebir contain matter first
written later than 1798 and therefore might conceivably represent
a change in his attitude, I have made a point of indicating the later
date.
51 Haller, The Early Life of Robert Southey, pp. 111, 101–3.
52. Cf. ibid., p. 109.
53 L and C, Feb. 24, 1796, to G. Bedford.
54 Preface to Joan of Arc for the 1837–38 collected edition, in The
Poetical Works of Robert Southey, introduction by Henry T.
Tuckerman, 10 vols. (Boston, 1864), I, 14.
55 Poetical Works, intro. Tuckerman, I, 17. This passage (not in the
1796 edition, but printed in the 1837–38 edition with the date
November, 1795) cannot be taken as a definitive statement of
Southey's views in the 1790's. His views were inconsistent even
during the period when Joan was written. For one thing, the poem
does actually contain some of the devices Southey sneers at, which
may indicate that the disclaimer was partly rhetorical, like Milton's
in Book IX of Paradise Lost. And shortly after the poem was published Southey referred to the Preface as inane hodgepodge and told
Grosvenor Bedford that the remarks on the epic had been so hastily
composed that Southey forgot to draw from them the conclusion
which he had intended to state. See L and C, Feb. 24, 1796.
56 Preface to Joan of Arc, p. vi.

57 1837 Preface to *Joan of Arc*, in *Poetical Works*, intro. Tuckerman, I, 12.

58 It is also possible that the arms found in the old tomb, unrusted and ready for Joan's use, are an echo of the provision of new armor for Achilles, Aeneas, and Tasso's Rinaldo, and that the miraculous signs which convince the skeptics of Joan's divine mission are adaptations of the epic omen (III.486–501; IV.118–39).

59 Later Southey came to believe that such a tour de force might make a poem effective in its own day but would not bring lasting fame. *L and C*, Feb. 3, 1809, to Ebenezer Elliott.

60 Sir Richard Blackmore had also defended the use of a female hero. But this precedent and that of Chapelain were anomalies, and one review of Southey's *Joan* questioned its choice of subject, saying that Chapelain and Voltaire had made it ridiculous. See Swedenberg, *Theory of the Epic*, pp. 23–24, 74, 132.

61 *Works*, XIII, 350.

62 Preface to *Gebir*, *Works*, XIII, 343.

63 1800 Post-Script to *Gebir*, *Works*, XIII, 351.

64 Note on *Gebir*, III.40, *Works*, XIII, 347; cf. *Aen.*, II.428.

65 An 1803 note on *Gebir*, I.15, justifies the author's fanciful derivation of *Gibraltar* from the name *Gebir* by appeals to Virgilian linguistic precedent (*Works*, XIII, 2), and another 1803 note, to VI.173, defends a hyperbolical description of Mt. Etna by defiantly citing the *Georgics* (*Works*, XIII, 349). About Miltonic influence Landor was even more self-conscious. He deleted after the 1798 edition a casual statement in his Preface implying an analogy between his own choice of blank verse and Milton's (*Works*, XIII, 343), and in the 1800 Post-Script he insists vehemently, in response to a critic's charges, that *Paradise Lost* was not a model for *Gebir* (*Works*, XIII, 350–51). On the other hand, the 1800 Post-Script is for the most part an elaborate defense of literary allusiveness and creative imitation as distinguished from plagiarism, a preoccupation that strongly implies that Landor was conscious of having used older poems as models in some sense.

66 The games are Landor's own invention, as is the idea of omitting the earlier events of the story and starting in the middle; see Stanley G. Williams, "The Story of Gebir," *PMLA*, XXXVI (1921), 624, 628. Also, the line (II.186) "In our affliction can the Gods delight" is an obvious echo of Virgil's *tantaene animis caelestibus irae*.

67 1800 Post-Script to *Gebir*, *Works*, XIII, 352.

68 Herbert Lindenberger, in his book *On Wordsworth's "Prelude"* (Princeton, 1963), pp. 117–18, describes Landor's epic devices in *Gebir* and also Wordsworth's groping efforts in *The Prelude*, Book I, to find a heroic theme as symptomatic of a troubled yearning for vanished epic possibilities. Although I admire Lindenberger's book, I think he is wrong here, about Landor because he misses the irony of the reversals of epic precedent and about Wordsworth because groping exploration of heroic themes is, owing to Milton's precedent, an affirmation of the heroic tradition.

69 See Williams, "The Story of Gebir," pp. 625–28. The connection with the older epics is also strengthened by the parallel relationships of queen and confidante between Charoba and Dalica in *Gebir* and Dido and her sister Anna in Virgil.

70 *Odyssey*, X.487–540; *Aen.*, VI.124–55, 236–63.

71 Landor's underworld is divided into a place of suffering and a place of happiness, and in its description of a kind of purgatorial refining (III.45–50) it recalls *Aen.*, VI.724–51.

72 *GL*, XV.vi–xxxv.

73 *Poems*, p. 460.

Chapter Three

1 *The Early Letters of William and Dorothy Wordsworth (1787–1805)*, ed. Ernest De Selincourt (Oxford, 1935), March 21, 1796, to William Mathews; this work is hereafter abbreviated as *EL*. For the later letters I have used the following, also edited by De Selincourt: *The Letters of William and Dorothy Wordsworth: The Middle Years*, 2 vols. (Oxford, 1937)—hereafter abbreviated as *LMY*; and *The Letters of William and Dorothy Wordsworth: The Later Years*, 3 vols. (Oxford, 1939)—hereafter abbreviated as *LLY*.

2 Abbie Findlay Potts, *Wordsworth's "Prelude": A Study of Its Literary Form* (Ithaca, 1953). I shall discuss the relationship between this essay and Miss Potts's book later in the chapter.

3 *LMY*, II, 633. Another reference to Dennis occurs in a letter to Catherine Clarkson written slightly earlier (*LMY*, II, 617, Dec., 1814); here we find Wordsworth in agreement with Dennis again, this time on the nature of poetic passion. But Wordsworth makes few such references to neoclassic critics.

See Swendenberg (above, ch. 1, n. 1), *Theory of the Epic*, pp. 340–42, for an index to and summary of English neoclassic theory on verse form in the epic.

I have no certain evidence that Wordsworth knew Camoëns during early or middle life, but his generally strong admiration for W. J. Mickle, who published his well-known translation of the *Lusiad* in 1776, makes it very likely that he did. See Wordsworth's letters to W. Mathews, *LLY,* III, 1334, Oct. 24, 1795, and to Allan Cunningham, *LLY,* Nov. 23, 1823. On Nov. 15, 1844, Wordsworth wrote a letter to John Adamson, the biographer of Camoëns, expressing his interest in Portugese literature, stating that Southey and Wordsworth's son-in-law, Edward Quillinan, had made Wordsworth familiar with the country and its literature. In this letter, as it happens, Wordsworth criticizes Mickle's translation sharply. See E. H. A., "Letters of Wordsworth," *Notes and Queries,* 8th series, XII (July 1, 1897), 86. But just when he first read the translation is uncertain.

4 *LLY,* March 9, 1840, to Edward Quillinan.
5 *LLY,* Jan. 21, 1824; Potts, *Wordsworth's "Prelude,"* p. 337.
6 The identification is made by De Selincourt in a note to the letter.
7 *Charlemagne; or The Church Delivered,* trans. Samuel Butler and Francis Hodgson, 2 vols. (London, 1815), I, xiv–xv.
8 See, for example, *LLY,* Nov. 23, 1823, to Allan Cunningham; *LLY,* Nov. 16, 1824, to Alaric Watts.
9 See, for example, *LMY,* I, 458d, Jan. 18, 1808, to Walter Scott; *LLY,* April 20, 1822, to Landor.
10 See, for example, *EL,* March 21, 1796, to W. Mathews; *EL,* Oct. 17, 1805, to Sir George Beaumont; *LLY,* Jan. 18, 1840, to Thomas Powell. George McLean Harper mentions that Wordsworth took with him a copy of *Orlando Furioso* during his 1790 tour through the Alps. *William Wordsworth: His Life, Works, and Influence,* 2nd ed., 2 vols. (New York, 1923), II, 43.
11 As explained later in this chapter, the text except where otherwise indicated is the 1805 version, in *The Prelude,* ed. Ernest De Selincourt, rev. Helen Darbishire (Oxford, 1959).
12 *LLY,* Jan. 21, 1824, to Landor; *LLY,* I, 506–7, to Henry N. Coleridge, 1830. It is true, of course, that Dante's reputation was not quite so high a century and a half ago as it is today, admired though he was by most of the Romantics.
13 For the 1804 letters see *EL,* p. 355 (exact date uncertain, to Francis Wrangham) and *EL,* p. 370, March 6, 1804, to Thomas De Quincey. For the letter to Beaumont, see *EL,* p. 497, June 3, 1805. The letter to Beaumont uses the phrase "narrative Poem of the Epic kind"; the other two letters mention a "narrative" poem without adding the epic label. But the similarity in context implies strongly

that all three letters refer to the same projected poem. Nor is it at all likely that the narrative poem is *The Excursion,* which later appeared as part of *The Recluse,* that is, part of the philosophic poem which Wordsworth in the letters distinguished explicitly from the narrative-epic one. Furthermore, *The Excursion* can hardly be called a narrative work. Most students of Wordsworth have missed this sharp distinction between the narrative and philosophic poems.

14 See, for example, Arthur Beatty, *William Wordsworth: His Doctrine and Art in their Historical Relations,* 2nd ed. (Madison, 1927), pp. 234–36; Elizabeth Sewell, *The Orphic Voice: Poetry and Natural History* (New Haven, 1960), p. 302.

15 See, for example, Lascelles Abercrombie, *The Art of Wordsworth* (New York, 1952), esp. pp. 41–42; Sewell, *The Orphic Voice,* p. 302–9; Karl Kroeber, *Romantic Narrative Art* (Madison, 1960), pp. 78–112; Herbert Lindenberger, *On Wordsworth's "Prelude"* (Princeton, 1963), pp. 9–15. (In a more casual way *The Prelude* has been called an epic countless times.) Most of these treatments emphasize the epic theme while admitting or implying that *The Prelude* fails to achieve epic shape or texture. Miss Potts's study (above, n. 2) is an exception, as I shall indicate in a more appropriate place.

16 Herbert Lindenberger (*On Wordsworth's "Prelude,"* p. 110) sees in this passage the demoralized sensibility of the modern poet—"procrastinating, self-analytical, recoiling from the burden of his task"—and contrasts it with Milton's sensibility as revealed in the invocations of *Paradise Lost.* But Milton too had been apprehensive that the greatness of his theme, "sufficient of it self" to raise his name, might succumb to the handicaps of "an age too late, or cold/ Climat, or Years" (*PL,* IX.44–45), and it is even more important to recognize that Milton's literary "autobiography," which Wordsworth knew thoroughly, represents Milton too as groping hesitantly, not only toward a theme but in many ways toward a form as well. The passage from Book I of *The Prelude* which we have been discussing invokes Milton's precedent through echoes of "Lycidas" and therefore shows a sense of kinship with the epic tradition rather than alienation from it. See the following note.

17 Wordsworth's discipleship to Milton is a familiar topic, but even so readers are likely to underestimate the extent of parallelism between the two poets in their views and especially in their self-images. The principal documents of Milton's literary autobiography molded Wordsworth's conception of his own literary evolution in powerful

and very specific ways, of which the gradual channeling of diffused ambition into a particular theme is only the most obvious. The beginning of *The Prelude* shows Wordsworth retiring from the city and his "unnatural self" to espouse what, in heroic and monastic terms, he calls "The holy life of music and of verse" (I.23, 50–54); here the situation and ascetic emphasis suggest Milton's address to Diodati in "Elegy VI," ll. 9–78. The mention of a romantic tale "by Milton left unsung" recalls the kind of subject which Milton first considered and then rejected, as we learn from *Mansus,* the *Epitaphium Damonis,* the *Apology for Smectymnuus,* and the Cambridge MS. if the order of subjects listed there is significant. (One wonders whether Wordsworth had seen the Milton MS. at the university.) The passage about the Druids in *Prelude,* XII.312–54, resembles the lines (41–43) about the Druids in *Mansus;* here both Wordsworth's and Milton's contexts celebrate the national past and the universal bond which unites poets. Wordsworth's distrust of his poetic powers has precedents not only in "Lycidas" but also in Milton's hint that his first difficulty in treating a heroic theme was stylistic (*Epitaphium Damonis,* ll. 155–60). The poet's *apologia* for himself near the end of *The Prelude* and subsequent distinction between earthly love and a higher kind (XIII.128–65) is, especially as expanded in the 1850 version, much like Milton's defense of himself against charges of licentiousness and his panegyric on Platonic love in the *Apology for Smectymnuus* (Columbia ed., III, 301–6). Wordsworth liked to apply to his own poetry and views the famous passage from Book Two of *The Reason of Church-Government* (III, 235–41); see *LMY,* April 28, 1814, to Poole; *LLY,* Sept. 3, 1821, to Landor. In the same passage Milton, like Wordsworth (*Prelude,* VI.64–69), tells of having felt great literary ambition for the first time in an academic setting. Milton's embarrassment about autobiographical intimacy and defense of it are strikingly like Wordsworth's sentiments in *Prelude,* XIII.386–90, and Milton's statement that the poet should teach, though by indirect means, is close to the view once expressed by Wordsworth (*LMY,* June 5, 1808, to Wrangham) and implied in Wordsworth's poetry in general. And, of course, it is in the *Church-Government* passage that Milton declares his view that the hero should be a model Christian and the poet's life itself a poem.

18 Although Wordsworth may have been thinking of a Biblical subject, another possibility is a tale, like some of those listed in the Cambridge Milton MS., derived from the English chroniclers. But

Professor Carl Woodring has suggested to me the likelihood that Wordsworth, under the influence of the English republican writers of the seventeenth century, had in mind an unsung hero modeled on Algernon Sydney or some such figure. For a discussion of Wordsworth's intellectual debt to the English republican writers, see Z. S. Fink, "Wordsworth and the English Republican Tradition," *JEGP*, XLVII (1948), 107–26.

19 Miss Potts (*Wordsworth's "Prelude,"* p. 295) cites the precedent of Spenser for this pastoral-to-epic motif in *The Prelude*.

20 See *ibid.*, p. 336.

21 *The Prelude*, pp. 568–69.

22 The words "now that I must quit this theme" would seem to say that the theme Wordsworth announces is not at all the general theme of the poem but rather the theme of the first books. But by "quit this theme" Wordsworth is on the simplest level implying no more than that he is closing out an episode in his life and beginning another. Immediately afterward he writes, "Enough: . . . A Traveller I am, / And all my Tale is of myself." The phrase "quit this theme" is one of almost countless modulating phrases by means of which Wordsworth shifts back and forth between private statement and generalization about man. I shall have more to say later about the structural function of the whole passage.

23 *EL*, pp. 120–21, June, 1794, to W. Mathews.

24 *EL*, p. 296, June, 1802, to John Wilson.

25 *LMY*, June 11, 1816, to John Scott.

26 Z. S. Fink distinguishes between Wordsworth's temporary conception of himself as divinely appointed leader and lawgiver, and the opposite, Burkean view according to which institutions arise through a long process of historical evolution. In *The Prelude* Wordsworth places himself in the tradition which held that "states were best contrived when they were made all at once by a single great institutor or legislator whose disinterestedness was guaranteed by the fact that he had no place in the government which he set up and retired from the scene once the state was established." "Wordsworth and the English Republican Tradition," pp. 119–22.

27 See De Selincourt, ed., *The Prelude* (1926 ed.), pp. xxxv–xxxviii. Book III was probably written partly during the years 1801–3 and partly in 1804 before March 24. But on March 29, 1804, Wordsworth had not worked on the poem for nearly three weeks, and on March 6 he had completed four books and still believed that one more would conclude his poem. Almost certainly, then, all of Book

III had been written by March 6 or a few days later, and very possibly long before that date.

28 Mario Praz, in his stimulating book *The Hero in Eclipse in Victorian Fiction* (New York, 1956), pp. 41–53, sees in Wordsworth's apparent retirement from the world of action and revolutionary zeal a symptom of typically *bourgeois* values later characteristic of the Victorians: sentimentalism, cozy domesticity, the sense of duty, the stress on the beauties of nature, the belief in humble life as somehow heroic. There is a sense in which these remarks are valid, and in that sense Wordsworth might have shamelessly pleaded guilty to the charges; he knew where his ideas led. We cannot, therefore, beg the very questions that Wordsworth was raising by simply condemning him peremptorily as a proto-Victorian; he might well have answered, *"Et donc?"* But it is even more important to recognize that in *The Prelude* Wordsworth's most important ideal, the Imagination, has little to do with class milieu or special environment, whatever he may say about his own debt to nature. He does not idealize nature and cozy domesticity for their own sakes; they are, rather, favorable conditions for what he considers the noble life of Imagination, which life as he depicts it far transcends *Gemütlichkeit* of the Victorian or any other variety. Wordsworth did, in Praz's phrase, turn from the world of the Revolution to "the little world of his own childhood" (p. 43), but the spiritual and psychological dimensions which he gives to that world are anything but little. Finally, we must recognize his championing of domestic life in the country as in part a rhetorical device used to dramatize the distinction between inner heroism and superficial activism.

29 This chapter was written before my belated discovery of R. A. Foakes's *The Romantic Assertion* (New Haven, 1958), which states (pp. 57–79) that the structure of *The Prelude* is founded on the metaphor of a journey. A few small points in Foakes parallel my own discussion, but otherwise his argument and mine have little in common; he claims that *The Prelude* is only superficially epic, and that it lacks the architectonic quality of *Paradise Lost* (p. 59). Part of my argument is that even the apparent meanderings which have always provoked criticisms of the structure of *The Prelude* are related to the epic pattern.

30 See n. 17 to this chapter.

31 George Wilbur Meyer observes that Wordsworth's personal history was "a miracle wrought by mysterious powers whose ways are dark and hidden from all but favored eyes." *Wordsworth's Formative*

Years, Univ. of Michigan Publications, Language and Literature, Vol. XX (Ann Arbor, 1943), p. 4, and cf. p. 35. Abbie Potts (*Wordsworth's "Prelude,"* pp. 335–36) mentions briefly the function of Nature as supernatural machinery. I am not aware that anyone has pointed out the less obvious but explicitly parallel function of Books.

32 This personal quality is mentioned briefly by Abbie Potts (*Wordsworth's "Prelude,"* p. 335) and compared to the relationship between Fatherhood and Sonship in the Gospels and in Milton.

33 The 1850 version has a more explicitly theological emphasis, but it does no more than clarify the half-explicit reference in the original text. The late version reads:

> Such dispositions then were mine unearned
> By aught, I fear, of genuine desert—
> Mine, through heaven's grace and inborn aptitudes.
>
> (VI.168–70)

34 Potts, *Wordsworth's "Prelude,"* pp. 307–8, 335.

35 Cf. C. M. Bowra, *From Virgil to Milton* (London, 1945), pp. 24–26.

36 Although Wordsworth generally reinforced in later revision the patterns we are examining, he deleted this passage. Perhaps he believed (rightly) that he had emphasized more than was necessary the distinction between moral lapses and imaginative ones, and was fearful of sounding merely complacent.

37 So I read this syntactically obscure passage.

38 "Io non Enëa, io non Paolo sono," Dante protests when he learns that he has been singled out by Grace for special visions and a special mission. Aeneas and Paul had been vouchsafed such experiences, Dante reasons, because of the high imperial and religious consequences which were to spring from their work. *Inf.,* II.13–33.

39 Potts, *Wordsworth's "Prelude,"* p. 19. Miss Potts seems (at least sometimes) to think of the French episodes as the part of the poem which is specifically epic, and to consider the ordeal pattern as primarily grounded in a liturgical tradition (pp. 11, 23, 112, 323, 359). I am trying to show that these patterns comprise a single whole in *The Prelude.*

40 On the other hand, the Red Cross Knight is similarly prostrated and passive when he is rescued by Arthur and Una. One could draw a neat parallel between the three helpers to whom Wordsworth explicitly attributes his recovery—his machinery Nature and the two

human persons Dorothy and Coleridge—and the Knight's three helpers—God acting through Arthur and Una. The parallel is very probably strained, but it is not entirely impossible that Wordsworth was thinking in some such terms.

41 See Kenneth MacLean, "The Water Symbol in *The Prelude* (1805–6)," *Univ. of Toronto Quarterly*, XVII (July, 1948), 372–89; Foakes, *Romantic Assertion*, pp. 69–74.

42 Cf. Foakes, *Romantic Assertion*, p. 69, where he too cites XIII.172–84.

43 See M. H. Abrams, "The Correspondent Breeze: A Romantic Metaphor," *Kenyon Review*, XIX (1957), 113–30, esp. 116–17.

Incidentally, Wordsworth's invocation soon modulates into the description of a storm, in his case a creative one: "A tempest, a redundant energy / Vexing its own creation" (I.46–47). Although this parallel too, like the one in n. 40, may seem far-fetched, I cannot help wondering whether Wordsworth had in mind the storm to which Virgil modulates after his invocation (*Aen.*, I.81 ff.). Wordsworth's knowledge of Virgil was microscopically thorough.

44 De Selincourt (*The Prelude*, pp. lxviii, 565) argues that the addition seriously falsifies Wordsworth's early views.

45 Raymond Dexter Havens, in *The Mind of a Poet* (Baltimore, 1941), p. 542, points out the resemblance to *PL*, IX.996–1014; *Iliad*, VIII.69–72; XXII.209–11; *Aen.*, XII.725–27. Potts (*Wordsworth's "Prelude,"* p. 301) suggests possible indebtedness to Spenser.

46 The parallel with Milton is noted by Potts, *Wordsworth's "Prelude,"* p. 323.

47 Harper (above, n. 10), *Wordsworth*, II, 151.

48 There are two passages from Wordsworth's letters which throw light on the Snowdon passage. The first is from a letter to Lady Beaumont (*LMY*, May 21, 1807) in which Wordsworth quotes *PL*, IV.604–9, to illustrate the importance of a single dominating image and the necessity of subordinating the details of a scene to the end of unity. A similar domination is exerted in the Snowdon passage by the "mighty Mind" there symbolized. Wordsworth's association of Snowdon with aesthetic theory is again illustrated in a letter to Jacob Fletcher (*LLY*, Feb. 25, 1825), where the poet describes a plan to make Snowdon "the scene of a Dialogue upon Nature, Poetry, and Painting—to be illustrated by the surrounding imagery."

49 *Par.*, XXII.127–54.

50 This is a major point in Jacques Barzun's *The House of Intellect* (New York, 1959).

51 *LMY*, I, 170, Jan. or Feb., 1808, to Sir George Beaumont. In 1794 he saw his projected periodical, *The Philanthropist*, as "a vehicle of sound and exalted Morality" whose aim was to "instruct and amuse mankind," partly through the edifying biographies of champions of liberty (*EL*, May 23, 1794, to W. Mathews; *EL*, June, 1794, to W. Mathews). *The Recluse* was to "do good" (*EL*, April 29, 1804, to Richard Sharp). His collected poems were "to console the afflicted, to add sunshine to daylight, . . . to teach the young and the gracious of every age, to see, to think and feel, and therefore to become more actively and securely virtuous" (*LMY*, May 21, 1807, to Lady Beaumont). He condemned *Don Juan* because he believed that it would "do more harm to the English character than anything of our time" (*LLY*, I, 254, probable date 1822, to unknown correspondent).

52 Cf. Bowra, *From Virgil to Milton*, pp. 31–32. Bowra's point is that the epic poet always writes at the end of a great age in order to preserve the threatened and dying values of that age. My emphasis is somewhat different; I see the standard epic poets as less elegiacally retrospective, more conscious of themselves as progressive links between past and future.

53 *Aen.*, VI.788–97; *GL*, I.iv–v; *Lus.*, I.xv–xvii.

54 The tone of elaborate compliment in apostrophes to Coleridge is also exemplified by II.479–84 and VI.326–31.

Chapter Four

1 I do not mean to beg the vexed question of whether *Epipsychidion* (or *Adonais*, for that matter) takes a thoroughly idealist position. I simply take for granted what most readers admit, that the Shelley of 1821 was a more convinced idealist than the Shelley of 1817.

2 The distinction between the "millenial" and "apocalyptic" strands in Shelley's thought, convincingly developed by Milton Wilson, seems to me one of the best helps toward grasping Shelley's protean ideas and images. *Shelley's Later Poetry* (New York, 1959).

3 A number of scholars have in passing described it as an epic or an attempt at one—for example, A. Clutton-Brock, *Shelley: The Man and the Poet*, 3rd ed. (London, 1924), p. 154; Benjamin P. Kurtz,

The Pursuit of Death: A Study of Shelley's Poetry (New York, 1933), p. 111; A. M. D. Hughes, *The Nascent Mind of Shelley* (Oxford, 1947), pp. 210, 212, 215.

4 *Mary Shelley's Journal,* ed. Frederick L. Jones (Norman, Okla., 1947). This is the most helpful single guide to Shelley's reading after July, 1814. Pp. 218–31 contain a summary of it as recorded by Mary, arranged both by author and chronologically.

5 *The Complete Works of Percy Bysshe Shelley,* ed. Roger Ingpen and Walter E. Peck, Julian ed., 10 vols. (London and New York, 1926–30). Except where I state otherwise, all my references to Shelley's poetry, prose, and letters are based on this edition, hereafter abbreviated as *"Works."*

6 Letter to Mary Shelley, Aug. 11, 1821.

7 Letters to Leigh Hunt, Dec. 8, 1816; to Byron, July 9, 1817; to Keats, July 27, 1820.

8 *Works,* VII, 91; much of this passage was later repeated almost verbatim in *A Defence of Poetry.*

9 See his letter to Peacock, Oct. 8, 1818.

10 Letter to Mary Shelley, Aug. 9, 1821.

11 Mary's journal (pp. 55, 60–61, 65, 68–69, 78–83) reveals that during the six months or so prior to writing *The Revolt* and during its composition Shelley read assiduously Spenser and the *Iliad,* besides doing some reading in Milton, Tasso, and Virgil. In *The Examiner* of Oct. 10, 1819, Leigh Hunt states that, at the time we are here concerned with, Shelley was often seen with a copy of "some Greek author or the *Bible";* see Newman Ivey White, *The Unextinguished Hearth* (Durham, N.C., 1938), p. 149. It is perhaps significant that two of the works alleged to be sources for Shelley's poem—Peacock's abortive Zoroastrian poem *Ahrimanes* and *La Araucana,* by the Spanish poet D'Ercilla—are epics; see Kenneth Neill Cameron, "Shelley and *Ahrimanes," MLQ,* III (1942), 287–95; Ben W. Griffith, Jr., "Another Source of *The Revolt of Islam," Notes and Queries,* CXCIX (Jan., 1954), 29–30.

12 Letter to Charles and James Ollier, Sept. 6, 1819.

13 He told Elizabeth Hitchener that *The Curse of Kehama* was his favorite poem and recommended *Joan of Arc* to her (letters of June 11, 1811, and July 25, 1811); see also *Mary Shelley's Journal,* pp. 15, 16, 32, 226, and the references to Southey in Shelley's letters indexed in *Works,* Vol. X.

14 In one of the most famous anecdotes about Shelley, Hogg relates

that he once had to interrupt Shelley's reading of *Gebir* aloud by snatching the book and throwing it out the window. *The Life of Percy Bysshe Shelley* (London, 1858), I, 201–2.

15 The Homeric quality in Shelley's scene is very distinct; there is the same atmosphere of silence and of darkness broken by the flickering light of the campfires (V.i–ii; VI.i).

16 *Aen.*, III.137–42; *Iliad*, I.8–12; *PL*, XI.477 ff.; *GL*, XIII.lii ff.; *Lus.*, V.lxxxi-lxxxii. I do not know of any certain evidence that Shelley had read the *Lusiad* by 1817, though on the general grounds of his wide reading the assumption seems safe. He comments on Camoëns' epic in *A Defence of Poetry*, of course.

17 See, for example, Charles W. Lemmi, "The Serpent and the Eagle in Spenser and Shelley," *MLN*, L (1935), 165–68, and the convenient index to scholarship on this point in Carlos Baker's *Shelley's Major Poetry: The Fabric of a Vision* (Princeton, 1948), p. 73*n*.

18 Wilfrid S. Dowden, "Shelley's Use of Metempsychosis in *The Revolt of Islam*," *Rice Institute Pamphlet*, XXXVIII (April, 1951), 70.

19 I.xxix; IV.xiii; V.liii; X.xliv.

20 *Shelley's Major Poetry*, p. 73.

21 Clutton-Brock, *Shelley*, p. 158; Carl Grabo, *The Magic Plant: The Growth of Shelley's Thought* (Chapel Hill, 1936), p. 225; Newman Ivey White, *Shelley*, 2 vols. (New York, 1940), I, 529, 530.

22 White, *Shelley*, I, 530.

23 Letter to "a publisher," Oct. 13, 1817.

24 *Shelley's Major Poetry*, pp. 64, 70.

25 The serpent is associated with the tyrannical Sultan (V.xxv), his senate (XI.xxv), fear and lust (II.iv), hate (VIII.xxi; X.xxxii), custom (VIII.xxvii), guile (X.xxxii), and wrath (XII. vii). On the other hand, the eagle is applied emblematically to the freedom-loving United States (XI.xxiii), and in prophesying the golden future Cythna declares, "From its dark gulph of chains, Earth like an eagle springs" (IX.xxv).

26 Laon's resumption of the first-person pronoun in the fifth stanza of Canto XII is distinctly a shock, especially in view of the repeated *his* in the third stanza.

27 Cf. Ded., iii–v, with II.ix–xv.

28 Cf. Baker, *Shelley's Major Poetry*, pp. 84–85.

29 *GL*, XV.iii–xliii; *Gebir* (1803 text), VI.130–289.

30 Letter to Godwin, Dec. 11, 1817.

31 Dowden, "Shelley's Use of Metempsychosis," pp. 62–66.

32 Southey's influence on *The Revolt of Islam* is treated briefly by Dowden, *ibid.*, pp. 61–62, and by Baker in *Shelley's Major Poetry*, p. 79. For Southey's influence on Shelley's poetry in general, see A. M. D. Hughes (n. 3, above), pp. 88–90. See also n. 13, above.

33 See II.xxxvi; IV.xxii; VII.v–vi. Shelley was as vehement as Southey in his condemnations of lust and obscenity. In *A Defence of Poetry* he calls obscenity "blasphemy against the divine beauty in life" and claims that it becomes, in periods of social decay such as the Restoration age, "a monster for which the corruption of society for ever brings forth new food, which it devours in secret" (*Works*, VII, 122). In "A Discourse on the Manners of the Antient Greeks Relative to the Subject of Love" he attacks Catullus, Martial, Juvenal, and Suetonius as "brutally obscene"—text as reprinted in James A. Notopoulos, *The Platonism of Shelley* (Durham, N.C., 1949), p. 412.

Chapter Five

1 As later parts of my chapter will show, I disagree with Bernard Blackstone's view, as expressed in *The Consecrated Urn* (New York, 1959), pp. 227, 244, that Keats's description of *Hyperion* as "abstraction" implies an attempt to escape reality, misery, and his own emotions. See also my more general remarks on Blackstone's book in n. 30 to this chapter.

2 For Keats's poems I have used H. W. Garrod, *The Poetical Works of John Keats*, Oxford Standard Authors ed. (London, 1956).

3 *The Letters of John Keats, 1814–1821*, ed. Hyder Edward Rollins, 2 vols. (Cambridge, Mass., 1958), I, 403. Hereafter referred to as *Letters*.

4 *Letters*, I, 278–79, May 3, 1818, to J. H. Reynolds. Keats originally wrote "epic passions," then crossed out the final *s*.

5 Keats's schoolboy translation of the *Aeneid* is mentioned by Charles Cowden Clarke and Charles Brown; see Hyder Edward Rollins, *The Keats Circle*, 2 vols. (Cambridge, Mass., 1948), II, 147, 55. For a discussion of the influence of Fairfax's Tasso on Keats's style, see Walter Jackson Bate, *The Stylistic Development of Keats* (New York, 1958), pp. 33–42, 201–2 (originally published 1945). The books in Keats's library, as catalogued by Brown, are listed and described by Rollins in *The Keats Circle*, I, 253–60.

6 *Letters*, Jan. 23, 1818.

7 Quoted from *Letters*, I, 214–15, Jan. 23, 1818, to George and Tom Keats.

8 *Letters*, I, 331, July 13, 1818, to Tom Keats.

9 *Letters*, Sept. 20, 1818, to C. W. Dilke.

10 *Letters*, I, 370, about Sept. 22, 1818.

11 Cf. Preface to *Prometheus Unbound*, *Works*, Julian ed., II, 173: "As to imitation, poetry is a mimetic art. It creates, but it creates by combination and representation. Poetical abstractions are beautiful and new, not because," etc.

12 See *Letters*, II, 12, Dec. 18, 1818, to George and Georgiana Keats.

13 *Letters*, II, 62, Feb. 14, 1819, to George and Georgiana Keats.

14 *Letters*, March 8, 1819, to Haydon.

15 Woodhouse's note written on the MS of *Hyperion*, quoted in Amy Lowell, *John Keats*, 2 vols. (Boston, 1925), II, 226.

16 *Letters*, II, 101–4, April 21, 1819, to George and Georgiana Keats.

17 *Letters*, June 9, 1819, to Sarah Jeffrey.

18 *Letters*, II, 80–81, March 19, 1819, to George and Georgiana Keats.

19 *Letters*, July 25, 1819. Although some scholars disagree, it has generally been accepted (since the discovery of the "lost letter" to Woodhouse—*Letters*, II, 169–75, Sept. 21–22, 1819) that the reference in the letter to Fanny Brawne is to *The Fall*; if this is true, it weakens the argument that Keats's earlier references to *Hyperion* as an abstract poem are a confession that he is writing an escapist poem. One argument that the July letter refers to the second version can be found in John Hawley Roberts, "The Significance of *Lamia*," *PMLA*, L (1935), 556–57.

20 *Letters*, II, 144, to John Taylor. A day later he expressed similar ideas in a letter to J. H. Reynolds; *Letters*, II, 146–47.

21 *Letters*, II, 167, Sept. 21, 1819, to J. H. Reynolds.

22 *Letters*, II, 212, Sept. 21, 1819, to George and Georgiana Keats. Also written on this day was that part of the letter to Woodhouse which contains the "Ode to Autumn" and excerpts from *The Fall of Hyperion*; *Letters*, II, 169–73.

23 Rollins, *The Keats Circle*, II, 72. For another bit of evidence that Keats continued to work on *The Fall* during the later autumn, see M. R. Ridley, *Keats' Craftsmanship: A Study in Poetic Development* (Oxford, 1933), p. 298.

24 *Letters*, Nov. 17, 1819, to John Taylor.

25 In discussing *Hyperion* I have followed Keats's precedent and ignored the distinction between Giants and Titans.

26 Occasional statements by Keats indicate a general belief in progress; see *Letters,* I, 278–82, May 3, 1818, to Reynolds; *Letters,* II, 193, Sept. 18, 1819, to George and Georgiana Keats. But the idea is not very prominent in Keats's letters. Furthermore, in his "Soul-making" letter (*Letters,* II, 101) Keats passionately rejects the doctrine of perfectibility, substituting for it the idea of progress or growth in the lives of individual human beings.

27 See James Ralston Caldwell, "The Meaning of *Hyperion,*" *PMLA,* LI (1936), 1086.

28 Claude Lee Finney, in *The Evolution of Keats's Poetry,* 2 vols. (Cambridge, Mass., 1936), II, 407–538, 710–19, reads *Hyperion* as an expression of Miltonic-Shakespearean "humanism" and what most readers call *The Fall of Hyperion* as an expression of Wordsworthian "humanitarianism," though he also claims (II, 505) that at a certain stage of the poem's composition Keats intended *Hyperion* to express an idealistic belief in the evolution of the world toward ultimate perfection. Caldwell ("The Meaning of *Hyperion,*" pp. 1089, 1095–96) entirely rejects the progress interpretations and sees the poem as expressive of Keats's conflicting leanings toward passion, or intense experience, and endeavor, or humanitarian concern with one's fellow men.

29 This interpretation has been suggested by John Middleton Murry, *Keats and Shakespeare* (London, 1926), p. 86, and by D. G. James, *The Romantic Comedy* (London, 1948), pp. 128, 139–40.

Two discussions of Keats which are not concerned mainly with *Hyperion* are especially relevant to my views on the poem. The first is Lionel Trilling's excellent introduction to *The Selected Letters of John Keats,* Doubleday Anchor ed. (New York, 1956). Keats's statement in the "Ode on a Grecian Urn" that truth is beauty is, Trilling claims, "an accurate description of the response to evil or ugliness which tragedy makes: the matter of tragedy is ugly or painful truth seen as beauty" (p. 29). Keats's attempt to find an answer to the problem of evil, an answer which would sanction a commitment to life and beauty, connects him with Milton, who tried to justify God's ways, and with Shakespeare, especially the Shakespeare of *King Lear* (pp. 37–40).

The other essay is John D. Rosenberg's "Keats and Milton: The Paradox of Rejection," *Keats-Shelley Journal,* VI (1957), esp. pp. 93–95. As I do, Rosenberg reads *Hyperion* as a poem in which Keats re-interprets the Miltonic *felix culpa* solution of the problem of evil in accordance with the ideas expressed in the "Soul-making"

letter. A good deal of the present chapter is an expanded version
of Rosenberg's view, though I am, of course, ultimately interested
in the general epic status of *Hyperion*.

30 It was not until I was making my final revisions of this chapter that
I read Bernard Blackstone's discussion of *Hyperion* and *The Fall of
Hyperion* in *The Consecrated Urn* (New York, 1959) and Stuart
Sperry's article "Keats, Milton, and *The Fall of Hyperion*," *PMLA*,
LXXVII (1962), 77–84. My reading of *Hyperion* is in its essen-
tials identical with that in my doctoral dissertation. "The English
Romantic Poets and the Epic" (Madison, 1959). I make the point
not in order to quibble about who got where first, but to reassure
the reader that I have not perversely tried to turn other men's opinions upside down simply by reversing their own arguments. The
fact is, however, that although both Blackstone and Sperry treat
some of the same questions I am concerned with and often use
similar evidence, my conclusions are almost diametrically opposed
to theirs on fundamental points.

I cannot describe both briefly and adequately Blackstone's very
interesting piece of criticism, but among his points are the following, all of which, as this chapter will make clear, I disagree with
in whole or in part: 1) *Hyperion* is an escapist poem, a retreat
from painful reality into ideal abstraction; 2) *Hyperion* is a poem
about growth in the universe, a cosmogonic poem (I believe that
Keats's interest in cosmic history is part of his general attempt to
give epic amplitude to his very human theme); 3) *Hyperion* is Miltonic mainly in technical rather than thematic ways, and both it and
The Fall, when they do draw on Miltonic themes, reflect mainly the
sensuous Milton of *Comus* and of *Paradise Lost*, Book V; 4) the
epic age had passed when Keats wrote and even when Milton did;
5) Book III of *Hyperion* moves from epic to lyric personal statement which is alien to epic (I have in fact used Blackstone to re-
fine my own ideas on this question). I must emphasize, however,
that I have found Blackstone's reading stimulating and that I am
far from disagreeing with all his important points.

Sperry's article, in effect, reads *The Fall of Hyperion* almost
exactly as I read both it and *Hyperion*, and on the basis of the same
kind of evidence. But I think Sperry is wrong in believing that the
two poems have different themes, that *Hyperion* does not assimi-
late Milton's Fall theme, and that *Hyperion* is a superficially optimistic poem. Like Blackstone, Sperry finds only Miltonic *texture*
in the first version, and again like Blackstone, he sees Keats as

making a fairly firm distinction in *The Fall* between the poet and the dreamer. I do not accept these views.

31 See nn. 29 and 30 of this chapter.

32 Ernest De Selincourt, ed., *The Poems of John Keats*, 5th ed. (London, 1926); Bate (above, n. 5), pp. 66–91. De Selincourt is most helpful in pointing out verbal echoes; Bate emphasizes more general and technical matters, especially prosody. He demonstrates that in most though not all ways *The Fall of Hyperion* systematically attempts to remove the Miltonic style of the earlier version.

33 See Robert Bridges, *John Keats: A Critical Essay* (n.p., 1895), pp. 33–34; James, *The Romantic Comedy*, p. 141. De Selincourt praises the subject, but on negative grounds, because the "remote heroic theme gave little scope to the weaker side" of Keats's genius; *The John Keats Memorial Volume*, issued by The Keats House Committee (London, 1921), p. 11.

34 *Letters*, II, 103.

35 Finney, *The Evolution of Keats's Poetry*, II, 494.

36 Ridley, *Keats' Craftsmanship*, p. 77. The preceding lines in Milton make the parallel with Keats even more striking:

> "Goe whither Fate and inclination strong
> Leads thee, I shall not lag behinde, nor erre
> The way, thou leading, such a sent I draw
> Of carnage, prey innumerable, and taste
> The savour of Death from all things there that live:
> Nor shall I to the work thou enterprisest
> Be wanting, but afford thee equal aid." (*PL*, X 265–71)

37 See *Letters*, I, 343, July 22, 1818, to Benjamin Bailey.

38 Robert Gittings, *The Mask of Keats: A Study of Problems* (London, 1956), pp. 19–23; compare *Inf.*, XIV.103–4. Gittings remarks (p. 43) that the *Inferno* and *Paradise Lost* fulfilled for Keats those moods wherein he felt the need for epic stature.

39 See C. H. Grandgent, ed., *La Divina Commedia*, rev. ed. (New York, 1933), p. 127.

40 *The Vision: or Hell, Purgatory and Paradise of Dante Alighieri*, trans. Henry Francis Cary, 3 vols. (London, 1814), *Inf.*, XIV.89–108.

41 *Letters*, March 24, 1818, to James Rice.

42 Quoted from *The Poetical Works and Other Writings of John Keats*, ed. Harry Buxton Forman, 4 vols. (London, 1883), III, 19.

43 *Poetical Works*, ed. H. B. Forman, III, 20. It is noteworthy than an-

other marginal comment in Keats's copy of *Paradise Lost* mentions Milton, Dante, and Shakespeare—probably the three most vital influences on *Hyperion:* "There are two specimens of a very extraordinary beauty in the Paradise Lost; they are of a nature as far as I have read, unexampled elsewhere—they are entirely distinct from the brief pathos of Dante—and they are not to be found even in Shakespeare." The two passages are *PL,* IV.268–72; VII.32–38. *Poetical Works,* ed. Forman, III, 27–28.

44 *Ibid.,* III, 21.

45 *Letters,* II, 101–2.

46 Gittings, *The Mask of Keats,* pp. 20–23.

47 Sperry (n. 30 of this chapter) argues (p. 82) that in *Hyperion,* as distinguished from *The Fall,* Apollo is deified through the knowledge he reads in Mnemosyne's face, whereas in *The Fall* Keats reads a lesson of pain and sadness in Moneta's face. But to make such a clear distinction ignores the *content* of Apollo's vision, which is intended to represent an education in pain just as agonizing as in the second version. Not only is Apollo's anguished metamorphosis described in explicit and forceful detail, but its emphatic seriousness is further reinforced by its echoing of Ovid and of the anguished serpent-transformations in Dante (*Inf.,* XXIV–XXV) and Milton (*PL,* X.504–84). It is interesting that the Miltonic passage ends with a comparison of the story of Eve with the myth of Saturn, Ops, and Jove. In addition, Apollo's critical agony is almost certainly meant to parallel the serpentine agony of Hyperion in I.259–63. In short, the transformation of Apollo in Book III is tightly knit into the pattern of the first two books and the pattern of the Dantean and Miltonic sources which Keats has been using thematically from the outset.

48 *Letters,* I, 280–81, May 3, 1818, to J. H. Reynolds.

49 See De Selincourt's note (*Poems,* pp. 496–97), which mentions the significance of Keats's *"King Lear"* sonnet.

50 I believe Keats's attempt to make this point corroborates Robert Langbaum's argument in *The Poetry of Experience* (London, 1957), ch. 1, that the early stage of Romanticism is escapist but the later stage an attempt to confront empirical knowledge of life.

51 *Letters,* I, 192, Dec. 21, 27(?), 1817.

52 *Letters,* I, 209, Jan. 23, 1818, to Bailey.

53 *Poetical Works,* ed. H. B. Forman, III, 28.

54 Finney (above, n. 28), II, 526.

55 See n. 27 of this chapter.

56 Other references to the Titans' new passionate nature and their new ability to suffer mortal distress are in I.70–71, 93–94, 135–39, 158–63, 213, 222–26, 231–33; II.24–28, 339–40.
57 *Letters*, I, 207, Jan. 23, 1818.
58 *Letters*, II, 102, April 21, 1819.
59 It is true that Oceanus draws a contrast not only between the doves and the eagles but also between the forest itself and the eagles. Thus he does suggest a kind of progress; the eagles excel the forest as the forest excels the soil from which it sprang. But certainly the contrast between the forest and the eagles does not suggest any triumph of progress over barbarity. And Keats, through Oceanus, gives the impression that the doves (romance, prettiness) are what would naturally be associated with the old forest, whereas the eagles are something new and unprecedented. In other words, pastel romance (beautiful itself in a limited way) is associated with the Titans, but the eagles represent a level of experience which is completely unknown to them. The "progress" is from the beauty of childhood to the beauty of manhood.
60 See my comment (n. 47 of this chapter) on the parallel agonies of Apollo and Hyperion.
61 See n. 30 of this chapter.
62 The argument for omitting the disputed lines has been put best by J. Middleton Murry in *Keats* (London, 1955), pp. 238–49. See also Brian Wicker, "The Disputed Lines in *The Fall of Hyperion*," *Essays in Criticism*, VII (1957), 28–41. Wicker agrees that Keats intended to cancel the lines but claims that they are important to an understanding of the poem. Blackstone (above, no. 30), *The Consecrated Urn*, pp. 251-52, interprets Moneta's apparently scathing denunciation of the supplicant as an ironic baiting which is part of the whole challenge to the narrator, who then responds in kind with ironic self-abasement. I find this unconvincing, though I would admit that Keats in the disputed passage was trying to rescue poetry from his own suspicions of it. But to rescue it meant contradicting his ideas in the rest of the poem.
63 There is still some disagreement. See, for example, Blackstone, *The Consecrated Urn*, p. 241.
64 *Letters*, II, 167, to Reynolds; II, 212, to George and Georgiana Keats.
65 This is nearly the same point Sperry makes, though he finds very little or no Miltonic quality in the first version other than "an unimaginative reliance on the structure and method of Milton's epic"

("Keats, Milton, and *The Fall of Hyperion*," p. 78). See n. 30 of
this chapter.
66 *Letters,* Aug. 16, 1820.

Chapter Six

1 See Andrew Rutherford, *Byron: A Critical Study* (Stanford, 1961),
p. 141, and compare George Ridenour, *The Style of "Don Juan"*
(New Haven, 1960), p. ix. Ridenour considers more seriously
than other critics of Byron the epic elements in *Don Juan,* and
a number of my points in this chapter are closely related to his.
For the most part Ridenour treats the epic elements in the poem as
metaphors which draw their force from their associations in the
traditions of rhetorical theory. This is a good point, but I believe
Don Juan uses the epic in other, sometimes larger, ways too. It is
very likely that I have been influenced by Ridenour's book, however, and I have tried to acknowledge such influence on particular
points as well as other important parallels between his study and
this one. I have found this difficult, partly because I had developed
independently many of the ideas he develops—in my University of
Wisconsin doctoral dissertation "The English Romantic Poets and
the Epic" (Madison, 1959)—and partly because Ridenour's approach to Byron, for all its incisiveness, strikes me as somewhat un-
clear.
2 I use the variorum text: *Byron's "Don Juan,"* ed. Truman Guy
Steffan and Willis W. Pratt, 4 vols. (Austin, 1957). Vol. I, *The
Making of a Masterpiece,* is by Steffan; Vols. II and III, the variorum text, are by Steffan and Pratt; Vol. IV, *Notes on the Variorum Edition,* is by Pratt. I use the abbreviation *Variorum* in references to any or all of the four volumes.
  On the inconsistencies in Byron's political opinions, see Rutherford, *Byron,* pp. 182–97.
3 Rutherford has a penetrating and generally convincing discussion
(*Byron,* pp. 159–65) of this subject, one of the oldest and most
fundamental for an understanding of Byron as a person.
4 Ridenour (*The Style of "Don Juan,"* p. xiii) calls *Don Juan* "a
beautiful, exciting, touching, and rather terrifying vision of a personal and cultural dead end" and says that, although the poem
would have disastrous effects as the statement of a practical program, its negativeness need not be an aesthetic disadvantage. Later

he implies that the unity of *Don Juan* does not arise from a system of ideas, but from Byron's "elaborately coherent" vision (p. 20), which seems to mean that Byron repeatedly uses certain metaphors, including that of the Fall from Eden and the concept of high and low styles. Except in the early mock-epic clowning, I do not think one can validly apply to *Don Juan* this kind of distinction between substantial message and literary purpose, nor (it seems to me) does Ridenour himself observe the distinction faithfully; for example, he writes, "we are to be persistently reminded that 'My poem is epic,' and the implications of that statement are at least as much moral as literary" (p. 17).

5 In its combination of seriousness with radical inconsistency of tone, no work seems to me more like *Don Juan* than Montaigne's *Apology for Raimond Sebond*.

6 Steffan's analysis of Byron's revision of and additions to *Don Juan* seems to have convinced many students of Byron that he was a careful artist after all. But even in Canto I, which Byron revised more carefully than he did later cantos, most of the original lines were never altered at any stage of composition. For even the most meticulous artist to have made fewer changes than this, especially in a verse form which uses only three rhyme-sounds in eight lines and which he has not yet mastered, would require of him an incredible facility which no one could ever have reasonably attributed to Byron. I doubt that the most cynically and rapidly composed greeting-card verse is written without blotting half the lines. Steffan's own judgment, I should point out, is more moderate; he admits that Byron was generally a "fast, careless writer," and claims only that in the first-draft manuscripts of the first five cantos Byron "did a little mental sweating" (*Variorum*, I, 102, 105).

7. *The Works of Lord Byron: Letters and Journals*, ed. Rowland E. Prothero, 6 vols. (London and New York, 1898–1901), Dec. 25, 1822, to John Murray. This edition is hereafter abbreviated as *L & J*.

8 *L & J*, Sept. 19, 1818, to Thomas Moore.

9 *L & J*, August 12, 1819.

10 *L & J*, Feb. 16, 1821.

11 See Steffan, *Variorum*, I, 33.

12 *L & J*, April 23, 1820.

13 *L & J*, Jan. 19, 1821, to Murray.

14 *L & J*, Aug. 12, 1819, to Murray.

15 *L & J*, April 6, 1819, to Murray.

16 Thomas Medwin, *Journal of the Conversations of Lord Byron* (New York, 1824), pp. 111–14, quoted in Elizabeth French Boyd, *Byron's Don Juan: A Critical Study* (New Brunswick, N.J., 1945), p. 165.

17 This account, which appeared anonymously in Leicester F. C. Stanhope, *Greece in 1823 and 1824* (London, 1825), was written, according to Ernest J. Lovell, Jr., by James Hamilton Browne, who knew Byron during the summer of 1823. Quoted in Lovell, *His Very Self and Voice: Collected Conversations of Lord Byron* (New York, 1954), p. 597.

18 James Hamilton Browne, "Voyage from Leghorn to Cephalonia with Lord Byron," *Blackwood's Edinburgh Magazine*, XXXV (Jan., 1834), 62–65. Quoted in Lovell, p. 398.

19 Sir Arthur Quiller-Couch considered *Don Juan* as second only to *Paradise Lost* among English epics—"Byron: A Study," in *Byron, the Poet*, ed Walter A. Briscoe (London, 1924), p. 23. But most critics have shrugged off the epic elements in the poem. Elizabeth Boyd calls them "subordinate architectural ornaments" (*Byron's Don Juan*, p. 34), and Steffan (*Variorum*, I, 87) writes that when Byron "dabbled in such pleasantry in some addendum stanzas near the end of Canto I (200–3) the gesture was urbane and clever. After that it became a trifling formula."

20 My remarks beg many tangled questions about the nature of "statement" in literary art; here, however, I simply wish to say that for the Byron of *Don Juan* the difference between statement and objective creation scarcely existed if it did so at all. This does not mean that in *Don Juan* there is no posing, but I suspect it is the kind of posing that Byron—or almost any person, for that matter—might have exhibited in conversation, social intercourse, or any other area of actual life. That is, Byron may well have been trying to create a definite, calculated, even a consciously false, impression; but I believe that the impression created was to be of him, Byron, and not of a character recognized by the reader to be fictional. I labor the point because some criticism of *Don Juan* uses the term "persona," a practice that strikes me as seriously misleading, whereas to write something like "Byron claims in *Don Juan* to worship women but actually patronizes them" is, in its choice of the term "Byron," usually merely ambiguous and harmlessly so, since the reader can interpret it in accordance with whatever views he may cherish about poetry as statement or impersonal artifact.

21 Steffan seems to miss this point. He writes, "It is a little strange

that Byron, who tried so hard for animation, should have nodded so drowsily when he let his accretive habit overburden the very beginning of his poem" (*Variorum*, I, 71). Elizabeth Boyd (*Byron's Don Juan*, p. 22) observes that the passage is a mocking echo of Tasso's list of possible heroes. Ridenour (*The Style of "Don Juan*," p. 91) notes the echo of Virgil's "I sing of arms and the man" and states that in his uncertainty about his hero Byron is undermining not only his own age but the entire idea of the warrior-hero.

22 The point that Southey was for Byron a representative figure and not just an object of personal detestation has been made by Karl Kroeber, *Romantic Narrative Art* (Madison, 1960), p. 136, and by Ridenour, *The Style of "Don Juan*," p. 1. Kroeber is referring specifically to *The Vision of Judgment*.

23 See Ded., 5–9, and Byron's canceled Preface to Cantos I and II, *Variorum*, II, 6.

24 See Pratt, *Variorum*, IV, 62.

25 Cf. *Inf.*, III.100–5:

> Ma quell' anime, ch' eran lasse e nude,
> Cangiar colore e dibattieno i denti,
> Ratto che 'nteser le parole crude.
> Bestemmiavano Dio e lor parenti,
> L' umana spezie e 'l luogo, 'l tempo, e 'l seme
> Di lor semenza e di lor nascimenti.

26 By Rutherford, *Byron*, p. 172*n*.

27 *Inf.*, XXVI.133–38.

28 Elizabeth French Boyd (*Byron's Don Juan*, p. 150) cites the parallel between Byron's incident and the episode of Latinus and his five sons in Tasso's *GL*, IX. She describes the Ismail cantos as an "anti-*Iliad*" (p. 148).

29 Ridenour, *The Style of "Don Juan*," pp. 70, 91.

30 *Ibid.*, p. 91.

31 See, for example, XI.88; XVI.2. The more frequent disclaimers of "fiction" include statements in VI.8; VIII.86; XIV.13.

32 Ridenour, *The Style of "Don Juan*," pp. 65–69. He states that Byron shares Blake's view (described by Northrop Frye) that war is a perversion of sex; on this premise the opposition in *Don Juan* "between lover and warrior, lover and tyrant, becomes clear, as does the close association between lust, sterility, tyranny, and war." See pp. 69–70 and, in a more general way, pp. 65 ff.

33 Keats once referred to *Don Juan* (Cantos I and II) as "Lord

Byron's last flash poem"—see *Letters,* ed. Rollins, II, 192, Sept. 18, 1819, to George and Georgiana Keats. During their voyage to Italy, Severn relates, Keats threw down a copy of the poem, saying: "this gives me the most horrid idea of human nature, that a man like Byron should have exhausted all the pleasures of the world so compleatly that there was nothing left for him but to laugh & gloat over the most solemn & heart rending [scenes] of human misery." He goes on to charge that Byron's poetry tends to be "based on a paltry originality, that of being new by making solemn things gay & gay things solemn." Keats also accused Byron of preaching "unmanly depravity." See Hyder Rollins, *The Keats Circle,* 2 vols. (Cambridge, Mass., 1948), II, 134–35. It is true, of course, that Keats was referring to the early cantos of *Don Juan.*

34 Shelley, *Works,* Julian ed., X, 303–4 (see ch. 4, n. 5); compare Steffan, *Variorum,* I, 211–13.

35 *Purg.,* I.22–27; *PL,* IX.41–47. Milton also mentions the personal handicap of "years"; he has been "long choosing, and beginning late." It is just possible that Byron's sorrowful or mock-sorrowful references to his own "old age"—i.e., his thirties—has a comic or other ironic connection with the apprehensions Milton confesses.

Ridenour, it seems to me, interprets the "Aurora Borealis" stanzas too optimistically. Byron's point as I understand it is not so much that the Northern Lights *illuminate* the chill wasteland below as that in their brilliance and beauty they are a mocking mirage, an *object* of sight. When Byron calls *Don Juan* itself an Aurora Borealis I believe he means to emphasize the kaleidoscopic, many-toned quality of his poem, which is an entertainment serving to divert readers' attention from the cold realities. Also, and perhaps more important, he is suggesting that *aspect* of *Don Juan* which holds up love and glory as noble ideals while explicitly acknowledging that they are remote and unrealizable by men. There is some inconsistency between my two readings, but such inconsistency is typical of the whole poem.

36 I omit discussion of *Don Juan* as a "real Epic"—a phrase Byron applies to *Don Quixote* with the implication that it also describes *Don Juan*—because Ridenour (*The Style of "Don Juan,"* pp. 99–123) has covered the ground thoroughly. The English cantos, he shows, are Byron's most sustained attempt at "real Epic," that is, at epic which is not merely fanciful but accommodated to the commonplaceness of modern upper-class life. Although I do not agree with everything Ridenour says in this part of his book, I have

probably been influenced in my remarks about "fact" and "truth" later in this chapter by his discussion of "real Epic," which discussion has helped me to expand certain ideas, similar to some of his, which I have stated in "The English Romantic Poets and the Epic" (n. 1 of this chapter).

37 Compare the relevant discussions of this matter in Steffan, *Variorum,* I, 262, 270, 274, and in Kroeber, *Romantic Narrative Art,* pp. 148–67. But that Byron wanted to distinguish his technique from the novelist's is suggested by the following lines:

> 'Tis strange—but true; for Truth is always strange,
> Stranger than Fiction: if it could be told,
> How much would novels gain by the exchange! (XIV.101)

38 X.73–74; XI.25; XI.9–10; XIII.55, 59–70.

39 XI.50; XII.33; XIII.8–11; XIV.71–72; XV.62, 67.

40 Note that this passage is not primarily an attack on the English for being unheroic; what they lack is color, which is only incidentally a part of heroism. The difficulty for the writer, Byron goes on to explain, is in the "common-place costume" of modern life, its uninteresting surface and style. Despite occasional sarcastic glances ("fleeced too in their fold"), the tone of the passage in general is detached rather than angry.

41 The only exceptions I know of are XVI.107–8, where Byron says that the "perhaps ideal" feelings re-awakened in Juan by Aurora Raby "Are so divine, that I must deem them real," and a somewhat similar passage in IV.18–19, where Byron expresses sarcasm toward the view that such perfect love as Juan and Haidée feel for each other is a "factitious state." (Byron thought of Haidée and Aurora as parallel figures.) Even in these passages, however, the context includes an even more insistent emphasis on the fleetingness of such experiences and feelings, which are subjective and explicitly associated by Byron with transitory youth. Both passages, significantly, have a tentative and defensive tone analogous to that in which, for example, a man today might say that he believed in ghosts.

INDEX